DIPLOMATS & ADMIRALS

From Failed Negotiations and Tragic Misjudgments
To Powerful Leaders and Heroic Deeds,
the Untold Story of the Pacific War from
Pearl Harbor to Midway

Dale A. Jenkins

Aubrey Publishing Co.
New York

DIPLOMATS & ADMIRALS
Copyright 2022 by Dale A. Jenkins

AUBREY PUBLISHING CO.

FIRST EDITION

Project Management by Marla Markman, MarlaMarkman.com

Cover Design by Peri Gabriel Design, PeriGabriel1.wixsite.com/mysite

Publisher's Cataloging-in-Publication Data:

Names: Jenkins, Dale A., author.

Title: Diplomats and admirals : from failed negotiations and tragic misjudgments to powerful leaders and heroic deeds , the untold story of the pacific war from Pearl Harbor to Midway / Dale A. Jenkins.

Description: Includes bibliographical references and index. | New York City, NY: Aubrey Publishing Co., 2022.

Identifiers: LCCN: 2022913753 | ISBN: 979-8-9865626-1-2 (hardcover) | 979-8-9865626-0-5 (paperback) | 979-8-9865626-2-9 (ebook)

Subjects: LCSH Coral Sea, Battle of the, 1942. | Midway, Battle of, 1942. | World War, 1939-1945--Naval operations. | World War, 1939-1945--Naval operations, American. | World War, 1939-1945--Campaigns--Pacific Ocean. | World War, 1939-1945--Aerial operations. | Aircraft carriers--History--20th century. | BISAC HISTORY / Military / World War II | HISTORY / Wars & Conflicts / World War II / Pacific Theater

Classification: LCC D773 .J46 2022 | DDC 940.54/5973--dc23

Printed in the United States of America

Front cover photos:
Franklin D. Roosevelt—*Photo courtesy of the Franklin D. Roosevelt Library archives*
Admiral Yamamoto Isoroku—*Photo Public Domain, commons.wikimedia.org*

TO SANDRA,

THE MOST LOVING AND LOYAL COMPANION

I COULD HAVE.

AND TO

DAVE, FRANCESCA, SUNNY AND GRACE.

PLEASE, MAY THEY, AND EVERYONE, LIVE IN PEACE.

Table of Contents

Preface

Diplomats and Admirals, after background perspective, focuses on events from July 1941 to June 1942. The story is told through the leaders who shaped events: President Franklin D. Roosevelt; Secretary Cordell Hull; Assistant Secretary Dean Acheson; Japanese Premiers Konoe and Tojo; Japanese Admirals Yamamoto; Nagumo, and Yamaguchi; U.S. Admirals Nimitz, Fletcher, and Spruance. These persons and others formulated the policies and strategies, and executed the tactics, that resulted in a changed world.

Most works covering this period largely fall into one of two camps: either a recounting of events based in economics and international relationships orchestrated by civilian leaders, or a military chronology of strategies and tactics commanded by senior officers of the armed forces. *Diplomats & Admirals* recognizes that the two are not independent but are very closely connected. One of the tragedies of this period was the abject failure of effective interaction and communications between the civilian leaders in Roosevelt's War Council and the commanders of the armed forces. The same occurred in the councils of the government of Japan.

We come away from this with the profound belief that the defining events of this period could have been very different. If there is a goal it is to offer this work in the hope that there may be something within it that could be useful when other people are responsible for monumental decisions.

The scholarship has been focused on resurrecting key source materials and original documents, such as those found in Foreign Relations of the United States Diplomatic Papers and Action Reports of commanders of fleets, task forces, ships, and squadrons written immediately after events.

Many important original documents were classified for extended periods after the war. With declassifications, it is possible to replace stories from aging memories with core documentation, and in that sense *Diplomats & Admirals* is a counter-revisionist work.

A large territory east of the major European countries has been known as Russia, then the Soviet Union as geography changed, then Russia again. For purposes of this writing those distinctions are not important, and the name Russia is used throughout. Other name changes have occurred over time, and we have attempted to be clear about these without being overly burdensome. In addition, following Japanese custom, surnames of Japanese individuals appear first, followed by given names.

Dale A. Jenkins
Tuxedo Park, New York
June 2022

CHAPTER 1

Roosevelt: The Beginning

In 1941, as the United States faced the threat of another horrific war, President Franklin D. Roosevelt was leading the nation from a wheelchair. Struck down by polio at age thirty-nine, he rehabilitated and marshaled himself, despite severe pain, to press on with his career in politics. Eleven years later, delivering his message of confidence and optimism, he was elected President of the United States.

Many people who lose a sense, like eyesight, compensate by developing keen hearing, touch, taste, or smell. In Roosevelt's case, his legs were paralyzed. Without assistance he could not move. Limited to thinking and speaking, he developed those capabilities to make himself one of the great communicators of his age.

Historians and others have groped to understand the inner person of Roosevelt. The only child of a wealthy and privileged family, he grew up in a large, spacious home in Hyde Park, New York, an exclusive enclave on the Hudson River north of New York City. His father, James Roosevelt, made a successful career in business. After the untimely death of his first wife, in 1880 at age fifty-two James married Sara Delano, then twenty-five and a young woman of independent means and initiative. They retired to the Hyde Park home where Franklin Delano Roosevelt was born in 1882.

Franklin's home was one in which both his strong-willed parents encouraged him to compete and excel at his studies and sports. Proud of his family and its history going back to the early seventeenth century in

America, broadened by frequent trips to Europe, he developed an inner confidence that he carried throughout his life. He never had siblings, and his early education was with private tutors. In this environment he developed an independence of mind, and while he would have many friends and acquaintances throughout his life, his innermost thoughts were his own.

He followed the classic path of sons of such families by attending Groton, a select boarding school, and then Harvard. At Groton he was heavily influenced by the headmaster, Dr. Endicott Peabody, a believer in hard work and discipline. The boys at Groton slept in doorless cubicles and were busy with studies, sports, and related activities from morning to night. It was a big change from the more genteel life of Hyde Park, and Franklin adapted quickly to the spartan life of Groton.[1] Peabody encouraged excellence from all students and was an advocate of civic responsibility by those who are more privileged. Franklin took these messages to heart. In civic responsibility he was influenced by his distant cousin Theodore Roosevelt, and from Theodore he developed an early interest in politics. Subtly competitive, he was "a young man intent on outdoing his classmates and establishing himself as the best at whatever he did."[2] Franklin's growth spurt occurred later than most and, even though he eventually would grow to more than six feet, at Groton his activities did not include the more highly esteemed competitive sports. A participant and sometimes an instigator of small insurrections, in most cases he shrewdly managed to avoid disciplinary action.

Bright scholastically but never one of the leaders of his class, his position in the school was somewhat enhanced when Assistant Secretary of the Navy Theodore Roosevelt came to address the students. Theodore became a model for Franklin's life. Already a dedicated small-boat sailor, his contact with his cousin focused his attention on the Navy. Becoming

---

1   David Kaiser, *No End Save Victory* (New York: Basic Books, 2014), 6.

2   Robert Dallek, *Franklin D. Roosevelt* (New York: Viking, 2017), 25.

a navy secretary was an early goal he set for himself. For the rest of his life, the Navy would be an area of key interest, in peace and war.

Like most Groton students of that era, he moved easily to Harvard. Immediately upon arriving, an excited eighteen-year-old freshman wrote a letter to his parents:[3]

Westmorly Court
September 25, 1900
Tuesday

Dearest Mama and Papa,

Here I am, in Cambridge and in twelve hours I shall be a full registered member of the Class of 1904. The journey from New York was uneventful, and I got off at the Back Bay Station to save the long distance from the Terminal, and arrived at our rooms at 9.15 finding Lathrop (Lathrop Brown, roommate) in an agony of correspondence. I have already seen a number of fellows I know & came out on the trolleys with Jimmy Jackson . . . Tomorrow afternoon I shall go to Boston to get my trunks & do general errands. I am hoping to hear of the "Half-Moon's" (family yacht) arrival & do hope Papa will not get too tired in New York. I will try to drop another line some time tomorrow.

It's late & I must make my bed. With a great deal of love to you both

I am ever your affectionate son

FRANKLIN

The Harvard that young Franklin attended was in the fourth and final decade of the presidency of Charles W. Eliot. During his tenure, Eliot had transformed Harvard from a small, regional college to a

---

3   Elliott Roosevelt, ed., *The Roosevelt Letters, Vol. 1.* (London: George G. Harrap & Co., 1949), 365.

major, world-class university. He had attracted to the faculty some of the preeminent thinkers of the time, including William James, Josiah Royce, George Herbert Palmer, George Santayana, George Lyman Kittredge, and Charles Copeland.

Shortly afterward, Franklin wrote another letter to Mama and Papa:[4]

> *I have three courses today, and of course the real work does not begin until Monday . . . Our Groton table is great fun & quite informal . . . I am very well & Lathrop awfully busy.*
>
> *No more for now*
>
> *Loads of love to you both. Ever your affectionate son*
>
> *F.D.R.*

His signature evolved from "Franklin" to "F.D.R.," where it remained.

The tutor who helped young Roosevelt plan his first-year courses was Archibald Cary Coolidge, a respected diplomat and scholar. Later in his time at Harvard, Franklin formed an important relationship with Roger B. Merriman, a young instructor in history who in many ways supplemented the education and insights from Coolidge. He was to have a heavy influence on Roosevelt's worldview. Merriman was an advocate of the study of history through biographies and how students needed to place the present within the context of Western history. The focus on the importance of understanding personalities and character in the context of events made a lifelong impression on Franklin.

Franklin's life up to that time had been confined to a narrow slice of the American population, and from these two scholars in particular Franklin gained important perspectives. His worldview was enhanced by the great works of humanism—the respect for individuality and the inherent worth of human life. These ideas were instrumental in

---

4   Roosevelt, *Letters*, 366.

expanding Franklin's understanding and respect for other cultures and people from backgrounds different from his own. His 1941 speech on the Four Freedoms would reflect those insights. In the same year, at the Atlantic Conference with British Prime Minister Winston Churchill, the Atlantic Charter would contain a clear statement reflecting their joint beliefs that "they (the United States and Great Britain) respect the right of all peoples to choose the form of government under which they live."

In December of Franklin's freshman year his father died. James Roosevelt had lived with a steadily weakening heart, and by November there was serious concern for his life. When his health became critical, Franklin made the trip back to Hyde Park, and he and his mother were with James on December 8, 1900, when he died. Christmas that year was mournful, and Franklin and his mother decided to make a trip to Norway and the rest of Scandinavia the following summer.

Beyond academics, Franklin worked at the daily college newspaper, *The Harvard Crimson.* He typically spent four hours a day at the Crimson offices. Positions on the Crimson staff were highly sought, and as a result of his diligence he was selected to be a permanent staff member. In his junior year, he became managing editor, and then president in his senior year, 1903-1904. The Crimson was his first experience managing an organization and drafting public communications.

His other primary area of interest revolved around his social club. Harvard students who join clubs are elected to membership during the fall semester of their sophomore year and remain members for the next two and a half years of undergraduate life. "Frank," as he was known by his classmates, was elected to the Fly Club. Cousin Theodore had been a member of the Porcellian Club, and Franklin wanted to follow Theodore there, but the faint utterance that wafted down from the cloistered Porcellian aerie above Massachusetts Avenue hinted that Franklin's circle of acquaintances was a bit too broad. The Fly Club turned out to be an excellent choice for Franklin.

Because of his interest in rare books, he took on the responsibility for the Fly Club's library, where he made significant contributions to its collection and care. A letter to his mother at the end of his junior year announced he was the head librarian of the Fly Club:[5]

THE HARVARD CRIMSON

A.F. Nazro '03, President	*C.H. Derby '03, Business Mgr.*
F.D. Roosevelt '04, Mg. Editor	*A.C. Travis '05, Secretary*

Cambridge
May 6, 1903
Wednesday

Dearest Mama –

Just a scrap to say that I am alive and well. I had a most delightful all night dance last Friday, a subscription affair & went to Gloucester Saturday to Monday to stay with Dr. Andrew, Professor of Political Economy . . . Last night I became head librarian of the Fly for the ensuing year. This between ourselves. I have been working like several canines. I sent home my best purchase yet – the best possible set of Morte d'Arthur *& very hard to get. I have had an order for it for over a year . . . Will write by Friday sure*

Ever lovingly

F.D.R.

The Fly Club, just off Mt. Auburn St., has a library with floor-to-ceiling shelves of books in the main room and in a small alcove at one

---

5   Roosevelt, *Letters*, 419.

side. It also has a comfortable area of leather chairs with a fireplace at the far end. It was in this room, with an inviting wood fire burning on snowy winter nights, where he and his fellow Fly Club members had many discussions about events of the day and the prospects for their own lives.

Years later, as president, he spoke to the nation from the White House thirty times, from March 12, 1933, to June 23, 1944, in what were described as Fireside Chats. It is likely that the many discussions with his friends in the library of the Fly Club formed the basis for the friendly, confident, and inclusive tone that characterized the Fireside Chats with his fellow Americans. During the Fireside Chats, half the country tuned in on their radios, and it was said that on hot summer nights when people had their windows open, one could walk through the residential downtown of a large city and hardly miss a word.

In 1939 Roosevelt became the first president to create a presidential library to house the papers of his administration. The scope of such a creation was far beyond his endeavors as the self-appointed head librarian, and perhaps the only librarian, of the Fly Club. His sense of the importance of not just using library materials but also of assembling, categorizing, and caring for written works may have been formulated and enhanced as a college undergraduate "head librarian."

Franklin had arrived at Harvard with credits from Groton for advanced standing, and by the end of his junior year he had completed enough credits to graduate. In his senior year, he was free to pour his considerable energy full time into the Crimson, where he was the undisputed choice to be president. He was very busy, as his activities show, but he always found time to write his mother:[6]

---

6 Roosevelt, *Letters*, 445.

THE HARVARD CRIMSON

F.D. Roosevelt '04, President   P. Dana '04, Business Mgr.

W.R. Bowie '04, Mg. Editor   C. Burlingham '06, Secretary

Cambridge
December 16, 1903
Wednesday

Dearest Mama

Yesterday I bought lots of books for the Fly Club. Dined at the Fly with Dr. Hale, Prexy Eliot, Dean Hurlbut, and A. Lawrence Lowell (future president of Harvard) – most interesting. Then had a meeting, wrote an editorial & at 11 appeared at the Bigelow's Ball at the Somerset – a huge affair . . .

F.D.R.

His editorials were described as noncontroversial. In one there was a hint about his circle of acquaintances, apparently too broad for Porcellian, with whom he would surround himself as president:

January 26, 1904

A large acquaintance means that many persons are dependent on a man and conversely that he himself is dependent on many. Success necessarily means larger responsibilities, and responsibility means many friends . . . the successful man of business makes his friends not after the hard work is over, but while it is going on . . .[7]

---

7   Roosevelt, *Letters*, 452.

The need for others to realize success would find tangible application as he overcame his polio attack. Franklin's worldview was not confined to his Harvard studies and travels. At the urging of Theodore, he became immersed in the writings of Alfred Thayer Mahan. Mahan was a U.S. Navy captain whose advocacy of sea power as the key to world power became a strong factor in geopolitics throughout the world. At the end of the nineteenth century, Mahan wrote a treatise entitled The Influence of Seapower on History, 1660 to 1783. Mahan asserted that a concentrated force of battleships was the most potent possible naval force, and such a force would be victorious over any other naval configuration. The ultimate victor in battle would be the fleet that achieved a concentration of force over an opposing fleet. A battleship fleet must always operate as a single, concentrated unit.

He pointed out the recurring mistakes of naval commanders who divided their fleets, allowing an opposing commander with a weaker force to hunt down a stronger force by attacking a weaker portion of the stronger force, then defeating it in piecemeal stages. Concentration of force—focusing all one's strength on the vital component of the enemy's force—is the key to the destruction of an enemy fleet. Without destroying the enemy fleet, one's own fleet is always in danger. Mahan's work had a huge impact on military leaders and geopoliticians all over the world. He was recognized as the god of naval strategy. It was compulsory reading in the Royal Navy, and it became a catechism for officers in the Imperial Japanese Navy. It also was widely read in the Netherlands, Italy, and Germany. These concepts would influence events when war broke out.

Roosevelt, Age 22.
Photo courtesy of the Franklin D. Roosevelt Library archives.

Fly Club Library—Genesis of the Fireside Chats

CHAPTER 2

The Rising Sun

On the other side of the world, in 1904, the same year that Franklin Roosevelt was graduated from Harvard, a young cadet was graduated from the Imperial Naval War College of Japan. Two years younger than Roosevelt, Takano Isoroku would distinguish himself in his navy career and, after an adoption, become Yamamoto Isoroku, the commander-in-chief of the Combined Fleet. The Combined Fleet essentially was the entire offensive force of the Imperial Japanese Navy.

Isoroku was born the son of a former samurai who, like Roosevelt's father, became a widower, remarried, and was in his fifties when Isoroku was born to his second wife. The Meiji government had eliminated the samurai system of regional fiefdoms, each with their own mercenary samurais, and this led to difficult times for Isoroku's father. Isoroku was able to get a specialized education that emphasized science. Much later he was adopted into the wealthy Yamamoto family, a practice not uncommon in Japan in which a family without a son will adopt one from another family with a son to spare to carry on the family line.

His excellent educational record led to an appointment to the spartan Imperial Naval War College at age seventeen, allowing him to escape his previous impoverished life and begin a career in the navy. He was small even by Japanese standards, an impediment for sports and other activities that required physical strength. He compensated by developing himself in gymnastics and martial arts, where technique and skill could offset the size and strength of his opponents. Upon graduation from the Naval War College, and after additional underway training, he was assigned to the cruiser *Nisshin*.

Ten years before Ensign Takano reported aboard *Nisshin*, there was a conflict between China and Japan known as the Sino-Japanese War. Japan took over Taiwan (Formosa) from China and added Korea incrementally from a protectorate to full annexation in 1910. Japan also took over the Liaodong Peninsula in the Yellow Sea from China, including the city of Port Arthur. As a result, Russia and Japan became competitive for influence and control in the northwest Pacific. Japan's goal was to secure natural resources. Russia controlled territory ranging from the Bering Strait south to Vladivostok but lacked a twelve-month warm-water port on the Pacific Ocean. Port Arthur was such a port, and Japanese control of it and the entire Liaodong Peninsula became a matter of contention between Japan and Russia. The European powers, at Russia's request, forced Japan to give up the peninsula, but instead of it reverting to China it was quickly annexed by Russia.

These tensions motivated Japan to seek a European ally as a counter to Russia. In 1902 that ally was Great Britain, which saw Japan as an emerging country that could strengthen its interests in the Far East. The Anglo-Japanese Alliance was formed that year. In 1904 a sudden move by the Japanese navy destroyed the Russian Eastern Fleet at Port Arthur and, sending in troops, Japan again took over Port Arthur and the Liaodong Peninsula. That led to a Russian declaration of war, a conflict that became known as the Russo-Japanese War.

It was at this time that Ensign Takano joined the ship's company on the *Nisshin*. In response to the attack on Port Arthur, the Russian Baltic Fleet navigated 18,000 miles through the Baltic, around Europe and Africa, across the Indian Ocean, the South China Sea, and the East China Sea to confront the Japanese in their home waters. On May 27, 1905, the two fleets met in the Tsushima Strait between Korea and Japan. Employing superior tactics and the new twelve-inch guns imported from England for its battleships, the Japanese fleet under Admiral Togo

Heihachiro achieved a victory that would be emulated for the next thirty-seven years. The Japanese fleet destroyed or captured almost all the Russian ships with trifling losses to themselves. It was the largest naval battle in the world since Trafalgar, 100 years earlier, and the only decisive gunnery battle of steel ships. Tsushima was a demonstration of superior armaments but, because the Japanese were outnumbered, the victory also resulted from superior tactics and training. This was not lost on Takano. The Treaty of Portsmouth in 1905 concluded the Russo-Japanese War. Japan took control of Korea and the Liaodong Peninsula and achieved its economic and political goals in southern Manchuria.

During the Battle of Tsushima, Takano was severely wounded, particularly in the legs, by shrapnel from an exploding shell or gun. He lost two fingers from one hand and made a difficult recovery over more than two months. Had he lost a third finger he would have been considered unfit for duty and discharged from the navy. Takano's early career in the Japanese navy took place against the overall background of economic developments in Japan and the buildup of Japanese power. In the latter decades of the nineteenth century, Emperor Meiji hired the best foreign industrialists to develop the economy, including shipyards, railroads, foundries, spinning mills, and port facilities. As each industry developed, it was sold to a Japanese family. Prosperity followed from an integrated economy and trade with the United States and its Asian neighbors. Bright students went to Europe and the United States to study shipbuilding, law, medicine, and business.[8]

For fifty years, including the end of the nineteenth century and the beginning of the twentieth, the US and Japan enjoyed a compatible and mutually productive commercial relationship. Japanese prosperity, in turn, allowed the country to build a formidable army and navy. After a token participation in the Great War on the side of the victorious Allies,

---

8   Craig Nelson, *Pearl Harbor* (New York: Scribner, 2016), 22.

Japan gained control of the former German island colonies in the Pacific
north of the equator—the Marianas except for Guam, the Carolines, and
the Marshalls.

Now adopted by the Yamamoto family, Isoroku's career continued on
an upward trajectory as his talents and skills were recognized. He served
on several capital ships, then moved to the advanced gunnery program at
the Naval Staff College in 1916. He came to the United States and became
a student at Harvard in 1919—fifteen years after Roosevelt had received
his degree. He was introduced to bridge and poker and quickly became
an expert at both. He traveled extensively around the United States and
developed an appreciation for the size and power of modern assembly-line
manufacturing, He compared it to the personalized craftsmanship of
Japanese manufacturing and realized its efficiency and strength. He also
studied the oil industry because he knew that without oil a modern navy
was inoperable. Japan imported 90 percent of its oil, and the United States
was by far the most significant source. He also realized that modern
warfare would be fought by airplanes.

Even while Japan developed modern and powerful armed forces, its
military ethic was still rooted in ancient beliefs. Beginning in the twelfth
century, the samurai became the elite warriors in the internal conflicts
between the shoguns, or warlords. The samurai embodied the spirit
of *bushido*, the glorious way of the warrior, which demanded unquestioned obedience and loyalty, and valued honor above life itself. Glori-
fication of war and the warrior remained a central ethic in the army.
Defeat brought intolerable shame. Although Emperor Meiji unified the
country and modernized the economy, the spirit of the samurai and
bushido lived on. It was consistent with another ancient belief: *hakku
ichiu*, bringing the eight corners of the world under one roof—that roof
being Japan.[9]

---

9   Samuel Eliot Morison, *The Rising Sun in the Pacific*, Vol. 3 (Annapolis, MD: Naval Institute
Press, 1948), 5-6.

As defined in the Japanese Constitution of 1889, the ultimate power in the country resided in the emperor. In the Shinto religion, the Meiji emperor was descended from gods, and there was glory in dying in battle for him. A cabinet of government ministers headed by a prime minister formed and executed policy. Each minister was deemed to be an appointee of the emperor. Dismissal from the cabinet could not be effected by the prime minister alone—the entire cabinet had to resign and a new government formed without the excluded former minister.

If the army minister resigned for any reason, only the Imperial Japanese Army had the power to appoint another one. A vacancy in the cabinet caused the government to fall, and there could not be a new government unless the army agreed to appoint a new minister. As a result, when there was a disagreement between the civilian government and the military, the army could heavily influence, if not control, decisions and events by the threat of withdrawing its minister.

The Imperial Japanese Navy also had a minister, but the navy was a junior power by tradition and lacked the army's centuries-old militaristic beliefs. This lasted until Japanese expansion outside the core islands in the early twentieth century brought the navy into a role of greater importance and power. However, the rigid and assertive traditions of the army still guided its mentality, and this in turn heavily influenced the government.

During this same period, the Qing Dynasty of China, known primarily outside China as the Manchu Dynasty, was in decline. European powers, including Great Britain, France, and Germany, carved out colonies on the coast of China. Sun Yat-sen overthrew the Manchu Dynasty in 1911 but brought in recently communist Russia for support. This move led to the introduction of communism into China. In 1927 Chiang Kai-shek succeeded Sun Yat-sen and outlawed communism in China. The result was a political division between communists led by Mao Tse-tung and the Kuomintang party under Chiang. Many years later, Mao emerged the victor and controlled all of mainland China.

It was at this time that the works of Kita Ikki, a Japanese philosopher and geopolitician, became relevant in Japan. Born in 1883, Kita was a student in Tokyo and spent time in China, where he participated in the overthrow of the Manchu Dynasty. Returning to Japan, Kita's stated goal was a just world, free from one nation or race exploiting another. He declared that Great Britain was a landlord nation and used the people of India as pack animals. He accused the Lenin government in Russia of greed by monopolizing the barren spaces of eastern Siberia. Kita advocated that a nation has a right to initiate a war, not just for self-defense, but when unprincipled and exploitative nations suppress others. He cited as examples the right to wage war for the independence of India or to protect China from colonizing powers. Kita also asserted that a nation has a right to launch a war against another nation that illegally occupies territory and ignores the mutual coexistence of nations. He claimed that Japan had a right to launch a war against the "illegal" Russian occupiers of Manchuria and eastern Siberia. His writings became highly influential in Japan and became a rationale for aggression by the Japanese army.

In response to the developments in China, the army moved to control all of Manchuria and create a buffer for Japan between communist Russia and the communist forces of China. In September 1931, a small detachment of Japanese soldiers, part of the Kwantung Army, detonated explosives near the Manchurian city of Mukden. They then claimed the explosives were planted by the Chinese to destroy a Japanese railroad line. The civilian government in Tokyo was unaware of these events at the time, and, despite efforts by the government to contain the army, the matter escalated. With the introduction of more troops, Manchuria came under army control, and Japan set up a puppet government called Manchukuo. Although there were international protests about these developments, there were no military countermoves.

Kita's philosophy was a prime motivator for the "Manchurian Incident." It also marked the revival of *hakku ichiu* in the Japanese military. His followers became known as Kodo-Ha, or the Imperial Way. In the decade after the Great War and the formation of the League of Nations, the world had moved toward democracy and peaceful diplomacy.[10] Although the government tried to suppress Kita's book, it was widely circulated, and several secret societies such as the Black Dragon were organized to promote his teachings.[11] Japanese expansion during this period not only added important territory but also communicated a policy of Asia for Asians—but an Asia ruled by Japan.[12] Other countries in Asia could have looked to Japan for positive leadership in the efforts to free themselves from the colonial impositions of European countries. However, in the confrontations with colonialism, Japan's overbearing attitudes diminished the possibilities of a more united front throughout Asia.

Lt. Yamamoto Isoroku
Photo AP Images

---

10   Morison, *Rising Sun*, Vol. 3, 8.

11   Morison, *Rising Sun*, Vol. 3, 10.

12   Morison, *Rising Sun*, Vol. 3, 12.

The Mikasa, flagship of Adm. Togo at the Battle of Tsushima
Photo Naval History and Heritage

CHAPTER 3

War Games

The clandestine, suspicious field of war planning and war gaming—what a country will do to wage war or defend itself if attacked—is a highly secretive art carried out in the bowels of war ministries and defense departments all over the world. Individual countries plan what they will do in the event of war with potential adversaries. Major powers, like the United States, Russia, Great Britain, China, and Japan (prior to WWII) go through painstaking evaluations, create alternative scenarios in great detail, and do it all with a high level of sophistication and expertise. The major powers consider every conceivable situation and possible adversary. Spy networks and cryptographers make major contributions. Prior to World War II, US war game plans were given color codes, with different colors used to designate the various potential adversaries. Germany was black, Japan was orange, and even Great Britain was assigned a color: red. All too often, these games have a way of becoming self-realizations.

There were no sets of strategies more keenly developed over the first decades of the twentieth century than those of the United States and Japan. The Japanese victory at Tsushima in 1905 established Japan as a power to be recognized, and US war gamers began to make serious plans to counter its offensive capabilities. In the decades that followed, War Plan Orange, the strategy against Japan, went through many revisions.

The first comprehensive War Plan Orange was initiated by Rear Admiral Raymond P. Rodgers in 1911. This plan contemplated a mobilization of

US naval forces from bases on the West Coast, followed by an advance westward across the Pacific to Pearl Harbor, Midway, Wake, Guam, and the Philippines. Later iterations of the plan, as aircraft became more significant, included support by aircraft at every stage. Each revision contemplated that the Philippines, and possibly Guam, might be under siege by Japanese forces. The westward movement would relieve those islands. Each revision assumed a consolidation of the fleet at Manila Bay, the only harbor west of Pearl Harbor large enough for a fleet anchorage. Finally, the US fleet would engage the Japanese fleet in a classic showdown battle, as envisioned by Alfred Mahan.

Mahan wrote his seminal book before there were aircraft carriers, or even aircraft. The Battle of Tsushima Strait in 1905 took place less than two years after the first airplane flew at Kitty Hawk. The inconclusive Battle of Jutland in World War I was fought in the North Sea in May 1916 between two huge British and German fleets. In that battle a single reconnaissance floatplane flew from a British seaplane tender, HMS *Engadine*, to reconnoiter the German fleet. While not particularly meaningful, this was the first flight from a ship by a heavier-than-air aircraft in a naval engagement. The idea of aircraft flying from a ship at that time was a novelty, possibly useful for scouting or spotting for battleship gunfire. Even the early days of World War II prior to Pearl Harbor had seen only small operations.

The first significant carrier attack prior to Pearl Harbor was the British carrier raid on the Italian naval base at Taranto in November 1940. In that engagement, twenty-one Fairey Swordfish torpedo biplanes from the British carrier *Illustrious* flew 180 miles in two waves to attack ships in the Italian naval base at Taranto. Torpedoes dropped from the Swordfish planes sank or heavily damaged three Italian battleships tied up at piers in the Italian port. This successful raid, with the loss of only two Swordfish, was a triumph of British naval aviation and allowed the

British battleship fleet to maintain naval control in the Mediterranean.[13] In the open Atlantic Ocean, the Swordfish, flying from the carrier *Ark Royal*, dropped torpedoes that resulted in damage to the propellers, steering mechanism, and rudders of the German battleship *Bismarck*. The damage made the ship uncontrollable and resulted in *Bismarck* being sunk by gunfire from the pursuing British battleship fleet.

The Washington Naval Treaty of 1922 set ratios limiting the size of capital ships among the major protagonists. The treaty also prevented the United States from fortifying bases at Guam and the Philippines and the British from further fortifying Singapore. However, there was nothing to prevent the Japanese from fortifying their Pacific islands, which they proceeded to do.

Between 1923 and 1940, the US Navy carried out exercises, known as Problems, to build proficiency in their forces and to practice tactics likely to be employed in a future war.[14] These were major fleet events employing large numbers of battleships, cruisers, destroyers, and, later, aircraft carriers. Routine training exercises were conducted throughout the Atlantic Ocean by US naval forces based in Norfolk, Newport, and other Atlantic ports. Fleet Problems were executed in the Caribbean or the eastern Pacific and occurred approximately once each year. The problems were identified by Roman numerals; Problem I was held in 1923, and Problem XXI in 1940.

Problems were differentiated from exercises by the inclusion of a battle scenario. The fleet was divided into two opposing forces: an aggressor force and a defending force that met and countered the aggressor. Senior admirals commanded each force. Since aggressor moves were not disclosed in advance, confrontations required admirals in command to be spontaneous and innovative. Mock battles with presumed hits and ships sunk

13   Richard Humble, ed., *Naval Warfare, An Illustrated History* (New York: St. Martin's Press, 1983), 226-28.

14   Albert A. Nofi, *To Train the Fleet for War* (Newport, RI: Naval War College Press, 2010), xi-xii.

were scored by a senior admiral umpire. Problems involving amphibious operations had Marine or Army generals as force commanders.

In the 1920s, Problems had an average duration of one week, but as greater complications were introduced in the mid- and late 1930s, the Problems required four to seven weeks to complete. The first several Problems were more tactical in nature and essentially were maneuvers of the battleship line. Later Problems explored the complexities of operating a task force that integrated aircraft carriers, amphibious operations, underway replenishment, and anti-submarine units.[15]

By 1927 the Navy had succeeded in converting two battle cruisers to aircraft carriers, which were renamed *Lexington* (CV-2) and *Saratoga* (CV-3). Carriers were named after famous battles in American history, or the ships that fought them. After 1929 these carriers joined the fleet, which allowed tactical developments with flight operations. After 1935 tactics were developed employing two carriers.[16] Problems from the mid-1930s onward required a year to prepare, execute, and evaluate. The resulting training and expertise greatly enhanced the capabilities of all participants, from seaman to admiral.

Even though many of the Problems were conducted in the Caribbean or the eastern Pacific, the unnamed enemy in every case was the Imperial Japanese Navy. Problem XIII in 1932 included an amphibious attack on the Hawaiian Islands.[17] Plans for Problem XXII contemplated a major engagement across the expanse of the Pacific Ocean, a prescient forecast of events to come. Scheduled for 1941, Problem XXII was never held because the increasingly tense international situation required naval units to be ready for actual combat.[18]

Problem XIII, the first Problem to use aircraft extensively, showed the huge potential power of aircraft when operated from fast carriers.

---

15   Nofi, *To Train the Fleet*, 279.

16   Nofi, *To Train the Fleet*, 288-89.

17   Nofi, *To Train the Fleet*, 151.

18   Nofi, *To Train the Fleet*, 267.

However, actual carrier construction was limited and the transition to operations built around carriers was slow. Building plans were in place for more carriers, but *Ranger* was not added until 1934, *Yorktown* in 1937, *Enterprise* in 1938, and *Wasp* in 1940. *Hornet* was under construction in 1941 and the Essex class was just in the planning stage. While these developments were taking place, the Navy built the *North Carolina* class of two battleships and the four battleships of the *South Dakota* class. In 1939 the Navy began the procurement of four *Iowa*-class battleships, built to spearhead the execution of War Plan Orange.

Perhaps because fliers trained in the warm weather of Pensacola, Florida, or carrier operations were associated with the warm weather of the south Pacific, the officers who were qualified for flight operations were more frequently associated with the tan summer uniform. This uniform included brown shoes, and these officers became known as "brown shoe" officers. Black shoes were part of the dress blue uniform, and the term "black shoe" became associated with surface warfare officers. Despite these informal designations, all officers wore either uniform depending on the order given on a particular day, the location of a ship, or time of year.

In the early months of the war, the US Pacific Fleet was hampered by obsolete torpedo planes and hopelessly ineffective World War I torpedoes. Built prior to the expansion of naval aviation, the torpedoes had been designed to be launched from destroyers and submarines, not airplanes. Manufacturers attempted to modify these torpedoes to aerial torpedoes, but the modifications were not effective. Tests, even against moored ships, showed that the torpedoes were grossly deficient. Torpedoes deviated from course, ran too deep or too shallow, or failed to explode when targets were hit.

The only modern and effective weapon in the carrier arsenal was the Dauntless dive-bomber. In Problem XIII the power of the dive-bombers was shown to dramatic effect. The dive-bombers had a hit effectiveness of 18 percent as a function of all bombs dropped. By comparison, level bombers dropping bombs from 8,000 feet scored 5.6 percent—about a third as effective as the dive-bombers. At the Battle of Midway in 1942, against high-speed, maneuvering Japanese carriers, the dive-bombers achieved 27.5 percent hits, versus 0 percent for both level bombers and torpedo planes.[19]

Meanwhile, the Japanese had been working hard on tactics and strategy since the 1920s. In contrast to the US Problems being conducted in the warm waters of the eastern Pacific or Caribbean, Japanese forces trained in remote areas of the north Pacific Ocean where they would not be observed by other naval forces, and where their sailors would be toughened by the elements. Casualties and lost sailors were accepted as necessary to achieve the level of proficiency required. Fleet units left home ports in January and carried out training exercises until April. During this time "there was hardly a day of rest . . . where one drill followed another with no time for sleep." Following the intense training period there would be "two or three days at anchor for recreation." The second half of the year would consist of divisional, type and fleet training, followed by a fleet problem similar to those of the U.S. Navy.[20]

Both the United States and Japan worked to develop fighter aircraft that would dominate the skies over a battle area. Grumman, the primary Navy aircraft builder, had developed the F4F fighter through several stages in the late 1930s. In 1940 the F4F-3 became fully developed, and in 1941 Grumman announced the plane would be called the Wildcat— the first of a long line of feline names for its planes. The Navy wanted to accommodate more planes into the restricted space on its carriers, and experiments with folding wings produced the F4F-4. This model reduced the wingspan from 38 feet to slightly more than 14 feet when folded, with the result that many more Wildcats could fit into the hangar decks of carriers. The F4F-4 model of the Wildcat gradually replaced

19   Nofi, *To Train the Fleet*, 33-34.
20   Morison, *Rising Sun*, Vol. 3, 24-25.

the F4F-3s throughout 1942. The F4F-4 Wildcat was powered by a 1,200-horsepower Pratt & Whitney engine and weighed almost 8,000 pounds fully loaded. It had a top speed of 318 mph, climbed at 1,785 feet per minute, and had a range of 830 miles. Armament was either four or six Browning .50-caliber machine guns mounted in the wings.

Mitsubishi was the original prime developer of the A6M Zero fighter for the Imperial Japanese Navy. The plane went through several evolutions before arriving at the A6M2 Model 21. The outer 20 inches of wing folded to a vertical position to avoid damage when the plane was hoisted and lowered on carrier elevators. Nakajima also produced the plane and supplied most of the 950 hp Sakae-12 engines used. The plane, fully loaded, weighed just over 5,300 pounds. It had a top speed of 331 mph, a range of 1,160 miles, and the ability to climb at 3,000 feet per minute. The climbing ability of the lighter plane was almost 50 percent faster than the Wildcat.

The basic Japanese battle strategy was offense, not defense, and the emphasis of the A6M2 Zero design was on speed and maneuverability. To achieve this, the plane was constructed with the lightest possible metals and sacrificed every conceivable extra weight, including any protection for the pilot or its fuel tanks. Armament was two 7.7 mm machine guns mounted in the engine cowling, timed to fire through the moving propeller, and two wing-mounted 20 mm cannons with exploding shells. The Fairey Swordfish was still flying from British carriers, and its contribution to the sinking of *Bismarck* was not to be easily dismissed. However, compared to the 331-knot Zero fighters and the deadly dive-bombers and torpedo planes being developed for Japanese carriers, the Swordfish, flying at 85 knots with a tailwind, was a joke.

Japanese strategists devised an action plan they believed would bring about victory if war broke out with the Americans: the Gradual Attrition Strategy. The Gradual Attrition Strategy involved comprehensive reconnaissance in the central Pacific for early detection of an enemy advance. A network of long-range land-based aircraft operated from airfields in their extensive Pacific island holdings. Large four-engine Mavis seaplanes with a total range of more than 2,500 miles operated from remote islands where, landing in harbors and coves, they could be refueled from surface ships and submarines. Submarines with extensive ranges themselves operated throughout the Pacific. Battleships and cruisers were built to accommodate floatplanes that were catapulted into the air. A special class of cruisers was modified to launch up to five floatplanes from each ship for long-range reconnaissance. Last, and by no means least, all Japanese planes, including all carrier planes, were designed with long-range capabilities that allowed them to strike an enemy ship when enemy planes were still out of range.

Destroyers and cruisers carrying the new, deadly, forty-nine-knot Long Lance oxygen-fueled torpedoes were ready to respond to the advance of US forces when discovered by the reconnaissance units. Submarines were to be ready in positions of ambush. Highly developed Japanese night-fighting capabilities allowed the destroyers and cruisers to close the range and sink American battleships with the Long Lance torpedoes.

The Japanese war plan developed during the 1930s was to meet the American battleships carrying out War Plan Orange, first with their cruisers and destroyers weakening the American battleships, then with a Japanese battleship fleet at least equal in strength to the reduced American fleet. Carrier operations were to protect the surface forces of the Gradual Attrition Strategy. In a massive battle in the western Pacific, perhaps around Taiwan, and ideally at night, the Japanese fleet would destroy the US Pacific Fleet.

Plans changed when Admiral Yamamoto assumed command of the Combined Fleet. He was one of the few officers in any country's navy to realize in the 1920s the potential power of carrier-based aircraft. In 1924, while still a captain, he learned to fly and changed his specialty to aviation. This led to his command of the carrier *Akagi* and, as a rear admiral, command of the First Carrier Division. He wanted more carriers and opposed the construction of the 74,000-ton super-battleships *Yamato* and *Musashi*, but the Japanese "gun club" of senior admirals had their way and those ships were built.

Yamamoto saw the future of Japan in the resource-rich Pacific islands, nicely offshore from the Asian continent. He was opposed to the war in China and to the Anti-Comintern Pact, an alliance with Nazi Germany and Fascist Italy in 1936. In 1940 he opposed the Tripartite Pact with the same parties. Because the army waged war in China and favored an alliance with Germany, he was the object of violent opposition from the Army. To spare him a very probable assassination. Navy Minister Yonai Mitsumasa assigned him to command of the Combined Fleet, where he would operate from his flagship based in the Inland Sea of Japan. Yamamoto took command of the Combined Fleet on August 30, 1939, and hoisted his flag on the battleship *Nagato*.

Yamamoto was considered, both in Japan and the US, as intelligent, capable, aggressive, and dangerous. Motivated by his skill as a poker player and casino gambler, he was continually calculating odds on an endless variety of options. He played bridge and chess better than most good players. Like most powerful leaders he was articulate and persuasive, and once in a position of power he pushed his agenda relentlessly. Whether he would push his odds successfully in the Pacific remained to be seen.

Yamamoto, like other naval officers around the world at that time, was schooled in the doctrines of Alfred Thayer Mahan. The Battle of Tsushima was a victory both for Japanese battleships and the Mahan strategy of concentration of forces. The Japanese fleet was able to concentrate its forces when it "crossed the T" of the Russians. In this tactic, the Japanese fleet passed ahead of and perpendicular to the Russian battle line, and in so doing fired broadsides, with most of the guns of its battle line firing on the first or second Russian ships. The Russian ships could fire only their forward guns on the Japanese. In this way, a fleet crossing the T can concentrate the force of its broadsides on a few ships at a time and can sink an opposing fleet one by one.

Yamamoto saw two serious problems with Japan's Gradual Attrition Strategy. The first was that it did not force action. It depended on the Americans to initiate action at a time of their choosing. That time could be when the United States, with its huge industrial capability, waited until it built an overwhelming force that could defeat the Japanese fleet even after it had suffered losses brought about by the Gradual Attrition Strategy. Second, the leading naval powers were developing carriers, and carrier planes could strike at much greater range than cruisers and destroyers. Striking at greater range meant that carrier planes could sink cruisers and destroyers employed in the Gradual Attrition Strategy before they got within range to use their guns and torpedoes. That, in turn, meant that Japan would have to deploy its own carriers to protect its cruisers and destroyers from enemy carrier attack, and that would lead to a different confrontation—carriers versus carriers.

Was it, therefore, not better to go on the offensive and destroy an enemy fleet before it could do the same to one's own fleet? As a result, Yamamoto superseded the Gradual Attrition Strategy with a new concept built around large, fast-moving fleet carriers. This was an aggressive force that could destroy the US Pacific Fleet without waiting for that fleet to move across the Pacific Ocean.

What Yamamoto created was a naval blitzkrieg, a lightning war at sea. As the German army in 1939 and 1940 had employed fast-moving tanks and other mechanized vehicles, supported by dive-bombers and other aircraft to deadly effect, fast carriers with dive-bombers and torpedo planes were the naval equivalent. The Japanese developed carrier operations and armaments that were, at that time, the most advanced in the world. The highly maneuverable Zero fighters and the long-range torpedo planes, nicknamed "Kates" by Pacific Fleet fliers, were the most advanced in any navy. The best US attack plane was the Dauntless dive-bomber, and the Japanese equivalent, nicknamed the Val, achieved a greater range but with lighter munitions. The Japanese carrier pilots and deck crews had been trained to a peak level of expertise. Carrier commands perfected their operations to allow full deck loads of planes to be launched in a matter of minutes. They developed operations for coordinated launches, formations, and attacks by multiple carriers, a skill the U.S. Navy would not match for several years. By the end of 1941, the First Carrier Striking Force would consist of six carriers—three carrier divisions, each division with two carriers—and was the most powerful naval force in the world.

CHAPTER 4

The Crisis Builds

While still at Harvard, Franklin Roosevelt and his fifth cousin Eleanor found each other, and in the spring of 1905 they were married at a private home in New York City. Eleanor was the niece of President Theodore Roosevelt. Since Eleanor's father was not living, her uncle Theodore stood in to give away the bride. The couple would have six children, five of whom reached majority.

After his graduation from Harvard, it was off to Columbia Law School, and after law school he went with the firm of Carter, Ledyard & Milburn in New York. His engagement letter with the firm defined the arrangements:

June 10, 1907

Mr. F. Roosevelt,
135 East 36th Street,
New York City

Dear Mr. Roosevelt:

I have talked over with Mr. Ledyard the question of your coming to our office, and I find that we can arrange to have a place for you at such time as you may wish to come here in the autumn, not later than October 1st, preferably a week or so earlier.

*In case you come to us the arrangement with you will be the
same as we usually make in such cases, that is to say, you will
come to us the first year without salary, and after you have
been with us for a year we would expect, if you remain, to pay
you a salary which, however, at the outset would necessarily be
rather small.*

Very truly yours,
s/ Edmund L. Bayliss[21]

In 1910, after three years as a lawyer and realizing his real love and
motivation was in public service, at the age of 28 Roosevelt left the
law firm to run for the New York State Senate. He ran as a Democrat
in a predominant Republican district that included his home at Hyde
Park, and he campaigned in a red open car. Advised by some that
this portrayed him as a rich playboy, Roosevelt thought otherwise.
He believed it showed him as unlikely to be corrupted and, with an
engaging common touch in his personal appearances, he won.[22] As a
state senator, he achieved recognition as a reform officeholder opposing
New York City's powerful political machine of Tammany Hall.

He served in the New York State Senate until 1913, when President
Woodrow Wilson, whom he had supported in the 1912 presidential
election, appointed him Assistant Secretary of the Navy. This was the
same position that Theodore Roosevelt had held years earlier and may
have resulted from someone's suggestion. Roosevelt held this office
throughout the Great War of 1914-1918. He took time off in 1914 to run
for the US Senate from New York, the first year that US senators were
on the ballot instead of being selected by state legislators. Even though
his campaign was unsuccessful, it gave Roosevelt statewide recognition

---

21   Edward Ellis, Francis M., and Clark, *A Brief History of Carter, Ledyard & Milburn* (Portsmouth, NH: P.E. Randall, 1988), 40.

22   Dallek, *Roosevelt*, 42-44.

throughout New York State, an investment of time and energy that would pay off in a few years.

His experience as assistant secretary deepened his knowledge of the navy and acquainted him with bright, rising naval officers, including Lieutenant Commander William Leahy. Leahy at the time was the effective head of the Department of Navigation, which, despite its name, had the responsibility and authority to order commands and duty assignments throughout the officer list of the Navy. Roosevelt took a keen interest in command assignments, and this brought the two men into frequent contact. Leahy dispatched his responsibilities with aplomb, and Roosevelt came to respect the young officer's steadiness and maturity. Roosevelt and Leahy also had many discussions about Mahan and general naval strategy, including their mutual advocacy for a larger, stronger navy.

In 1920, at age 38, Roosevelt resigned his position in the Navy Department to run for vice president on a ticket with James M. Cox of Ohio. Defeated by Warren G. Harding and Calvin Coolidge, Roosevelt was considering his next move when, in 1921, polio cost him the use of his legs. Rehabilitation in Warm Springs, Georgia, was a huge undertaking. He was in severe pain, but he was determined to withstand it with all his strength. Through it all, Roosevelt never wavered in his commitment to politics. He supported Al Smith in his successful 1922 campaign for governor of New York and in his two unsuccessful runs for the presidency in 1924 and 1928. In that latter year, Roosevelt himself was elected governor of New York and was reelected in 1930. In 1932 he ran for president during a very serious depression and, with his optimistic spirit and policies of economic and social reconstruction, soundly defeated incumbent Herbert Hoover.

March 4, 1933, was the inauguration of Franklin D. Roosevelt as President of the United States. Eight days later, confronted with the banking crisis, he broadcast by radio the first of the Fireside Chats to the nation. In a tone of confident inclusiveness, seeking support for his actions, he said:

I want to talk for a few minutes with the people of the United States . . . I want to tell you what has been done in the last few days, why it was done, and what the next steps are going to be . . . I know that when you understand what we in Washington have been about I shall continue to have your cooperation as fully as I have had your sympathy and help during the past week . . .

He then proceeded to explain the basics of banking. He wanted the public to understand that their money, when deposited in a bank, was not put into a vault, but was invested in loans, securities, and other assets that allowed businesses, including farms, to expand and prosper. In that way, banks were at the core of the entire economy. Because of the investments made by a bank, only a small portion of the bank's assets were held on hand in the form of currency. Roosevelt declared that all banks would be closed—called the Bank Holiday—to confirm that the banks could still function and serve depositors. Confidence in the banking system could be restored. He explained the procedures by which the banks would be reopened, and the faith necessary to have a sound banking system. In closing:

It has been wonderful for me to catch the note of confidence from all over the country. I can never be sufficiently grateful to the people for the loyal support they have given me in their acceptance of the judgment that has dictated our course . . . Together we cannot fail.[23]

In 1936, with the country still in depression, he was re-elected by a substantial margin. Several months after his second inauguration, on October 12, 1937, seeking support for his message of united national will and general prosperity, he delivered another Fireside Chat to the nation, first declaring his own responsibilities as President:

---

23   Franklin Roosevelt, *The Fireside Chats* (Brooklyn, NY: Sheba Blake Publishing, 2017), 5-7.

My Friends,

*This afternoon I have issued a proclamation calling a
special session of the Congress to convene on Monday,
November 15, 1937.*

He reviewed the economic problems of the nation and the measures
he was taking to regain prosperity. He then summarized his own views
on his responsibilities as president:

*For a President especially it is a duty to think in national
terms. He must think not only of this year but of future years,
when someone else will be President. He must look beyond
the average of the prosperity and well-being of the country, for
averages easily cover up danger spots of poverty and instability.
He must not let the country be deceived by merely temporary
prosperity, which depends on wasteful exploitation of resources
which cannot last . . .*

Aware of growing threats from Europe, he stated:

*He must think not only of keeping us out of war today, but also
of keeping us out of war in generations to come. In a world of
mutual suspicions, peace must be affirmatively reached for.
It cannot be just wished for. And it cannot be just waited for
. . . The development of civilization and of human welfare is
based on the acceptance by individuals of certain fundamental
decencies in their relations with each other. The development of
peace in the world is dependent similarly on the acceptance by
nations of certain fundamental decencies in their relations with
each other.[24]*

---

24   Roosevelt, *Fireside Chats*, 59-64.

In a particularly revealing personal comment he made in a later
Fireside Chat on April 14, 1938, he said:

> *I always try to remember that reconciling differences cannot*
> *satisfy everyone completely. Because I do not expect too much,*
> *I am not disappointed. But I know that I must never give*
> *up – that I must never let the greater interest of all the people*
> *down, merely because that might be for the moment the easiest*
> *personal way out.*[25]

Beginning in 1935 Congress had passed a series of Neutrality Acts,
approximately one each year for four years, to prevent a repeat of the
involvement of the United States in the Great War. The Acts prevented
aid to any "belligerents" without distinction, even in the face of a rising
Nazi Germany. In 1937 Roosevelt made a speech in Chicago that became
known as the Quarantine Speech. With Japanese expansion in China and
German involvement in the Spanish Civil War in mind, he stated:

> *Innocent peoples, innocent nations, are being cruelly sacrificed*
> *to a greed for power and supremacy which is devoid of all sense*
> *of justice and humane considerations . . .If those things come*
> *to pass in other parts of the world, let no one imagine that*
> *America will escape.*[26]

He warned that neutrality "cannot insure ourselves . . . against the
dangers of involvement." He referred to war as a "contagion" and, like a
disease, a "quarantine" was necessary to isolate the violators of peace. Even
this subtle shift drew outrage from the opponents of US involvement in
another European war. His speech created anxiety, and many telegrams
arrived arguing against overseas involvements that could lead to war.

---

25   Roosevelt, *Fireside Chats*, 65-72.
26   Dallek, *Roosevelt*, 290.

Also in 1937 the appointment of the next Chief of Naval Operations (CNO) of the US Navy was due, and Roosevelt turned to the officer he had held in particularly high regard for many years, now the commander of the Pacific Fleet Battle Force, Vice Admiral William Leahy. Leahy assumed the CNO post and promotion to four stars.

Within a year of the beginning of Roosevelt's second term, an incident occurred in the Pacific that was one of the precursors of trouble with Japan: the unprovoked attack on December 12, 1937 by Japanese aircraft against the gunboat USS *Panay* on the Yangtze River. Several sailors were killed and others wounded. The Japanese apologized profusely for the *Panay* action. Reflecting on his early contacts with the Japanese in the Pacific, Leahy's reaction was to mobilize the Navy to be ready for battle. Although Roosevelt was unwilling to take any action that could provoke further shooting, the incident led to support for increased shipbuilding. Construction of the carriers *Yorktown*, *Enterprise*, and *Wasp* had started in the 1934-1936 period. As appropriations were made in 1937, Leahy advocated for overall expansion of a balanced fleet, and this led to appropriations for the *Iowa* class of battleships. Leahy also advocated for a major sea-air buildup on Guam, but when Congress could not be persuaded the idea was dropped.

Roosevelt involved himself in the fine details of the Navy, as indicated in a memorandum to his naval aide, Captain Daniel J. Callahan, USN:[27]

The White House

May 10, 1939

Memorandum for Captain Callahan:

Will you ask Admiral Leahy to pursue this further—i.e., two 8,000 ton light cruisers to carry four 11" guns plus as many 5"

---

27   Roosevelt, *Letters*, 262.

dual purpose guns as possible? What chance is there of a three-gun light turret or the 5" dual purpose guns, in order to save weight. In other words, such a ship would have a good chance of standing up against the German pocket battleship type. I still think an 8,000 ton light cruiser, mounting only ten 6" guns, provides too light an armament for this tonnage.

F.D.R.

On August 1, 1939, Leahy retired from the Navy and was succeeded by Admiral Harold Stark. Roosevelt did not want Leahy to disappear into retirement and appointed him Governor of Puerto Rico, only a few flying hours from Washington. The possibility of war was growing almost by the day, and Roosevelt decided that Leahy was the one person in the government he wanted by his side. However, in November 1940 he assigned Leahy to be ambassador to Vichy France, an appointment that kept him away from Washington as the crises developed that led to war. Leahy, as a highly regarded retired admiral and Roosevelt confidant, just might have been the person who could have built communications between civilian officials and senior officers of the armed services that was lacking when ultimate decisions were made.

By 1939 the concerns of the country had shifted from domestic problems to the massive Nazi war machine that had rolled over Poland, and in 1940 was conquering Western Europe. Roosevelt was concerned by the aggressiveness of Japan, but its long-term capabilities seemed limited by its relatively small industrial base. Nazi Germany, on the other hand, posed a lethal danger to the free world. The support Roosevelt could provide the Allies fighting the Nazis was limited, not only by the demilitarization that had occurred immediately after the Great War of 1914-1918, but by the powerful isolationist movement in the US.

The isolationist movement had its origins in the aftermath of the Great War as questions arose about the wisdom of the decision to involve the United States in that war. The agonies over the deaths of 116,000 fathers, sons, and brothers were still fresh. At least twice that number had been wounded, many with afflictions they would carry the rest of their lives. Now, with a resurgent Germany posing a new threat, those terrible sacrifices appeared to have been wasted.

The isolationists argued that if the United States had stayed out of the Great War, or, as it later became known, World War I, there never would have been a World War II. By 1917 the warring protagonists—Britain, France, Germany, Austria, and others—had suffered millions of casualties and were exhausted. The German populace was starving. The isolationists believed that a resolution was inevitable without US involvement, and we could have avoided the seething resentment in Germany over the terms of the Wilson–George-Clemenceau armistice (not surrender) that led to Hitler. The isolationists argued that if the United States had stayed out of the Great War, no one would ever have heard of Adolf Hitler.

In August 1939, Hitler and Russian leader Joseph Stalin executed the Molotov-Ribbentrop Pact, bearing the names respectively of the Russian and German foreign ministers. A shrewd move by Joachim von Ribbentrop and Hitler, the nonaggression pact between Russia and Germany secured the Germany's eastern front, and at the same time killed any chance of an Anglo-French-Russian alliance. On September 1, in the aftermath of the pact, Hitler and Stalin both invaded Poland, dividing the country. Germany took the western portion, including Warsaw, and the Russians took the eastern part. Britain and France declared war on Germany within days.

In response to the invasion of Poland, Roosevelt took to the radio again for a Fireside Chat on September 3, 1939:

> Tonight, my single duty is to speak to the whole of America. Until four-thirty this morning I had hoped against hope that some miracle would prevent a devastating war in Europe and bring to an end the invasion of Poland by Germany.
>
> It seems to me clear, even at the outbreak of this great war, the influence of America should be consistent in seeking for

humanity a final peace which will eliminate, as far as it is
possible to do so, the continued use of force between nations . . .

He emphasized the problems inherent in maintaining a position of
neutrality:

It is easy for you and for me to shrug our shoulders and
to say that conflicts taking place thousands of miles from
the continental United States . . . do not seriously affect the
Americas. . . . [P]assionately though we may desire detachment,
we are forced to realize that every word that comes through the
air, every ship that sails the sea, every battle that is fought does
affect the American future.

He nonetheless established a position of neutrality for the United States:

Let no man or woman thoughtlessly or falsely talk of America
sending its armies to European fields. At this moment there is
being prepared a proclamation of American neutrality. This
would have been done even if there had been no neutrality
statute on the books . . . We seek to keep war from our own
firesides by keeping war from coming to the Americas.

But he also made an assertion of individual rights:

This nation will remain a neutral nation, but I cannot ask
that every American remain neutral in thought as well. Even
a neutral has a right to take account of facts. Even a neutral
cannot be asked to close his mind or his conscience . . . I hope
the United States will keep out of this war. I believe it will.
And I give you assurance and reassurance that every effort of
your government will be directed toward that end.[28]

---

28   Roosevelt, *Fireside Chats*, 81-83.

Great Britain and France declared war on Germany but failed to carry out any offensive actions on Germany's thinly defended western border in the fall of 1939. Following the carve-up of Poland, the German army loaded its tanks, artillery and infantry on trains and moved westward over the winter. Snug behind their Maginot Line, the French continued their bonhomie with fine cuisine, wine, and cabarets.

Now, with the threat of wider Nazi expansion, the isolationist movement grew louder. They continued to pound on the theme that entry of the United States into the Great War had been a huge mistake, and it was absolutely necessary that we not make that mistake again. The America First Committee was the most powerful group opposing US entry into the war. This organization, chaired by General Robert Wood, chairman of Sears, Roebuck, had broad popular and financial support, impressive lobbying force, and media backing from publications such as the *Chicago Tribune*. In response to the German threat, the Committee quickly grew to a listed membership of 800,000, operating in 450 chapters throughout the United States. Total public support was far broader. Prominent individual supporters were Tribune head Robert R. McCormick, Henry Ford, Ambassador to Great Britain Joseph Kennedy, aviator Charles Lindbergh, Norman Thomas, and several important members of the US Senate who had been longtime opponents of Roosevelt.[29]

In April, 1940 the Nazis invaded Norway and Denmark. Then in May and early June, the deadly tank army rampaged through the Netherlands, Belgium, and France. The British Parliament wrenched power from Neville Chamberlain and turned to Winston Churchill. In a Fireside Chat on May 26, 1940, Roosevelt described to the nation the terrible conditions of war in western Europe. He reminded Americans of the need to preserve democracy and the actions to be taken at home.

Tonight over the once peaceful roads of Belgium and France

---

29   Kaiser, *No End*, 164-170.

millions are now moving, running from their homes to escape
bombs and shells and fire and machine gunning, without
shelter, and almost wholly without food. They stumble on, not
knowing where the end of the road will be . . .

Let us sit down together again, you and I, to consider our own
pressing problems that confront us. There are many among us
who in the past closed their eyes to events abroad—because
they believed in utter good faith what some of their fellow
Americans told them—that what was taking place in Europe
was none of our business . . . that many hundreds of miles of
salt water made the American hemisphere remote . . . that
we could maintain our physical safety by retiring within our
continental boundaries. There are a few among us who have
deliberately and consciously closed their eyes because they are
determined to be opposed to their government. They have lost
the illusion that we are remote and isolated . . .

Reacting to the of panic and sudden demands for safety even at
the expense of constitutional liberties: It is whispered by some
that, only by abandoning our freedom, our ideals, our way of
life, can we build our defenses adequately . . . I do not share
those fears . . . Let us not be calamity-howlers and discount our
strength . . . We have spent large sums of money on the national
defense . . . It is my resolve and yours to build up our armed
defenses . . . between 1933 and this year, 1940, the fighting
personnel of the Navy rose from 79,000 to 145,000 . . .
we [recently] have commissioned: 12 cruisers, 63 destroyers,
3 aircraft carriers, [and] 8 new battleships . . . Patriotic
Americans of proven merit and of unquestioned ability in their
special fields are coming to Washington to help the government
with their training, their experience, and their capability.[30]

---

30   Roosevelt, *Fireside Chats*, 85-92.

In May 1940, on Roosevelt's order, the headquarters of the United States Fleet moved from San Diego to Pearl Harbor, Hawaii. (It would not be designated as the Pacific Fleet until February 1941.) The State Department, acting on the views of Stanley Hornbeck, Chief of the Far East Division, opined that the flee t's deterrent effect in Pearl Harbor was important and it should remain there.[31] In a memo to Hull on May 24, Hornbeck advised that the administration "make no change in the disposal of the United States Battle Fleet."[32]

Hornbeck had been a Rhodes Scholar, and later earned a PhD from the University of Wisconsin in 1911. He was initially an academic and had taught at several Chinese universities. From 1928 he served in the Department of State[33] where he became a policy adviser to Secretary of State Cordell Hull. Reflecting his experience as a scholar in China, he held strong views favoring that country.

The order by President Roosevelt to keep the fleet based at Pearl Harbor was made over the very serious objections of Admiral James O. Richardson, the commander-in-chief of the fleet, who argued that Pearl Harbor was not at that time equipped to handle a large fleet and that crew morale would suffer because they would be away from their families for extended periods. In addition, a prepared, well-serviced fleet in West Coast ports was a stronger deterrent than undermanned and unprepared ships at the end of a 2,000-mile logistical supply chain from the West Coast to Pearl Harbor. The admiral felt so strongly about this position that he visited Washington in July 1940 and again in October to impress his views on the president and the State Department.[34]

---

31 Kaiser, *No End*, 115.

32 William Langer and S. Everett Gleason, "The Challenge to Isolation, 1937-1940," *Political Science Quarterly* 67, no. 3 (September 1952): 397. As quoted in Roberta Wohlstetter, *Pearl Harbor: Warning and Decision* (Stanford, CA: Stanford University Press, 1962), 82.

33 Franklin L. Burdette, "Stanley K. Hornbeck 1883-1966: An Appreciation," *World Affairs* 129, no. 4 (January, February, March 1967): 222-24.

34 Morison, *Rising Sun*, Vol. 3, 47.

Admiral Richardson graduated from the US Naval Academy in 1902, and his first duty assignment as a young ensign was with the Asiatic Squadron. In 1922 he was commanding officer of the Yangtze River Patrol, and later as a flag officer he took part in formulating the Pacific War strategy. Throughout his career he was considered within the Navy as an expert on East Asian naval affairs and strategy. Fleet exercises in the 1930s showed the vulnerability of Pearl Harbor to air attack, and as fleet commander he instituted extensive air patrols to the west of Oahu.

As a result of his conflict with the president, Admiral Richardson was relieved of his fleet command in January 1941. He retired from the Navy and from public life. The renamed Pacific Fleet was based at Pearl Harbor under the command of newly appointed Admiral Husband E. Kimmel. Admiral Richardson's retirement was a reminder that armed service officers have no constituency of their own and serve at the pleasure of the president.

Roosevelt realized that mobilizing support for Britain was crucial, as was the preparation of US defenses. The power of the anti-war isolationists was such that he had to move very carefully, particularly before the November 1940 election when he was running for an unprecedented third term. More extensive aid to Britain or other aggressive actions that could lead to war could result in his electoral defeat. The defeat of France earlier that summer had served notice of the threat of Hitler, and Roosevelt had succeeded in getting a major naval shipbuilding bill passed that would increase the total tonnage in the Navy by 70 percent. However, it would be two years before even the first ships would be in the fleet. Meanwhile, since 1935 Japan had been making an all-out effort to build the world's most powerful navy.

CHAPTER 5

The Lines Are Drawn

Over many years the US had built a series of possessions across the Pacific, some by acquisition and others by war. In 1867, in a brilliant and farsighted strategic move, the United States purchased Alaska from Russia. Alaska expanded US influence into the northern Pacific Ocean and provided the United States with a strategic position on the great circle route between the United States and Japan. The island of Attu in the Aleutian Island chain is only 1,700 miles from Tokyo, considered geopolitically close in the vast expanses of the Pacific. It also removed any Russian influence on the northwestern corner of the United States. Alaska and its Aleutian chain have had increased strategic importance since its acquisition.

As a result of its victory in the Spanish-American War of 1898, the United States, led by President William McKinley, took over the Spanish possessions in the Caribbean and the Pacific Ocean. Cuba was considered the most important acquisition at the time, but as events unfolded the Philippine Islands and Guam took on added significance. By participating in a revolt against the Hawaiian monarchy, in 1898 the United States was able to take over the entire Hawaiian chain. This territory stretched from the big island of Hawaii through Oahu to Midway, 1,300 miles away. Wake Island, between Midway and Guam, was annexed in 1898. The result was a 7,200-mile-long chain of islands stretching across the Pacific Ocean from California to the Philippines. Taken one leg at a time, large commercial amphibious flying boats and large military planes could leave California, hop from one island to another, and reach the Philippines in a matter of hours.

The next expansion in the Pacific, offshore the Asian continent, was by Japan. Japan had taken Taiwan in 1895, and during the Great War took advantage of Germany's commitment to the European continent to occupy its colonies in the Pacific. These included the Caroline and Marshall Island chains, all the islands in the Marianas except Guam, and the Shandong Province in the Yellow Sea west of Korea. After a modest participation with the victorious Allies in the Great War, the Paris Peace Conference conferred lawful control of the German colonies, called Mandates, to Japan.

In an effort to preclude future wars, the Allied powers convened a conference in Washington beginning in 1921. Known as the Washington Naval Treaty of 1922, three major agreements were established:

The Four Power Treaty amended an earlier agreement that had existed between Japan and Britain since 1902 that would have required Britain to support Japan in the event of a conflict between Japan and the United States. The revised treaty, by the agreement of Britain, Japan, and the United States, removed that requirement. France also was included as a party to the treaty.

The Five Power Treaty, the most important agreement of the conference, limited total tonnage of battleships to 500,000 for Britain and the United States, 300,000 for Japan, and 175,000 for France and Italy. The rationale for the 5-5-3 ratio, giving Britain and the US an advantage over Japan, was the assertion that those two countries had to cover the Atlantic and Pacific Oceans, whereas Japan was concerned only with the Pacific. (France and Italy were included in this treaty, but the Netherlands, which had naval forces in both the Atlantic and Pacific, was not). Although the Japanese diplomats reluctantly agreed to these limitations, the result of this secondary position for Japan caused resentment on the Japanese home front and added to Japanese frustration over policies limiting the rights of Japanese immigrants in the United States. Britain agreed to not build

Pacific fleet bases other than maintaining the existing base at Singapore. The United States agreed to forgo any naval bases west of Hawaii.

The Nine Power Treaty included all the participants of the Five Power Treaty plus the Netherlands, Belgium, Portugal, and China. This agreement confirmed the territorial integrity of China and the Open Door policy. The Open Door policy provided equal access to all countries wishing to trade with China and equal treatment regarding regulations affecting such trade. The Nine Power Treaty confirmed Japanese "dominance" in Manchuria, a clause that would become significant twenty years later. It also provided for the return to China of the Shandong Province.[35]

In response to the perceived slights, particularly in the Five Power Treaty, the Imperial Japanese Navy launched a program to build up its forces with modern ships and armaments to the limit allowed. The demanding fleet exercises brought their crews to peak performance levels, particularly in torpedo and gunfire night attacks. They introduced aerial torpedoes and found that dive-bombing was a highly destructive aerial weapon.

Powerful elements in the Japanese armed forces were preoccupied with a perceived conspiracy against Japan, the ABCD coalition: Americans in the Philippines, the British in Malaya, the Chinese to their south and west, and the Dutch in the East Indies, plus the French in Indochina and the Russians to the north. All these colonies and countries formed a perimeter around Japan, and the government used this threat of encirclement to mobilize support in the populace. Their perception of being forced into a weaker position by the Five Power Treaty and being surrounded created anxiety within some elements of the Japanese naval establishment and the government generally.

A second naval treaty followed eight years after the first. The London Naval Treaty of 1930 was intended to continue to limit naval buildup by

---

35   "The Washington Naval Conference, 1921-22," Department of State, Office of the Historian, https://history.state.gov/milestones/1921-1936/naval-conference.

extending the Washington Naval Treaty to include other naval armaments, particularly cruisers. Parties to the treaty were the same as in the Five Power Treaty: Great Britain, United States, Japan, France, and Italy. A key provision was the modification of the ratio of cruisers amongst the parties, so that Great Britain and the United States were at ten and the Japanese were at seven. This modest increase for the Japanese was in exchange for the United States insisting that light cruisers with main battery armaments up to 6 inches be allowed maximum displacement of 10,000 tons. The increased tonnage allowed the United States to have light cruisers with greater range that could effectively defend its series of islands from the West Coast to the Philippines.[36] Parties to the treaty exchanged ratifications on October 7, 1930, and the treaty was effective immediately.

A League of Nations commission in 1932 chaired by Lord Lytton of Great Britain condemned Japan for their occupation of Manchuria in 1931. In a dramatic meeting of the League in Geneva, the leader of the Japanese delegation, Matsuoka Yosuke, a Kodo-Ha advocate, made a powerful speech criticizing the United States and Great Britain for their condemnation of Japan. Matsuoka pointed out that there were no objections to the United States and Great Britain taking over territories, such as Panama and Egypt, respectively, and for those countries to criticize Japan for its actions in Manchuria was no different. Following this speech, Matsuoka summoned the other members of the Japanese delegation and walked out.[37]

Because Japan had been a founding member of the League of Nations, this was a dramatic and shocking event. It was followed by Japan withdrawing entirely from the League in 1933. The London Naval Treaty would expire in 1936. An attempt in 1935 to include the Japanese in an extension of the treaty failed when the Japanese, in the aftermath of their withdrawal from the League of Nations, walked out of the negotiations.

---

36   "The London Naval Conference, 1930," Department of State, Office of the Historian, https://history.state.gov/milestones/1921-1936/london-naval-conf.

37   Eri Hotta, *Japan 1941* (New York: Alfred A. Knopf, 2013), 62.

The Japanese began accelerating their naval buildup immediately. Matsuoka will surface again as foreign minister in 1940 and play a major role in critical events between Japan and the United States.

Expansion policy was being debated in Japan during this period. Japan had few natural resources of its own, but resources imported by Japan from Taiwan, Korea, and Manchuria resulted in prosperity. The imported oil, mostly from the United States, could continue indefinitely. General Ishiwara Kanji, a brilliant army officer who had been in command of the Kwantung Army in Manchuria when it was taken over, saw the current situation as one in which prosperity could continue without interruption—provided Japanese expansion stopped. In Ishiwara's view, to even consider confrontation with Russia was completely ill-advised. To expand further south was foolish and potentially disastrous, for four reasons:

First, the real enemy, the power that was already heavily invested in China and potentially threatening to Japan, was Russia. Ishiwara studied the defeat of Japanese forces by Russian troops in 1938 and 1939 at Nomonhan, at the intersection of the borders of North Korea, Manchuria, and Russia. He pointed out that Japan did not have the tanks and heavy artillery for such battles, so it should avoid further conflict with Russia. Russia had significant forces in Siberia ready to move if a situation developed that required action—or just presented an opportunity. The Trans-Siberian Railroad could ship additional forces to the Russian eastern frontier in short order. The occupation of Manchuria, intended to separate Soviet Russia and China, also served as a buffer against Russian moves against Japan. It was important to Japan that this buffer be maintained, not weakened by moving forces to other areas. The Japanese navy had destroyed the Russian navy in 1905, and that disaster had not been forgotten in Russia. Ishiwara instead proposed an East Asia League in partnership with China.

Second, an aggressive expansion southward threatened Britain in Singapore and, by extension, its ally the United States. Ishiwara argued that sooner or later such an expansion would result in a war with Britain and then the United States. The resources of those countries far exceeded those of Japan, and in the long run Japan would lose.

Third, the British, together with the Europeans, had significant problems in Europe, and the Americans showed no sign of aggression. Therefore, the threat of a combined envelopment, the "ABCD Envelopment," was not a serious threat and, according to Ishiwara, was a fraud.

Fourth, if Japanese southward expansion resulted in a war between Japan and a Britain-United States alliance, Ishiwara predicted that Russia would take advantage of Japan's involvement to attack Manchuria, Korea, and even Japan itself.

The strategy to invade China was led by Major General Doihara Kenji, a capable and aggressive officer. The Doihara element in the army had backing from some sympathetic government ministers. Japan was meager in certain important resources, and the increasing war threats in Europe made this a promising opportunity to exploit the resources in the colonies of the ABCD group.

Unbeknownst to the civilian government in Tokyo, in early 1937 Doihara was busy organizing units of the Kwantung Army to make incursions into northern China. The senior leadership of the army, including General Tojo Hideki, supported these moves, and General Ishiwara and his containment proposals were pushed into the background. As a rival to Ishiwara, Tojo was able to force his retirement. With Ishiwara out of the way, the China expansion began in earnest. An early opportunity to avoid the Pacific War and keep their empire was missed when Japan failed to adopt the Ishiwara strategy.

Japan was a strong proponent of the Asia for Asians movement. Many Asians resented the exploitation of their countries by the Europeans, creating further incentive and support for aggressive elements in Japan. Japan promoted itself as the nation that could take back territories controlled by European colonists. However, it was unlikely to surrender control once it had pushed out the Europeans. Whether administration of the colonial territories by the Japanese would be any more favorable to local populations than administration by the European colonizers was a question that had not surfaced at that time.

The Imperial Japanese Navy, however, opposed the military action in China. They saw expansion to the islands of the southern Pacific, with abundant resources, offshore from the teeming Asian continent, as the future of Japan.[38] But, as Ishiwara had pointed out, the problem with expansion to the south was the possibility of war with Britain and the United States. A China invasion appeared to be less risky, and the army followed that strategy. It would grow into a major war known as the China Incident—called an "incident" because Japan did not formally declare war. The Japanese government, led by Prime Minister Hirota Koki, showed itself unable to control the army's invasion into northern China, and Hirota resigned when the cabinet rebelled against him.

Hirota was followed in June 1937 by the unlikely choice of Prince Konoe Fumimaro. Prince Konoe was born in 1891 into the Fujiwara family, a clan that ranked second in honor and prestige only to that of the emperor. The Fujiwaras traced their lineage back 1,300 years to the time an ancestor first rose to power. With the early death of his father, Konoe inherited the aristocratic title of Prince at the age of twelve. In 1916 at the age of 25, he entered the House of Peers and, showing an early ability, was appointed a delegate to the Paris Peace Conference at Versailles in 1919.

Konoe submitted a racial equality proposal into the preamble of the League of Nations Covenant that failed to carry. Konoe took this as a personal humiliation, and it would not be forgotten by him, nor by the population of Japan. Konoe also authored an article critical of the preaching of pacifism by the Anglo powers, claiming that such doctrines were just methods to maintain the power of those who already possessed it. Recognized for his intelligence and grasp of events, he became president

---

38   Morison, *Rising Sun*, Vol. 3, 38.

of the House of Peers in 1933. He remained there until he accepted the responsibility to form a government in June 1937.

Prince Konoe was described as highly intelligent, reserved, sophisticated, highly discriminating, even elegant in his demeanor. He was very patient, listening to all sides of an issue. For a person with such a refined background, he was democratic in his views.[39] Konoe had originally said he preferred to remain as president of the aristocratic House of Peers, but in the end, at the young age of 46, he consented to be prime minister. His restrained aristocratic origins and his early reluctance were seen, in an odd way, as a qualification to deal with the turmoil in the government, particularly in its conflict with the army.

In July 1937, a month after Konoe formed his government, an exchange of gunfire near the Marco Polo Bridge outside Peking broke out between Chiang's Nationalist troops and a Japanese unit stationed there. After several attempts over a three-week period to control the confrontation, the fighting escalated on July 25, and the result was a war between China and Japan.[40]

The army sent General Katsuki Kiyoshi to the scene. Katsuki issued a proclamation that he was forcing punitive measures against Chinese troops, whom he described as taking actions derogatory to the prestige of the empire of Japan. This arrogance foretold the atrocities that lay ahead in China. War Minister General Sugiyama Hajime assured the government and the emperor that the Chinese would sue for peace within three months. This turned out to be an empty promise, and Prince Konoe, who originally was seen as the best person to avoid war, now headed a war government that was heavily influenced, if not virtually controlled, by the army. Konoe would serve three terms as prime minister. The first, which lasted nineteen months from June 1937, was characterized by the army's expansion into China and Konoe's inability to control these events.

39   Hotta, *Japan 1941*, 33-34.
40   Hotta, *Japan 1941*, 29-30.

As the army became increasingly unmanageable and atrocities in China continued, Konoe finally resigned in January 1939.

Relationships with the United States deteriorated during this period. As a result of Japanese military action in China, the United States stopped exporting aircraft to Japan in 1938. After Konoe left office, the United States gave notice in July 1939 of its abrogation of the Commerce and Navigation Treaty, to take effect in six months. This abrogation, which vacated a treaty that had been in effect since 1911, reduced the export of various US industrial products to Japan.[41]

After 17 months of failed premierships, in June 1940, Konoe returned to form another government. This government would endure for sixteen months until October 1941, including an internal reorganization after one year that was officially considered the formation of a new government. A fateful appointment by Konoe upon taking office for the second time was that of Matsuoka Yosuke as foreign minister, the same Matsuoka who had walked out of the League of Nations assembly at Geneva in 1932. Matsuoka was high energy, brilliant but arrogant, and grossly self-interested. The first twelve months of Konoe's second term could be considered the Year of Matsuoka, and actions during that time would define Konoe's premiership. Matsuoka initiated heavy involvements with Germany, Italy, and Russia that had serious international repercussions. These actions would lead to a highly contentious relationship between Japan and the United States, a situation in which attempts at reconciliation would be very difficult, and ultimately would fail.

Matsuoka Yosuke was born in 1880 in the southern part of Honshu into a once-prosperous family that had fallen on hard times. As a teenager he traveled to the United States, where his family had contacts, and his experience there would be the basis of his attitude toward that country. He received a law degree in the United States and returned to Japan at age twenty-two. At twenty-four he qualified for the Foreign

---

41   Hotta, *Japan 1941*, 23.

Service, a highly sought and prestigious position, and spent several years in China. He was appointed a delegate to the Paris Peace Conference in 1919, his first experience at a major diplomatic event, and where he first met Prince Konoe.

Finding ordinary bureaucratic diplomacy too boring, he quit the Foreign Service in 1921 to take a senior position in a Manchurian railroad company. In the aftermath of the Manchurian Incident of 1931 he was recognized for his knowledge of Manchuria and was welcomed back into diplomatic circles. Heading the 1932 delegation to Geneva in the aftermath of the Lytton Report, he delivered his spirited address and withdrew Japan from the conference. From 1936 to 1939, Matsuoka returned to the Manchurian railroad where he served as president. Having operated on the fringes of power for several years, he parlayed himself into Konoe's confidence as the prince formed his second government.

Once installed as foreign minister in June 1940, Matsuoka sprang into action. He immediately supported the army's invasion of the northern portion of Indochina. This move ostensibly resulted from negotiations with the French government, a government that continued to function as a thinly veiled accommodation to Hitler after the country's defeat by Hitler's armies and the occupation of Paris.

One might wonder why a refined and intelligent person such as Konoe, schooled in the ways of decorum and formal diplomatic relationships, would choose a highly aggressive, belligerent person such as Matsuoka to carry out the sensitive diplomatic work of his government. Perhaps he thought Matsuoka's more aggressive tactics would complement his own reserved style. Perhaps Matsuoka's obvious intelligence and aggressiveness would be put to work for the benefit of Japan. What Konoe failed to realize was that Matsuoka was interested, not in promoting the interests of Japan, but rather those of Matsuoka Yosuke. If Matsuoka could achieve a series of brilliant diplomatic and military successes, he saw a route for himself to be the next prime minister. For the chance to achieve that, he was willing to gamble the future of Japan and its seventy-seven million people.

Prime Minister Konoe
*Photo Public Domain,
wikpedia.org*

Matsuoka with Stalin - Soviet-Japanese Neutrality Pact
Photo Public Domain, wikpedia.org

CHAPTER 6

The War Council

The early years of the Roosevelt presidency had focused on domestic issues. By 1937 the aggressive policies of Hitler in Germany and the Japanese invasion of China had moved Roosevelt's focus increasingly to the geopolitical. His personal experience oriented him much more toward Europe than to the Far East. In addition, Japan was seen as far more remote and less threatening than Nazi Germany under Hitler, and few in the State Department had deep experience in Far East matters. Those who did, as would be discovered, had their own agendas.

Roosevelt's method of operating had become clearer over his first term in office. He had great personal magnetism and inspired loyalty in virtually everyone around him. In addition, he had great personal confidence and did not hesitate to make decisions—or to make subsequent decisions modifying, sometimes significantly, the first ones when that suited his purposes. Despite his expansive personal style, he was inwardly secretive and had an indecipherable agenda that he shared with no one. The personality he developed as a youngster at Hyde Park and as a student at Groton and Harvard still guided his actions. He was a genius at mass communications, and his speechwriters deferred to his reviews of their drafts, not so much because he was the president, but because when a text required the perfect word, the exquisite or incisive phrase, or exactly the right tone, he was the best. And when it came to delivery, he had no peer.

Certain members of Roosevelt's cabinet were beginning to coalesce together in what would become the civilian members of the War Council.

These were Secretary of State Cordell Hull, Secretary of War (Army) Henry L. Stimson, and Secretary of the Navy Frank Knox. A fourth person regularly involved in War Council discussions was Secretary of the Interior Harold L. Ickes. While not officially involved in foreign or defense policy, Ickes had been in the cabinet since 1933 and his judgment was respected by the president and the others.

Roosevelt had little regard for the Foreign Service, recognizing many persons there with backgrounds like his own but lacking in initiative or astuteness. Someone had to be appointed Secretary of State, and upon taking office in 1933 Roosevelt chose Tennessee Senator Cordell Hull. Very unlike Roosevelt, Hull had been born in a remote log cabin in Overton County, Tennessee. Descended from English immigrants, he grew up in that community, attended local schools and Cumberland Law School for a year. He was admitted to the Tennessee bar in 1891. Involving himself in politics, he was elected to the Tennessee House of Representatives and served as a local judge. In 1907 he began a career in the US House of Representatives that stretched to 1931, except for a brief interruption in the early 1920s. Hull had built a reputation as a solid party member, and in 1928 he was the Democratic candidate for vice president on the national ticket with Al Smith. Hull moved to the Senate in the 1930 election, and in 1932 was instrumental in Roosevelt's carrying several border and southern states. His reward, appointment as Secretary of State, gave the perception of someone other than another eastern establishment person entering that high office. The fact that he knew essentially nothing about foreign affairs was immaterial because Roosevelt had every intention of being his own Secretary of State. Hull was known for not making decisions, but as a legislator he knew how to identify issues that would be popular and advocate for them. Tall, erect, silver-haired, and of English descent, eleven years older than Roosevelt, Hull looked like a Secretary of State direct from central casting. He was just what Roosevelt wanted.

By 1939 Hull was sixty-eight years old, and although he kept it a secret, he was in deteriorating health. For years he had concealed a case of tuberculosis—during epidemics it was called the white plague—that was in remission and apparently no longer infectious to others. However, it had left permanent damage to his lungs that caused increasingly frequent periods of illness. In addition, he was diabetic. All told, he had serious health problems that were not obvious in his early years as secretary but would become very significant later at critical times.

Henry Stimson was seventy-four years old in 1941. A long-serving public official and cabinet member in the administrations of both parties, he first served in the public sector as a US Attorney under President Theodore Roosevelt beginning in 1906. In 1911 he was appointed Secretary of War by President William Howard Taft. President Calvin Coolidge appointed him Governor-General of the Philippines, where he served from 1927 to 1929. He then served as Secretary of State for the entire Hoover administration, 1929 to 1933. In 1940 President Roosevelt, to create a bipartisan cabinet and replace the isolationist Harry Woodring, brought him into his administration for a second tour as Secretary of War. When not in government he practiced law in New York and served on important commissions.

A graduate of Phillips Andover Academy, Yale College (Phi Beta Kappa), and Harvard Law School, he had sterling educational credentials. He was remembered for closing the Cypher Bureau, the US cryptanalytic unit, upon becoming Secretary of State in 1929 with the famous comment, "Gentlemen do not read each other's mail."[42] Other foreign ministers must have laughed at that statement. Between the wars he served on a disarmament and arms limitation commission. Stimson opposed Japanese aggression and established a diplomatic principle that became known as the Stimson Doctrine, a refusal to recognize

42   Olga Khazan, "Gentlemen Reading Each Others' Mail: A Brief History of Diplomatic Spying," *The Atlantic* (June 17, 2013), https://www.theatlantic.com/international/archive/2013/06/gentlemen-reading-each-others-mail-a-brief-history-of-diplomatic-spying/276940/.

territories or events that were the result of aggression. His experience in negotiations with the Japanese on arms limitations after the Great War helped form his opposition to Japan's expansion in the 1930s and his generally negative attitude toward Japan. Stimson, as early as December 1940, had advocated for a more aggressive policy toward Germany and "stop[ping] the German submarines by our intervention."[43]

The third member of the War Council, after Hull and Stimson, was Secretary of the Navy Frank Knox. Knox grew up in Grand Rapids, Michigan, and attended Alma College in Alma, Michigan. When the Spanish-American War broke out in 1898 he left college before graduation to enlist in Theodore Roosevelt's Rough Riders. He participated in the Rough Rider campaign in Cuba, then returned to Grand Rapids to become a newspaper reporter. His career in journalism led to his owning several newspapers. He advocated US involvement when war began in Europe in 1914, and when the United States declared war in 1917 Knox enlisted in the army again. In France he served in artillery and rose to the rank of major. He returned to the newspaper business after the war, and his involvement in Republican politics led to his unsuccessful candidacy for vice president with Alf Landon in 1936. Adding to the bipartisan coalition before the 1940 election, Roosevelt appointed him Secretary of the Navy. Although a latecomer to the small group who made up Roosevelt's inner circle from the beginning in 1933, his appointment as Navy Secretary brought him into the War Council, and his earlier acquaintance with Stimson brought him into an informal afternoon cocktail group with President Roosevelt.

Knox did not want to stay out of the war. In March 1941 he wrote to Roosevelt advocating for the seizure of approximately one million tons of Axis and neutral shipping in US ports, and for the Navy to convoy merchant shipping across the Atlantic.[44] Roosevelt realized the European

---

43   Kaiser, *No End*, 148.
44   Kaiser, *No End*, 181.

allies alone could not stand up against Hitler, and it was inevitable that at some point the United States would have to enter the war. He also knew Knox's recommendations would be denounced by the isolationists and create a huge political division. His positions also could precipitate a premature entry into the war before the naval shipbuilding program of 1940 could deliver ships to the fleet.

Harold L. Ickes grew up in Chicago and received BA and JD degrees from the University of Chicago. His practice of law was brief, and he spent the bulk of his career as a Republican working on progressive causes. Roosevelt saw in Ickes a person who could promote the New Deal and create a bipartisan cabinet. Ickes came into the administration in 1933 as Secretary of the Interior and served as Director of the Public Works Administration. As Interior Secretary, Ickes was responsible for petroleum reserves on public lands, and this led him to advocate for an oil embargo on Japan.[45] He became a close associate of other cabinet members, particularly Stimson, Hull, and Knox, and was aggressive in his attitude about stopping Germany and Japan. Known for his keen intellect and the ability to think quickly on his feet, Ickes became an unofficial, but important and influential, member of the War Council. In addition to Stimson, Knox and Ickes arguing for a hard line against Germany and Japan, Treasury Secretary Henry Morgenthau, Jr., who was highly respected by Roosevelt, held similarly aggressive views. Morgenthau had been treasury secretary since 1934.

Despite the hawkish views of his close advisers, Roosevelt realized that a war against Japan was to be avoided while the armed forces were still unprepared and Nazi Germany was an increasingly formidable power. The Atlantic theater was the crux of the Allied effort, and support for Britain was crucial. A shift of forces to the Pacific resulting from a war with Japan in 1940-1941 could have been fatal for Britain, and that country's defeat would have created a serious dilemma for the United States. To

---

45   Edward S. Miller, *Bankrupting the Enemy* (Annapolis, MD: Naval Institute Press, 2007), 186.

help the British war cause and benefit the US defense of the Western Hemisphere, and without inflaming the isolationists, Roosevelt made a brilliant move by trading 50 older World War I destroyers that had been considered for scrap in exchange for 99-year leases on British bases in the western Atlantic: Newfoundland, Bermuda, Jamaica, Antigua, St. Lucia, Trinidad, and British Guiana.[46] The destroyers filled a huge gap in British sea defenses.

Worldwide alliances were being formed by the primary players. Japanese atrocities in China had moved American sentiments away from its earlier constructive relationship with Japan and toward China. China eventually became a beneficiary of US aid. US Ambassador Grew was instructed to advise Japan against making an alliance with Germany, but the Japanese response was to demand that the United States abandon aid to Chiang Kai-shek. By mid-1940, the entire coastline of China was controlled by the Japanese military. Any aid to Chiang had to come over the Burma Road, a difficult trek over the Himalayas from Burma to Chiang's forces in Chunking (Chongquin).[47]

The Japanese expansion into China caused the US to revoke the Treaty of Commerce on July 26, 1939. In accordance with the terms of the treaty, which required a six-month notice, after January 26, 1940, the president and Congress would decide the new terms of trade with Japan. A provision was added to the US National Defense Act that provided for the embargo of strategic materials to Japan. Ambassador Grew in Tokyo had advised Hull as early as 1938 that implementing an embargo on oil would provoke a Japanese move against the Dutch East Indies.[48]

Meanwhile, developments were taking place in Europe that affected the western Pacific. Since the Russo-Japanese War, Japan had been jockeying for alliances in Europe in response to threats by Russia. In 1936 Russia agreed to sell arms to Japan's enemy China, causing the

---

46   Kaiser, *No End*, 95.
47   Morison, *Rising Sun*, Vol. 3, 42.
48   Morison, *Rising Sun*, Vol. 3, 36.

Russian threat to become acute. After the Anglo-Japanese Alliance of 1902 had been terminated, Japan still needed a European ally for support against Russia, and the best prospect at that point was Germany. Japan joined Germany and Italy to form the Anti-Comintern Pact of 1936, a defensive move against Russia and the Communist International.

Following the Anschluss of Austria in March 1938, the appeasement agreement of Munich in September of that year turned Czechoslovakia over to Hitler. Stalin interpreted these moves as a gathering of forces against Russia and entered the Molotov-Ribbentrop Pact with Germany in August 1939, not only to secure his western border but also to establish the basis on which the two countries would invade Poland and divide the spoils. Molotov-Ribbentrop offset the possibility of a triple alliance against Hitler, but to the Japanese it undermined the Anti-Comintern Pact. The Japanese then became concerned that the Russians, with a new alliance to protect their western front, might deploy troops to Siberia to threaten Manchukuo. Japan again perceived itself as vulnerable to a coalition of European powers, including Russia. Looking longer term, Germany, if successful in Europe, might even assert claims to its former Pacific island colonies that were now important parts of the Japanese empire.

The Japanese army believed a resurrected relationship with Germany was necessary to accommodate the new power structure created by the Molotov-Ribbentrop Pact. In addition, if the army could cement an alliance with Germany, it would be a powerful deterrent against the "Anglo-Saxons," as it would dissuade them from a conflict with Japan if they would have to cope with a powerful ally in Hitler. The army also thought a pact with Germany would lead to a geographic division of interests, providing Japan with easy targets of European colonies in Asia while their home countries were at war with, or defeated by, Hitler. By 1938 the Japanese army had committed 1.5 million troops to its "China Incident."[49]

---

49   Willmott, 55.

The Japanese navy took a different view. Having had contacts with Britain for shipbuilding over many decades, they foresaw a war ultimately between Germany and Great Britain, with the United States coming in on the side of Britain. Senior admirals warned that a future war between Germany and the US would, by one means or another, lead to war between Japan and the United States. In that conflict, Japan ultimately would be the loser. In addition, the navy viewed the army's bogged-down campaign in China as a total waste of Japan's resources that did nothing to meet the country's strategic needs.

Foreign Minister Matsuoka sided with the army. Without even waiting for a formal Tripartite Pact to be signed, as it would be on September 27, 1940, Japanese troops disembarked in northern French Indochina on September 19. The unwritten agreement among the Axis powers contemplated that Japan would control territories of the western Pacific, China, Manchuria and the Indian Ocean to the eastern border of India. Germany and Italy would control all territory west of India. India itself, in anticipation of an eventual agreement with Russia, would fall within the Russian sphere. Japan's commitment to the Tripartite Pact with Germany and Italy was intended to make it more difficult for the United States to take military action against any single member of the Pact. Matsuoka further calculated that forestalling actions by the United States would allow Japan to exploit the Pacific colonies of the Europeans.

The agreement was made despite the explicit objections of the Japanese ambassador to Germany, Kurusu Saburo. Ambassador Kurusu, a seasoned professional in the foreign ministry of Japan, was compelled to sign the agreement in Berlin and be photographed standing next to Hitler. Kurusu would emerge later at a crucial time in Japanese-American relations, when those photographs would prove to be a poisonous factor in the negotiations between Japan and the United States.

After a preliminary recitation pledging pursuit of peace and mutual prosperity among nations, the Tripartite Pact provided:

ARTICLE 1. Japan recognizes and respects the leadership of Germany and Italy in the establishment of a new order in Europe.

ARTICLE 2. Germany and Italy recognize and respect the leadership of Japan in the establishment of a new order in Greater East Asia.

ARTICLE 3. Japan, Germany, and Italy agree to cooperate in their efforts on aforesaid lines. They further undertake to assist one another with all political, economic and military means if one of the Contracting Powers is attacked by a Power at present not involved in the European War or in the Japanese-Chinese conflict [i.e., the United States].

ARTICLE 4. With a view to implementing the present pact, joint technical commissions, to be appointed by the respective Governments of Japan, Germany and Italy, will meet without delay.

ARTICLE 5. Japan, Germany and Italy affirm that the above agreement in no way affects the political status existing at present between each of the three Contracting Powers and Soviet Russia.

ARTICLE 6. The present pact shall become valid immediately upon signature and shall remain in force (for) ten years from the date on which it becomes effective. In due time, before the expiration of said term, the High Contracting Parties shall, at the request of any one of them, enter into negotiations for its renewal.

Berlin, Sept. 27, 1940[50]

---

50   "Three-Power Pact Between Germany, Italy, and Japan," The Avalon Project, Lillian Goldman Law Library, Yale Law School, https://avalon.law.yale.edu/wwii/triparti.asp.

The Tripartite Pact provided that the signatories would take no military action against each other for ten years. It was a revival of the Anti-Comintern Pact to the extent that it resurrected the relationship among Germany, Italy and Japan. After the signing of this pact, other nations joined over the next nine months, some as a result of German invasions: Hungary, Romania, Bulgaria, Spain, Yugoslavia, and Croatia (formerly part of Yugoslavia).

By 1940 aggressive elements in the Japanese army wished to continue the military expansion under the banner of eliminating the European colonial powers from Asia. Hitler's conquest of most of Western Europe presented an opportunity. Under pressure from Hitler, Marshal Philippe Pétain, leader of the Vichy French after the French surrender, consented to the "protection" of French Indochina by the Japanese. This resulted in a Japanese military occupation of northern Indochina. However, as General Ishiwara had pointed out, to expand their empire at the expense of colonies of the defeated or weakened Dutch, French, or British governments was dangerous because it could lead to war with Britain, the United States, or Russia.

Extensive negotiations took place immediately after the Tripartite Pact was signed between German and Russian diplomats for the purpose of expanding the Tripartite Pact to include Soviet Russia. Flush with his victories in Western Europe earlier in 1940, Hitler initially viewed negotiations with Russia in the context of the four potential allies dividing up the world. Because of the Molotov-Ribbentrop Pact and Germany's military successes, Stalin showed interest in joining the Tripartite Pact and creating a Quadripartite Entente. Foreign Minister Vyacheslav Molotov was sent to Berlin to negotiate a possible entry, and in October and November, discussions took place over Russian annexation of Finland and control over the various countries of the Balkan states.

Molotov was in Berlin to discuss how Germany and Soviet Russia would divide up Eastern Europe. During these discussions, Molotov insisted that Russia must annex Finland and all of Bulgaria, assume a greater role through the Bosporus into the eastern Mediterranean, and claim greater maritime rights in the Baltic Sea.[51] As discussions progressed on the formation of the Quadripartite Entente, Stalin insisted on being treated as an equal to Hitler.

Hitler, however, could not tolerate that thought. Acting on his hatred of communism and his maniacal demand for sole supremacy, he gambled that he could do what the Allies feared—conquer Russia. Invading Russia meant a complete revocation and betrayal of the Molotov-Ribbentrop Pact. It also meant squandering the potential power of a Quadripartite Entente. Even while negotiations were taking place with Russia in November, December, and January, Hitler secretly ordered his generals to prepare for an invasion of Russia. The second attempt to invade Britain, greatly feared by the British government and its armed forces command, was about to be deferred.

Also in September 1940, the US Army chief of staff, General George C. Marshall, made final an evaluation of the country's entire military establishment. The defense of the Western Hemisphere alone would require an army several times its existing size, as well as a much larger navy. Even with a significant rearmament program, Marshall concluded that the United States would not be prepared for military expansion beyond Western Hemisphere defense for eighteen months, or until early 1942.[52] Even at that point a more active involvement by the Navy in the Atlantic could be realized only at the cost of a drawdown of naval forces in the Pacific. The defense of Guam and the Philippines was considered impossible, and in a conflict with Japan they would be written off.

Because of Japanese warfare in China and its incursion into the northern portion of French Indochina, the United States in 1940 had imposed embargoes on gasoline and scrap metal to Japan. Marshall warned that further sanctions against Japan could result in their

---

51   John Keegan, "How Hitler Could Have Won the War," in *What If?*, ed. Robert Cowley (New York: Berkeley Books, 2000), 299.

52   Kaiser, *No End*, 121.

invasion of the Dutch East Indies, or even the Philippines or Guam. His evaluation concluded that the United States would not be ready for action by our armed forces in the Pacific "for several years."[53]

Meanwhile, the Joint Planning Committee, made up of the most senior US armed service officers, formulated a series of alternative strategies to deal with the developing situation. They came up with five possible scenarios:

A. *War with Japan in which the United States has no allies*

B. *War with Japan in which Britain is an ally*

C. *War with Japan, with Japan allied with Germany and Italy*

D. *War with Germany and Italy, United States allied with Britain, but not at war with Japan*

E. *Stay out of the war and fortify the Western Hemisphere*

The Joint Planning Committee concluded that the potential danger to the United States from Japan was limited, but the threat from Nazi Germany was potentially mortal. It was important to avoid becoming overextended into a two-ocean war. Admiral Stark summarized the position of the committee in a memorandum to President Roosevelt on November 12, 1940, recommending that the United States plan for Option D. Using military phonetics, it became known as Plan Dog.

In the 1940 election against Republican Wendell Willkie, there were no serious disagreements over foreign policy, and Roosevelt won his third term by a substantial margin. In the final months of 1940, Roosevelt was looking for additional ways to aid the Allied cause without the United States being involved in the European war. He devised a program called Lend-Lease. The bill provided that the president could transfer munitions to any foreign nation, provided that such transfer,

---

53   Kaiser, *No End*, 120.

in his judgment, would benefit the defense of the United States. The bill was attacked immediately by the isolationist members of Congress and by influential private individuals. In support of the bill, Secretary of War Stimson stated, "Defense of the US depended on assistance to Great Britain. The situation [now] was more perilous than the United States had faced in 1917."[54] A bill was submitted to Congress in January 1941 and signed into law in March.

Also in January 1941, Roosevelt sent an intelligence report to Churchill predicting an invasion of Britain, probably in February. Marshall's intelligence staff had evaluated Britain's position and concluded that it had one chance in three of surviving without US aid. The passage of Lend-Lease strengthened opposition to a US entry into the war. The United States was not ready for war, but Lend-Lease provided powerful support for Great Britain in its fight for survival.

Ambassador Grew had been the US ambassador to Japan since 1932 and, with the Belgian ambassador's retirement, had become the senior ambassador in Tokyo. Grew and Roosevelt were closely associated through Groton and Harvard, and that gave him special access to the president. He was one of the few people who could address a letter to the White House "Dear Frank." Grew foresaw the Far Eastern situation getting beyond the point where a nonconfrontational solution could be achieved, and he supported Roosevelt's mobilization. In a letter of December 14, 1940, he wrote:

It seems to me to be increasingly clear that we are bound to have a showdown [with Japan] someday, and the principal question at issue is whether it is to our advantage to have that showdown sooner or to have it later.

Commenting on the Japanese "invitation" by the Vichy French to occupy northern French Indochina in September 1940, Grew stated,

---

54   Kaiser, *No End*, 167-71.

The risks of not taking positive measures . . . are likely to be much greater than the risks of taking positive measures as the southward advance proceeds. The Germans here are working overtime to push Japan into a war with us. I have told Matsuoka point blank that his country is heading for a disaster . . .

Faithfully yours,
Joseph C. Grew.[55]

A managed oil export slowdown in January 1941, for example, could have produced a reevaluation among the expansionist elements in the Japanese government as they realized the power the United States held to curb their aggressions.

Ambassador Grew, through his very extensive contacts in the Japanese government, caught rumors that the Japanese navy was formulating plans to attack Pearl Harbor. In a message to Secretary of State Hull on January 27, 1941, he reported:

A member of the Embassy staff . . . had heard from many quarters, including a Japanese one, that a surprise mass attack on Pearl Harbor was planned by the Japanese military forces in case of "trouble" between Japan and the United States.[56]

In the monthly chronological report to Hull on the same date, Grew wrote,

There is a lot of talk around town to the effect that the Japanese, in case of a break with the United States, are planning to go all out in a surprise mass attack on Pearl Harbor. I rather guess that the boys in Hawaii are not

---

55   Joseph C. Grew letter to Roosevelt, Document 5, Papers as President: President's Secretary's Files.

56   "Foreign Relations of the United States, Japan 1931-1941," Vol. II, 1941, Message #80, Department of State, Office of the Historian, https://history.state.gov/historicaldocuments/frus1931-41v02/d80.

precisely asleep.[57]

This communication was passed on to Naval Intelligence. Naval Inelligence replied that no move against Pearl Harbor appeared imminent or planned for the foreseeable future.

In the early months of 1941, senior military officers in Britain and the United States anticipated a renewed German invasion attempt on Great Britain, occupation of a friendly Spain and Vichy French North Africa, and then an all-out fight over control of the Atlantic Ocean. It was in this circumstance that Roosevelt reassigned retired Admiral Leahy to be ambassador to the French government operating at Vichy.

Secretary Hull, in a memorandum to Roosevelt dated February 5, 1941, concluded with an appraisal of the Far Eastern situation. He recognized the stalemate of the China-Japan war and the desire of the Japanese to extricate themselves from the huge and continuing casualties there in favor of more fruitful alternatives:

> *It seems to me that, if through the good offices of this government an arrangement were worked out which would extricate Japan from its present involvement in China, the likelihood would be that Japan would extend and accelerate her aggressions to the southward rather than that Japan would change her present course of aggression to one of peaceful procedures.* [58]

There is nothing in this memorandum that recommended a course of action that would change the aggressive attitude or actions of Japan. In fact, it implies that the war in China, and the continuing heavy casualties on both sides, was useful because it precluded further Japanese expansion elsewhere.

---

57   Joseph C. Grew's Monthly Diary of January 1941. Entry of January 27, Line 4740. Papers of Ambassador Joseph C. Grew, Houghton Library, Harvard University, Cambridge.

58   Cordell Hull, Document 10, Papers as President: President's Secretary's Files, February 5, 1941. https://history.state.gov/historicaldocuments/frus1941v04/d17.

In a telegram to the State Department on February 18, 1941, Ambassador Grew reported that a reliable contact in the moderate element of the Japanese government had informed him that they believed Matsuoka, in his hostility to the United States, was taking actions that ultimately would benefit Russia. Russia would like nothing better than to see armed conflict between the United States and Japan that would provide an opportunity for Russia to stab Japan in the back.

A few months later, on April 13, 1941, Matsuoka was in Moscow to sign a Neutrality Pact with Stalin that provided for neutrality between Japan and Russia: if one of the parties to the pact became involved in hostilities with a third party, the other party promised to remain neutral. In addition, the pact provided that Russia would recognize Japanese control over Manchukuo, and Japan would recognize the Russian-dominated government of Mongolia. This agreement was desirable for both countries because it would free up their military forces at the Siberia-Manchukuo border in northeast Asia. Japan could move troops to the south, and Stalin gained some confidence that he could move forces away from his Siberian front when that became desirable.

Matsuoka had succeeded in stabilizing the Siberia-Manchukuo border in two steps. The Tripartite Pact provided Japan with allies in the event of a confrontation with Russia. Now, a few months later, the Neutrality Pact with Russia lowered the threat against Japan by making Stalin more comfortable about withdrawing troops from Siberia to help safeguard the western front against Hitler. The long-standing desire of Russia to stab Japan in the back was deferred. Despite the seeming security of the Molotov-Ribbentrop Pact and the ongoing discussions over the possibility of Russia joining the Tripartite Pact to form a Quadripartite Entente, Stalin still had deep concerns about Hitler.

In May, weeks after the signing of the Soviet-Japan Neutrality Pact, and at Hitler's urging, Matsuoka argued for an immediate attack on Singapore by the Imperial Japanese Army.[59] A Singapore invasion would assist the German efforts by cutting off support from British Empire entities in Asia and Australia-New Zealand. Royal Navy defense of Singapore would draw British naval forces away from the defense of the home islands, making it more probable that an invasion by German amphibious forces across the English Channel would succeed.[60] In addition, it would assist the German fight in the Mediterranean and ultimately the Atlantic. Matsuoka also calculated that a British defeat at Singapore would pave the way for Japan to dominate the southern Pacific and Indian Oceans. It assumed the United States would take no action in the event of an invasion of Singapore,[61] but there was no guarantee of that. In the end, the army, aware of Singapore's heavy defenses, was shocked at the aggressiveness of his proposal and refused to act.

Matsuoka's initial goal with the Neutrality Pact was to preclude the possibility of Japan being attacked by Russia. Now, turning his attention to the United States and moving ahead forcefully, in June Matsuoka's communication to Secretary of State Hull warned that US entry into the European war would "bring about tragedy." Matsuoka asserted that if the United States were to become involved in Europe, and Japan upheld its agreement with Germany under his interpretation of the Tripartite Pact, Japan would be at war with the United States. This was Matsuoka's misinterpretation of the defensive provisions of the Tripartite Pact. In addition, he asserted Japan's right to expand in Southeast Asia and proposed that the United States and Japan sign their own neutrality pact.

Hull rejected Matsuoka's claim that Japan had a right to further territorial expansion and brushed off the neutrality proposal as an absurdity. In an unusual diplomatic response, Hull served notice on the Japanese government that he considered the actions of its foreign minister to

---

59   Hotta, *Japan 1941*, 111.

60   Owen Matthews, *An Impeccable Spy* (London: Bloomsbury Publishing, 2019), 235.

61   Hotta, *Japan 1941*, 111.

be "illusory."[62] Matsuoka was insulted and infuriated by this criticism, declared that US involvement in the internal workings of the Japanese government was outrageous, and told his diplomats in Washington that the message should have been rejected immediately, even before it was forwarded to him. United State-Japan relations reached a new low.

The ultimate goal for Matsuoka, and the purpose of his trip to Moscow to form the Neutrality Pact with Stalin, was to see Russia join the Tripartite Pact to form the Quadripartite Entente.[63] This huge alliance of Germany, Italy, Russia, and Japan would be a formidable coalition against Britain and the United States. Matsuoka thought he was on the brink of an enormous victory. For his contributions to this mighty potential alliance, Matsuoka had visions of himself not only as the next prime minister of Japan, but as a major world figure.

Secretary of State Cordell Hull
Photo Library of Congress

---

62   Hotta, *Japan 1941*, 114.

63   Kiyoshi Aizawa, Military History Department, National Institute for Defense Studies.

Secretary of War Henry Stimson
Photo Public Domain, wikpedia.org

Secretary of the Navy Frank Knox
Photo Naval History and Heritage

Secretary of the Interior Harold Ickes
Photo Library of Congress

CHAPTER 7

The Axis Expands

The German assault on Russia had been scheduled for May 15 but was delayed by the invasion of Yugoslavia on April 6. Yugoslavia capitulated eleven days later and joined the Tripartite Pact. Seemingly just a quick blitzkrieg, this move nonetheless caused a six-week delay in Hitler's invasion schedule that would have large implications as the Russian campaign unfolded. On June 22, three million mechanized German troops, including thousands of tanks and planes, launched a massive, three-pronged attack against Russia, code-named Operation Barbarossa. The military experts in London and Washington predicted that Russia would be conquered in three months, followed by another invasion attempt against Britain in early 1942 and a ferocious fight over control of the Atlantic Ocean.

In addition to the German blitzkrieg, and despite the Neutrality Pact, Stalin was still worried about the possibility of a Japanese invasion of Siberia. It was acknowledged in the Kremlin, even in the first days and weeks of Barbarossa, that a two-front war against Germany in the west and Japan in the east would be catastrophic. "The very existence of the Soviet state depended on the Japanese resisting the temptation to invade the Soviet Far East."[64] It was not surprising that Stalin had been overjoyed with the Neutrality Pact in April and made the unprecedented

---

64   Matthews, *Impeccable Spy*, 289.

move to see Matsuoka off at the Moscow train station.[65] Whether that agreement would hold now remained to be seen.

By invading Russia, Hitler turned a potentially powerful ally into a deadly enemy that would sap the strength of his army. Having failed to conquer Britain in 1940, he now committed Germany to a two-front war. After invading Russia, the best result Hitler could hope for on the western front was to delay his invasion of Great Britain until 1942, and that assumed victory over Russia in 1941. Even in 1942 Hitler would be attempting to invade a Great Britain made stronger by increased aid from the United States, and even the possible entry of the United States into the war.

The Nazi blitzkrieg into Russia had moved 500 miles in seven weeks and was only 100 miles from Moscow by the beginning of August. The same Allied military minds were still holding to their estimate that Russia would be defeated by October, but in fact the German attack had been slowed substantially by the end of July.[66] Hitler had been second-guessing the tactics of his generals on the battlefield, and this was beginning to show. A failure in Russia would mean the German army would be bogged down on a 2,000-mile front and under air attack on the homeland from the US-supplied aircraft flying from the British Isles. A two-front war overextended Hitler's resources, just as a two-ocean war at that time would have overextended the United States. Had the invasion of Russia taken place on the original date of May 15 the German army presumably would have penetrated deeper into Russia before the weather closed in. The Battle of Moscow could have had a different outcome.

Former corporal Hitler, decorated for his service on the front lines of the Great War, may have believed he knew more about waging war than

---

65   Matthews, *Impeccable Spy,* 254.
66   Waldo Heinrich, *Threshold of War* (Oxford, UK: Oxford University Press, 1988), 136.

the Prussian generals. His successes as an infantryman, terrorist, diplomatic bully, and military victor in early 1940 had made him supremely confident. But, in reality, he was out of his depth. He already had failed to easily capture the British Expeditionary Force at Dunkirk in May 1940 and failed again a few months later in the Battle of Britain despite superior air power. Understanding the enormous potential of a comprehensive geopolitical strategy, such as the Quadripartite Entente, was beyond his capabilities and destroyed by his hatreds. While Germany was still powerful, the misjudgments in 1940 and the failure to conquer Russia in 1941 were taking a toll. Largely unrecognized at the time, the odds were beginning to shift away from Hitler.

The Russian invasion caused a drastic change in the circumstances underlying the Tripartite Pact. Under international law, a party to a treaty can withdraw from it when there has been a significant change in the circumstances under which the treaty had been established. Japan's alliance with Germany and Italy had been enacted in the Tripartite Pact, but this was followed by Germany's invasion of Russia. This major change constituted grounds for revocation of the pact by Japan. Prince Konoe wished to revoke it, but Matsuoka and Army Minister Tojo opposed him, and without their support Japan was forced to remain in the pact.[67] The actual effect of the Russian invasion was Japan's withdrawal from any coordinated strategy with Germany, as Japan had little to gain from participating in the Tripartite Pact now that war was expanding in Europe and Germany was committed to war on that front.

Not only was Hitler's invasion of Soviet Russia the end of any thought of a Quadripartite Entente, but it also destroyed Matsuoka's dreams of power on the world stage. In a state of surprise and shock following the invasion, Matsuoka became increasingly erratic. Maintaining his support of Germany, and perhaps feeling the pressure from Berlin, he advocated an immediate invasion of Siberia from Manchuria. He made

---

67   Hotta, *Japan 1941*, 118.

this appeal directly to the emperor, a highly improper act, and this followed only briefly from his earlier advocacy of a Singapore invasion.

The only possible beneficiary of a move against Siberia at that time was Germany, and the Japanese army had no desire to repeat the unhappy Siberian forays in 1938 and 1939 just to benefit Germany. A major military action against Russia could leave their troops bogged down in frozen Siberia, opposed by the heavy, armored Russian Siberian army. In addition, there were scarce economic benefits for Japan in such an invasion. The armed forces, both army and navy, now favored expansion into Southeast Asia for oil and other resources.

Matsuoka had advocated two unwise policies for Japan: the proposed early invasion of Singapore and, when events turned, an invasion of Russia through Siberia. Both were calculated to benefit Germany at the expense of Japan. Because on two occasions he had placed the interests of Germany ahead of those of Japan, Matsuoka showed himself to be a traitor to Japan. Prince Konoe was shocked by his latest proposal, and for his arrogance in going around him to address the emperor directly. He determined to rid himself of Matsuoka.[68]

A resignation of the cabinet and its reorganization without Matsuoka was a way to oust him, but this could be accomplished only with the support of the army and navy ministers. The armed forces, particularly the army, were focused on the current opportunity to expand in the south Pacific. To gather support in the cabinet against the formidable Matsuoka, Konoe went along with the expansion plans while mobilizing support to oust him.

On July 2, 1941, following an earlier liaison conference of military leaders, an Imperial Conference was held with much bravado, at which the takeover of the southern portion of Indochina was approved. An attack on Russia was also held up as a possibility, but only after they had realized their objectives in the south. Despite this, at a later liaison

---

68   Hotta, *Japan 1941*, 114.

conference on July 10 it became clear there were private misgivings amongst the senior military about the southern invasion strategy. Navy Minister Oikawa Koshiro reminded the assembled officers that the navy did not want a war with the United States, and the move south ultimately could lead to such a war. Every indication was that the United States also did not want war.

On July 14 Matsuoka drafted a note to Secretary of State Hull, stating that the United States should pressure Chiang Kai-shek to make peace with Japan. Arrogant notes such as this had been sent previously to Hull, and they aggravated relations between Japan and the United States. But this time Konoe took action. At a meeting of the cabinet on July 14, the entire cabinet, except Matsuoka, voted to resign. On July 16 a new cabinet was formed without Matsuoka, and the office of foreign minister was filled by Admiral Toyoda Teijiro. Thus ended the yearlong ministry of Foreign Minister Matsuoka.[69]

Matsuoka had played an aggressive diplomatic game, and his actions left Japan in a difficult and vulnerable position. His moves to create an alliance against the United States, behind which Japan could continue to expand, had a major flaw: Japan imported 90 percent of its oil, almost all of it from the United States, as well as other important strategic commodities. The United States could cut off the sale of oil to Japan at any time. Had no one in the Japanese government considered that? In addition, the powerful position of the United States in the worldwide banking system, and Japan's dependence on it, made Matsuoka's strategy of arrogant confrontation with the United States not just risky but reckless.

In addition, Matsuoka's timing was off. The world knew in 1940 that Hitler had squandered his opportunity at Dunkirk. When the massive air raid against London and other British cities on September 15 of that year failed to break British resolve, it was increasingly apparent that the Luftwaffe was about to lose the Battle of Britain. Matsuoka had two

---

69   Hotta, *Japan 1941*, 141.

weeks to evaluate the effects of that latest German reversal before he drew Japan into the Tripartite Pact on September 27. Matsuoka, who considered himself brilliant beyond peer, failed to realize the implications of Hitler's miscalculations. Tying Japan to the Tripartite Pact at that point would not increase its power or security and would become a dangerous impediment to diplomatic relations with the United States. Blinded by his ambitions, however, Matsuoka went ahead with the pact even though its benefits to Japan were doubtful at best, and ultimately would become a huge liability.

The Japanese cabinet should have known that invading southern Indochina and giving Japan eight new air bases and two naval ports, threatening Singapore, would cause great concern in Britain and, by extension, the United States. Instead, the armed forces, particularly Army Minister Tojo, were adamant that the decision of the July 2 Imperial Conference to invade southern Indochina be carried out. Konoe had needed Tojo's support to oust Matsuoka, and as a result the reconstituted cabinet forged ahead with its plan to take over all of Indochina.

Considering the hostile relationship that had existed between Matsuoka and Washington, the downfall of Matsuoka and appointment of Toyoda could have been an opportunity to reappraise Japan's entire diplomatic policy and form a fresh understanding with the United States. However, the Japanese cabinet's failure to reconsider Japan's expansion policy in the face of expected opposition from Great Britain and the United States was a huge lost opportunity to avoid a Pacific War. On July 24, Japanese troops landed in southern Indochina.

In the last months of 1941, the United States continued to mobilize its military and naval forces. German U-boats continued to cause heavy shipping losses in the Atlantic Ocean, and President Roosevelt initiated an undeclared "war at sea." The U.S. Navy would escort convoys as far as Iceland and attack any Axis U-boats or other ships they encountered. This undeclared war, extending over two-thirds of the Atlantic Ocean, could have resulted in an actual war with Germany, but Roosevelt gambled, correctly, that Hitler would not further extend his forces while engaged in a war with Russia. At the same time, Roosevelt calculated that the war at sea would not provoke US isolationists to the point that they would seriously undermine his support in Congress.

During this period, several U.S. Navy ships were attacked by U-boats, and one, destroyer USS *Reuben James*, was sunk with the loss of more than 100 officers and men. That loss was comparable to the 128 Americans lost (out of nearly 1,200 total lost) on the sinking of the *Lusitania* in 1915, and that incident was a significant factor in the US entry into the Great War. The *Reuben James* could well have resulted in Roosevelt asking for a declaration of war on Germany. Another particularly egregious action involved a torpedo attack by a German submarine on another destroyer, USS *Greer*, as it approached Iceland. The event is best summarized by the Fireside Chat of September 11, 1941:

> *The submarine deliberately fired a torpedo at the Greer,*
> *followed later by another torpedo attack . . . The United States*
> *destroyer, when attacked, was proceeding on a legitimate*
> *mission . . . This was piracy—piracy legally and morally. It*
> *was not the first nor the last act of piracy which the Nazi*
> *government has committed against the American flag in this*
> *war. For attack has followed attack.*

Roosevelt then recounted the record of German submarine attacks on five ships over the preceding few months. Four of the five were American. Two of the American ships were U.S. Navy warships. Placing the Greer incident in context, he said:

> *It would be unworthy of a great nation to exaggerate an*
> *isolated incident, or to be inflamed by some act of violence. But*
> *it would be inexcusable folly to minimize such incidents in the*
> *face of evidence which makes it clear that the incident is not*
> *isolated, but is part of a general plan . . . It is the Nazi design to*
> *abolish the freedom of the seas, and to acquire absolute control*

and dominion of these seas for themselves. For with control
of the seas in their own hands, the way can obviously become
clear for their next step—domination of the United States . . .

Then he called for Americans to be realistic about the threat of
Nazi Germany:

It is time for all Americans . . . to stop being deluded by the
romantic notion that the Americas can go on living happily
and peacefully in a Nazi-dominated world . . . No tender
whisperings of appeasers that Hitler is not interested in the
Western Hemisphere, no soporific lullabies that a wide ocean
protects us from him—can long have any effect on the hard-
headed, farsighted, and realistic American people . . . The
attack on the Greer . . . was one determined step towards
creating a permanent world system based on force, on terror,
and on murder.

Then he clearly stated what the United States must do:

One peaceful nation after another has met disaster because
each refused to look the Nazi danger squarely in the eye until
it had them by the throat. The United States will not make that
fatal mistake . . . when you see a rattlesnake poised to strike,
you do not wait until he has struck before you crush him.
These Nazi submarines and raiders are the rattlesnakes of the
Atlantic . . . American naval vessels and American planes will
no longer wait until Axis submarines lurking under the water,
or Axis raiders on the surface of the sea, strike their deadly
blow first . . . [O]ur patrolling vessels and planes will protect all
ships . . . engaged in commerce in our defensive waters.

Then, mobilizing support, he added:

I have no illusions about the gravity of this step. I have not taken it hurriedly or lightly . . . The American people have faced other grave crises in their history—with American courage and American resolution. They will do no less today.[70]

---

70   Roosevelt, *Fireside Chats*, 93-98.

CHAPTER 8

The Oil Embargo

Roosevelt had already stated that he did not want a war in the Pacific that would draw resources away from the greater danger in Europe. He also was looking for a policy that would make it difficult for the Japanese to continue their expansion without triggering a war with the United States. However, he decided that the southern Indochina invasion could not be tolerated. On July 24, the day the Japanese forces landed there, he announced a freeze of Japanese assets. He intended that the freeze would be regulated and flexible, depending on the Japanese response and any future understandings that might develop between the two countries.

The Japanese assets subject to the freeze were almost entirely US dollar-denominated funds held in US financial institutions. The order empowered the US government to block transfers of such funds, and without those funds the export of oil to Japan would be cut off. To implement it, Roosevelt ordered Under Secretary of State Sumner Welles to draw up an order regulating a partial financial freeze. Under the order, each application for a transfer of funds was unique and separate from any other application, so that Roosevelt could approve or deny each request to release blocked funds as he saw fit. He said he wanted Japan brought to its senses, not to its knees.

Immediately following this announcement, in a meeting with Japanese Ambassador Nomura Kichisaburo, Roosevelt proposed a radical policy:

declaring the entire Indochina peninsula neutral and withdrawing all Japanese forces:

> *If the Japanese government would refrain from occupying Indochina with its military and naval forces, or, had such steps actually been commenced, if the Japanese government would withdraw such forces, the president could assure the Japanese government that he would do everything within his power to obtain from the governments of China, Great Britain, Netherlands, and of course the United States itself a binding and solemn declaration, provided Japan would undertake the same commitment, to regard Indochina as a neutralized country in the same way in which Switzerland has up to now been regarded by the powers as a neutralized country.[71]*

To avoid complications, Roosevelt explicitly avoided any mention of the China War in this proposal. In addition, implicit in this declaration was a resumption, in terms to be defined, of trade between Japan and the United States, including oil.

While Nomura communicated the proposal to neutralize Indochina to Tokyo, in the United States plans for implementing the freeze order proceeded. The Treasury favored a partial financial freeze, but whether that would lead to an effective embargo was unclear. Rear Admiral Richmond Kelly Turner, head of the Navy's War Plans Division, stated his considered conclusion that if the United States embargoed all petroleum products, Japan would attack British Borneo, Malaysia, and the Dutch East Indies to replenish their oil supplies.[72] If the previously stated US policy of opposing such actions were followed, it would draw the United States into a war with Japan.

---

71   Hotta, *Japan 1941*, 144-45.

72   Miller, *Bankrupting*, 174.

Welles appointed Assistant Secretary of State Dean Acheson—a fateful choice—to complete the necessary documentation for a partial freeze. Welles specifically ordered Acheson not to launch a total oil embargo and told Hull adviser Stanley Hornbeck to prepare orders that would restrict some grades of oil exports and silk imports and impose a freeze on Japanese financial assets.[73] Acheson, Treasury General Counsel Edward H. Foley, Jr., and Assistant Attorney General Francis M. Shea, all lawyers, formed an interdepartmental committee that became known as the Foreign Funds Control Committee (FFCC). The committee would manage the US freeze policy under the control of Acheson.

Acheson came to this position, like Stimson, with sterling educational credentials. He had schooled at Groton, Yale (Phi Beta Kappa); graduated near the very top of his class at Harvard Law School; and from 1919 to 1921, clerked for Supreme Court Justice Louis Brandeis. When he joined the Roosevelt administration in 1941 he had been in private law practice at the Washington law firm of Covington & Burling for twenty years, except for a few months in 1933 as Under Secretary of the Treasury. Acheson was smart, self-confident, competitive, and belligerent. In two decades of high-powered legal practice for demanding, sophisticated clients, he had learned how to achieve maximum benefit for them by pressing matters aggressively, and he brought those capabilities to the job at the FFCC.

By August 1 there had been no reaction from Tokyo to Roosevelt's proposal to neutralize Indochina. There had not yet been much fighting, and in the face of US objections to their invasion of southern Indochina the Japanese army could have cloaked a withdrawal in a "mission accomplished" statement in order to save face and break the asset freeze. Unfortunately, such subtleties were not part of the Japanese

---

73   Miller, *Bankrupting*, 175.

army's mental functioning, and they threw away another opportunity to avoid the Pacific War.

It was at this time and in the context of important developments in both European and Far Eastern regions that President Roosevelt and British Prime Minister Winston Churchill met in the North Atlantic at Placentia Bay, Newfoundland. Placentia Bay is on the southern coast of Newfoundland, an island barely separated from the province of Labrador and the rest of Canada by the narrow Strait of Belle Isle. Roosevelt arrived on August 9 on the cruiser *Augusta*, which anchored in the center of the bay. General George Marshall, Admirals Harold Stark and Ernest King, and Army Air Force General Hap Arnold were the core of his military entourage. Roosevelt had left the sickly Secretary Hull behind in favor of bringing Under Secretary Sumner Welles, whom he favored in any event, to this important meeting.[74]

After a rough crossing from Britain that caused a day's delay, HMS *Prince of Wales* arrived with Churchill aboard. Harry Hopkins, also a member of Roosevelt's first team of foreign affairs advisers, had just returned from Moscow as far as Britain in time to join Churchill on *Prince of Wales*, and they made the crossing to Newfoundland together. Meetings between the two leaders and their military commanders were held on both ships over the following three days.

Roosevelt would do what he could to help Britain but was limited until the United States was ready to play a larger role. Being ready meant not only rearmament but also educating the US public on the danger of the Axis forces over the objections of America First isolationists. Roosevelt was resigned to the country's eventual entry into the war, but resisted Churchillian high oratory to persuade him to intervene immediately. He was deeply impressed with Churchill's courage and tenacity, his remarkable intellect, and his ability to place

---

74   Nigel Hamilton, *The Mantle of Command* (Boston: Mariner Books, 2014), 10.

the problems of the world within a wider historic and moral frame-
work.[75] Roosevelt and Churchill agreed to work closely together, which
was not a foregone conclusion. At the end of the meetings on August 12
their agreements were recorded in a document that became known as
the Atlantic Charter.

The position for Roosevelt to take in the Charter was a delicate
one. To state anything in the charter that could be seized upon as an
alliance with Great Britain would bring down the wrath of America
First. Beyond the commitment to fight the Nazi tyranny, Roosevelt
and Churchill agreed that at the end of the war all oppressed nations
would be restored to self-rule and have a democratic government of the
people.[76] Considering that the United States was not even in the war
at that point and that Nazi Germany was still riding high and possibly
victorious, it was a remarkable statement. They also agreed to oppose
territorial changes. Compared to the wholesale territorial changes
effected during the Paris Peace Conference of 1919 and the long-term
repercussions that followed, this was a fortuitous agreement.

Although never signed by either Roosevelt or Churchill, this "working
paper" thereafter became the policy of both nations for the conduct of
the war. Calculated to bolster the morale of British citizens and people
of occupied countries, the Atlantic Charter communicated a lofty
resolution: "the final destruction of the Nazi tyranny." The final draft was
edited by Roosevelt and Welles sitting together in the admiral's cabin
aboard *Augusta*.

Under Secretary Welles and Sir Alexander Cadogan, Under Secretary
of the Foreign Office and Welles' opposite number, had a conversation
on a matter that was not included in the Atlantic Charter and was undisclosed at the time. The United States became "fully aware that Churchill's
main purpose in crossing the Atlantic was to engage the United States in a

---

75   Hamilton, *Mantle of Command*, 27-28.

76   Kaiser, 273-274.

joint warning to Japan: if it continued its aggression, war would be inevitable."[77] Churchill wished to make Roosevelt aware that Britain's survival depended not only on the defense of the British Isles but on its worldwide network of supply lines. Britain could not withstand a Japanese attack on its Far East positions alone, and Churchill wanted a commitment from Roosevelt that the United States would go to war with Japan if Japan went to war with Britain. It was for that reason that he wanted the joint warning to Japan. Roosevelt preferred a parallel warning to a joint warning. He pledged that upon returning to Washington he would summon Japanese Ambassador Nomura and hand him a note detailing US actions leading to war if Japan continued its aggression. Even this parallel warning to Japan would commit the United States to counter Japan if it took military action against Britain's interests in the Far East.

In the absence of a reply from Tokyo regarding Roosevelt's proposal for a Japanese withdrawal from southern Indochina, Acheson began a total freeze on Japanese funds. This resulted in an effective embargo on the sale of oil to Japan. In violation of Roosevelt's policy and Welles' directive, the hyperaggressive Acheson used legal or other devices to ensure that funds from blocked dollar accounts were not released to complete any transactions, including purchases of oil. Acheson believed that pressure would force Japan to knuckle under to US demands. Secretary Hull, ill when the freeze began, was not aware of Acheson's actions until early September.[78] The British government and the Dutch government-in-exile, operating from London, also were persuaded to join the freeze. For the Dutch it meant violating an existing economic treaty with Japan which included the sale of oil from the East Indies.

The consensus among the cabinet members of the War Council was that a freeze ultimately would force Japan into a position of economic constriction and weaken their military prowess. A notable exception

---

77   Benjamin Welles, *Sumner Welles, FDR's Global Strategist*, St. Martin's Press, New York, 302.

78   Hotta, *Japan 1941*, 151.

to this view was Ambassador Grew in Tokyo. Grew informed the State Department that the Japanese government, in response to US pressure, was "converting into a state-directed economy" and the belief that "a war in the Far East could best be averted by sanctions or even a blockade was not supported by facts he observed."[79] Grew stated that it would not work in the short run because the Japanese government would impose sacrifices on the civilian sector that would allow the armed forces to remain viable. If the economic pressure continued, war was the likely result.

In Japan, news of the freeze and effective embargo of petroleum came as a surprise. On August 6 a reply came from Tokyo to Roosevelt's proposal of a neutralized Indochina. Japan would withdraw from Indochina upon settlement of the China Incident and asked for the "good offices" of the United States to help accomplish it. Japan also asked for a resumption of normal trade between the two countries, and neutrality for the Philippines. They asked that there be no buildup of US forces in the Pacific and requested that the United States advise the British and Dutch to take similar steps. The Japanese, now desperate to stop the endless casualties that were occurring in China, had foolishly tied the neutralization of Indochina to their China War problem. The reply constituted a rejection of Roosevelt's proposal.

Two days later, on August 8, Prince Konoe, acting through Ambassador Nomura to Secretary Hull, requested a summit meeting with Roosevelt. Coming on the heels of their rejection of the Indochina neutralization proposal, it was not clear what they had to discuss. However, one can surmise that the military members of the cabinet were behind the rejection, and that Konoe had not agreed with it. Konoe clearly realized that the invasion of southern Indochina had been a huge mistake, and he must make a major move to avoid further deterioration in Japan's relationship with the United States. He was unable to win in

---

79   Joseph Grew, "Monthly Report of Conditions During the Month of July, 1941," in Miller, *Bankrupting*, 225.

a confrontation with the generals, so he took the unprecedented step of moving outside normal diplomatic procedures to request a direct, one-on-one meeting with Roosevelt.

Prince Konoe had been part of the diplomatic world since the end of the Great War and knew, or had connections with, many of the important world figures. As a person from a high aristocratic background who moved easily in the world of trusted equals, he saw in the patrician Roosevelt someone with whom he could meet and resolve matters. Although both army and navy senior representatives would be part of a Japanese summit delegation, Konoe was sure he could find an opportunity to end-run the narrow-minded generals and reach an agreement with Roosevelt. Once such an agreement was reached it would not be overturned. Ironically, at the time of his request for a meeting with Roosevelt, Roosevelt himself was meeting with Churchill on ships of their respective navies in an atmosphere of trusted equals, similar to the one Konoe envisioned for Roosevelt and himself.

During much of this crucial period the sickly Secretary of State Hull was absent, and Roosevelt had departed on August 3 for two weeks to meet Prime Minister Churchill. Hull, staying in touch remotely, received the August 8 note from Ambassador Nomura and responded unenthusiastically to the request, stating that more junior officials of the two governments would have to agree on basic principles before any meeting of leaders could take place.[80]

Meanwhile, the Acheson oil embargo continued. Japan had two primary sources of dollar funds needed to complete oil purchases: dollars on deposit in US financial institutions, which could be transferred to pay for oil only with Acheson's approval, and the sale to the US Treasury of a portion of the sizable gold hoard in the vaults of the Bank of Japan in Tokyo. Sales of gold had taken place periodically in the past as shipments were sent across the Pacific by steamship.

---

80   Kaiser, *No End*, 279.

However, Acheson let it be known there would be no more purchases of gold. There was nothing partial or flexible about the freeze. He was determined to make it complete. Acheson intended to shut down the Japanese economy, both civilian and military, and move Japan into an economic and military crisis.

Roosevelt returned from his meeting with Churchill in mid-August and, upon being informed of the actions regarding the freeze, was reluctant to modify the practice without appearing to appease Japan. The Economic Defense Board, the senior entity to Acheson's FFCC, composed of cabinet officers and chaired by Vice President Henry Wallace, took no action. Roosevelt could have advised Wallace to investigate the matter while staying out of it himself, but he did not do so.

The Japanese government attempted to persuade the Netherlands government-in-exile to reconsider its revocation of the economic treaty. The sale of a modest amount of oil was a possible solution to the impasse between Japan and the United States. The Dutch East Indies was capable of supplying approximately twice the needs of Japan.[81] Because of the US-imposed asset freeze on Japan, such sales would have to be on credit, secured by a claim on the gold in the Japanese central bank. Repayment would be made when the asset freeze was modified or canceled.

It was fine for the United Sates to declare an asset freeze from distant Washington, but the Dutch East Indies were in the crosshairs of the Japanese armed forces. The Dutch might have considered that selling oil, even on credit, was preferable to the wholesale destruction and loss of thousands of lives that would follow from a Japanese invasion. No doubt feeling pressure by its exile location in the shadow of Downing Street, as well as by their relationship with the Roosevelt administration,

---

81   Miller, *Bankrupting*, 158.

the Dutch-in-exile rejected any discussion of an oil sale to Japan, despite the existing treaty.[82]

Willingness to allow a modest flow of oil could have precluded the Japanese invasions. It also would have removed the threat of Japanese economic collapse. The Japanese pro-war faction, which advocated striking quickly before their forces were immobilized for lack of oil, would have lost a key argument. The anti-war faction within the Japanese government might have won the internal debate. If the Dutch had avoided invasion by supplying a limited amount of oil, a scheduled withdrawal from southern Indochina, together with an agreement to resolve the war in China, was a logical next step. It also was a way to avoid the United States seeming to appease Japan by easing the embargo, and a more astute State Department might have lent covert support for this arrangement. The war between Japan and the United States might have been avoided.

A fallback possibility for Japan after everything else failed was a limited invasion of a minimum number of islands of just the Dutch East Indies, on the rationale that they were merely enforcing their treaty rights. In this circumstance, Japan would have made its movements known publicly, and their armed forces would have scrupulously avoided contact with the territory of any other nation or jurisdiction while they secured a limited amount of oil. Had they taken this action, the Roosevelt administration might have found it difficult to mobilize public opinion to defend the Pacific colony of a European country, particularly one operating in exile, and when there was the rationale of a previous treaty. Japan would have to accept the risk of intervention of their shipments near the Philippines, which was on the route between the East Indies and the home country. Even the risk of a possible intervention and loss of a ship would not be great in the larger context. However, none of this happened, and the Pacific nations moved toward war.

---

82   Willmott, 63, fn.

In a move best described as suicidal, the Netherlands government declared war on Japan on December 8, 1941, a day after the attack on Pearl Harbor. The Japanese invaded Borneo a week later and occupied the entire island, including North Borneo, Sarawak, and Brunei, that were protectorates of Britain. The rest of the island was a protectorate of the Netherlands. Within a matter of weeks, the Japanese also occupied the other Dutch islands, resulting in the predictable thousands killed and untold hardship and misery for the survivors during the years of Japanese occupation.

In the Inland Sea of Japan, Combined Fleet commander Admiral Yamamoto was doing his part for war preparations. Aware of the possibility of war with the United States since the signing of the Tripartite Pact in 1940, Yamamoto had prepared the forces under his command to create an option to be employed should that become the desired course of action. He was not in favor of war and did not think Japan could prevail in a long war with the United States. However, he believed that if war came, Japan's only chance for success was a big victory at the very outset to bring about negotiations.[83] The attack on the Pacific Fleet at Pearl Harbor by Japan's formidable carrier force was Yamamoto's plan for the big victory Japan needed. In late 1941 the last two of the six carriers of the Striking Force would join the fleet. If war came, all six carriers would be used in a powerful, devastating attack.

Ambassador Nomura was able to meet with Roosevelt and Hull on August 17, and because of the urgency communicated by Toyoda, they met on a Sunday afternoon. Nomura repeated the earlier message, requesting a summit meeting between Konoe and Roosevelt, and proposed Hawaii as a site. A meeting outside Japan for a Japanese prime minister, particularly on Hawaii, being US soil, was unprecedented, and was an indication of the urgency Konoe attempted to communicate. In reply, Roosevelt

---

83   Hotta, *Japan 1941*, 105.

expressed his displeasure with Japan's occupation of southern Indochina, and, as copied to Ambassador Grew, warned that:

> [I]f the Japanese Government takes any further steps in pursuance of a policy or program of military domination by force or threat of force of neighboring countries, the Government of the United States will be compelled to take immediately any and all steps which it may deem necessary toward safeguarding the legitimate rights and interests of the United States . . .[84]

Having made his point, Roosevelt replied that Hawaii was too far for him to travel and suggested they meet in Juneau, Alaska, instead. Juneau also would be closer for Konoe. By warning Japan in the formal note against any further military action, he was playing for time, as he had told Churchill at Newfoundland he would do. But, with Acheson's asset freeze in place, the warning he communicated to Nomura produced the opposite result he hoped for from the pro-war elements in Japan. Roosevelt was now convinced that Japan was going to attack the Dutch East Indies, and he had decided to go to war if they did.[85] Whether circumstances would change between the time he decided on such action and the time action was required could not be assured.

Secretaries Hull and Stimson disliked the idea of a Konoe-Roosevelt summit. Hull saw Konoe in deep conflict with the Japanese army and thought he lacked the power to effect a resolution at a summit with Roosevelt. He did not believe that a summit was a plausible way for Konoe to end-run the army and achieve a fait accompli that would bind the entire government, including the armed forces. Stimson, a committed China advocate, was concerned that Roosevelt, in a meeting with Konoe, would make concessions harmful to China.

---

84   Foreign Policy of the United States Diplomatic Papers, Vol IV, The Far East, Chapter III, 1941, Message 266.

85   Kaiser, *No End*, 279.

On August 18 Roosevelt briefed congressional leaders on the results of the Atlantic Conference. Among other points, he reported that the Russians had held out longer against the German invasion than originally expected, and this was a reprieve for the British. He saw Asia as the most likely area for military action involving the United States because it was likely that Japan might embark on further aggression.[86] The current spate of good news from the Russian front, however, did not change the overall strategy of recognizing Hitler as the primary threat. The best course of action was still to prevent the United States from getting embroiled in a conflict with Japan when a turn of events could produce a new crisis in Europe that the United States then would be less able to confront. This was a complicated and possibly conflicting set of priorities, as he perceived Asia as the more likely to see armed conflict but Europe still ultimately the greater danger.

The US oil embargo meant that Japan had to go south to the East Indies to get oil, and this presumably would preclude an invasion of Siberia. However, the pro-war army elements also knew a two-front war likely would finish Russia. Despite the army's rejection of Matsuoka's demand that they invade Siberia when Hitler invaded Russia in June, it did not eliminate the possibility of a Siberian invasion if circumstances changed. The possibility of finishing Russia was so attractive to the pro-war army elements that they could reverse their earlier aversion to Siberia and launch an attack. The army was watching the progress of the German offensive approaching Moscow, and, quite apart from the impending shortage of oil, a defeat of Russia in the west would be the signal for an attack on Siberia.[87]

A Siberian attack would have to begin by the end of August for troops to not be caught in the Siberian winter.[88] In mid-August the Kwantung Army ordered hundreds of thousands of Japanese troops loaded onto

86   Kaiser, *No End*, 280.

87   Matthews, *Impeccable Spy*, 313.

88   Matthews, *Impeccable Spy*, 304.

trains for Manchuria. Plans were made for shipping 100,000 tons of military arms and equipment. Movements of this magnitude could not be made secretly, and Stalin would have been aware of this development. August 1941 was the most perilous time for Russia in the entire war.

The most successful spy in the war on any side was Richard Sorge, a German and Nazi Party member operating as a journalist in Tokyo, but in fact working for Russia. Sorge was a wounded veteran of the Great War who had come to believe in communism, and this belief determined his ultimate loyalty. He built a small spy network in Tokyo, and through various sources uncovered the date of Operation Barbarossa, which he reported to Stalin.[89] Opinions differ on whether Stalin believed Sorge's information about Barbarossa, but when it turned out to be true it added credibility to other important information from Sorge. His standing with Stalin was enhanced, and Sorge established himself as a reliable source for later crucial intelligence transmissions.

Sorge was the potential target of three counterspy investigations. The German Gestapo was suspicious of his activities, and Colonel Joseph Meisinger, for good reasons known as the Butcher of Warsaw, was sent to Tokyo to investigate. The Russian NKVD was checking to determine the true loyalties of Sorge, and any significant suspicion would have resulted in Sorge's elimination. Finally, the Japanese secret police were aware of illegal coded radio transmissions, and its agents were suspicious of Sorge and other members of his network. Sorge was able to elude all these operations by complicated maneuverings, alcoholic seductions, and lies for several years, during which he played a crucial role in the outcome of the war.

Sorge had his circle of spies following the Japanese move to Manchuria, collecting every available scrap of information. Finally, on September 14, a member of the Sorge ring returned from Manchuria with the information that the Japanese buildup in Manchuria was being reversed. A

89   Matthews, 281.

message went to Stalin with that crucial information.[90] This was the most important intelligence information that any spy in the war obtained.

Exactly what produced this sudden turnaround by the Japanese army is not possible to identify exactly, but there had been earlier discussions in army circles that Japan would not invade Siberia until they were sure of a German win in the west. News of the slowing German advance may have reached the Japanese generals, causing them to pull back and not have their troops in Siberia be exposed to Russian eastward troop movements if the German attack in the west were stopped. The entire Japanese move to Manchuria may have been a feint to hold Russian troops in Siberia while the German army captured Moscow. If that was the motive, they did not hold their Manchurian position long enough. Stalin, with the information from Sorge and confident that no attack could be made after mid-September, began transferring his forces to the west. By the first week of December, 18 divisions of troops, 1,500 tanks, and 1,700 planes had been moved west to defend Moscow.[91]

---

90   Matthews, *Impeccable Spy*, 316-17.

91   Matthews, *Impeccable Spy*, 317.

Assistant Secretary of State Dean Acheson
Photo Public Domain, wikpedia.org

Ambassador Joseph C. Grew
Photo Library of Congress

CHAPTER 9

Muddled Diplomacy

In Tokyo, the cabinet held a meeting on August 27–28, 1941, to hear the conclusions of the Total War Research Institute.[92] The Institute, formed in April 1941, was composed of thirty-six of the brightest and most promising younger, midlevel persons from various government departments and agencies. Only four were from the armed forces—two from the army, two from the navy.

The purpose of the Institute was to analyze Japan's situation regarding the prospect of war with the United States and determine the most probable outcome. It was authorized to make observations and recommendations based on objective analysis, not politics. For the first several months, the members of the Institute researched Japan's industrial and economic position and that of potential adversaries. This was followed by visits to army and navy operating forces, including an underway exercise beginning in the Inland Sea on the Combined Fleet flagship of Admiral Yamamoto.

Returning to Tokyo, Institute members concluded that Japan might win some initial battles, but it could not prevail in a long war against the United States. The United States had an industrial capacity twenty times that of Japan. Even though in 1941 Japan had the world's most powerful navy, eventually it would be overwhelmed. To break the oil embargo, the Institute researchers speculated that Japan might be tempted to

---

92   Hotta, *Japan 1941*, 164.

invade the Dutch East Indies. Such an action would be repelled by the United States and make war inevitable. Russia would then exploit the situation for its own benefit. Therefore, going to war with the United States must be avoided absolutely. Diplomacy was the only option that would not result in a defeated Japan.

This sobering analysis was not just delivered in a summary report of final conclusions in a single one-hour meeting. On the contrary, over two days the members of the Institute reviewed the source data, analytical techniques, and methods of comprehensive integration that they used to reach their final conclusions. Their work was irrefutable. The serious conundrum facing Japan was the ongoing gradual strangulation from Acheson's total embargo of exports if they took no action, and an inevitable defeat by the United States if they fought to obtain alternative sources. Diplomacy was the only answer. Being obsessed with details, no one worked harder to understand this work product than Army Minister Tojo, who took copious notes over the two-day presentation. Prime Minister Konoe accepted this analysis and was determined to do everything in his power to achieve a one-on-one meeting with President Roosevelt.

Konoe realized that diplomatic relations had reached a climax. Not only was a meeting with Roosevelt the best chance to avoid a war with the United States, but his total commitment to scheduling such a meeting, should he fail, would probably result in the collapse of his government. What would happen after that was unknowable, but an assertive military dictatorship was the most probable. A summit with President Roosevelt was the best chance to avoid a Pacific War, but in the face of the intransigent War Council around Roosevelt, this opportunity would wither and die. Even Roosevelt himself, thinking of the developing mobilization of US forces, did not appreciate the full implications of the urgency, even desperation, of Prince Konoe's request for a summit meeting.

On August 28 Ambassador Nomura delivered a second message from Konoe to Roosevelt, this one in English. The message was not written in the usual stilted diplomatic prose, but rather in the first person singular. It began by stating that discussions between the diplomats of their two countries were not satisfactory in the rapidly developing circumstances. It continued:

> I consider it, therefore, of urgent necessity that the two heads of the Governments should meet first to discuss from a broad standpoint all important problems between Japan and America covering the entire Pacific area, and to explore the possibility of saving the situation. Adjustment of minor items may, if necessary, be left to negotiations between competent officials of the two countries. Because of the nature of the meeting as stated above, I prefer that it will take place as soon as possible.[93]

Roosevelt received the message warmly and again suggested Juneau as a meeting place. Nomura suggested September 21 to 25 as dates for such a meeting, and Roosevelt was impressed with "the tone and spirit" of the message, that he was "very hopeful," and that he was "keenly interested in having three or four days with Prince Konoe."[94] Nomura thought he had communicated the urgency of the matter to Roosevelt and had reason to believe a summit meeting of Roosevelt and Konoe would take place in Juneau around the dates suggested. Roosevelt trusted Hull to move forward with the summit arrangements.

Immediately after the meeting with Roosevelt, Nomura met with Hull. Instead of assisting Roosevelt with moving forward on a summit, Hull reverted to the traditional process of diplomacy. Before proceeding further, Hull wanted clarification of Japan's commitment to

---

93   "Papers Relating to the Foreign Relations of the United States, Japan, 1931-1941, Vol. II," Document 317, Office of the Historian, Department of State, https://history.state.gov/historicaldocuments/frus1931-41v02/d317.

94   Hotta, *Japan 1941*, 161.

the Tripartite Pact and Japan's troops in China and Mongolia, as well as Indochina. Despite Konoe's strong statement about the urgency of the matter and Roosevelt's initial agreement to meet, Hull wanted diplomatic officials of the two countries to schedule meetings to resolve details on these outstanding issues and come to agreements.[95] Once this had been accomplished the two national leaders would appear to ratify agreements that had been reached by the junior diplomats. Considering the positive tone of communications between Konoe and Roosevelt, and the emphasis on timely scheduling, this quash by Hull constituted a reversal of progress and lowered the prospect of a peaceful resolution between Japan and the United States.

In view of Konoe's persistent requests for a summit meeting with Roosevelt through the month of August and Roosevelt's agreeing in principle to meet in Juneau during September 21-25, why didn't Roosevelt insist on moving ahead with the summit instead of allowing Hull to crush it with procedural roadblocks? Roosevelt had stated to Churchill at their summit at Newfoundland earlier in August that he would "baby the Japanese along" as a way of playing for time. Despite the desperate tone of Konoe's most recent note, Roosevelt did not appreciate the very short time frame Konoe was attempting to communicate. The US armed services chiefs continued to emphasize that they needed time to build their forces, but they also stated clearly that a war with Japan was to be avoided. In these circumstances Delay became the policy, and having Hull handle it was acceptable because it would involve him going through the motions of formal diplomatic procedures. Delay also fit the agenda of Roosevelt's War Council, who were heavily biased toward China and were dismissive and seemingly unaware of the human and financial costs of a war with Japan.

An agreement that would settle issues with Japan would have been a better strategy than delaying matters that would result in escalations and

---

95   Hotta, *Japan 1941*, 162.

unpredictable actions. Delay was not a winning strategy, and Roosevelt was ill-served by the civilian War Council of Hull, Stimson, Knox, and their advisers. The pro-China, anti-Japan bias of Stimson and Hull and the pro-war sentiments of Stimson and Knox were powerful influences on Roosevelt that argued against accommodations with Japan—and that included a summit meeting with Prince Konoe. Roosevelt's style was not to confront others directly. Hull was not moved by the strongly stated messages from the Japanese prime minister and further articulated by the Japanese ambassador. He had expressed doubts about Konoe's power to effect a meaningful agreement, and this was consistent with the strategy of Delay.

The failure to recognize the sincere and urgent message from Prime Minister Konoe was a tragic oversight. In view of the total freeze of Japanese assets and effective embargo of oil, the time frame of conventional diplomacy, including consultations with allies, had no chance of success. Japan was heading for a crisis, and if Hull and his staff had evaluated the effects of the embargo on Japan, they would have known that. Ambassador Grew had consistently argued against postponement. Nomura could not explain more of the urgency of the Japanese situation without getting into military matters, and he himself was kept in the dark about specific plans. At one point Roosevelt and Konoe had agreed in principle to meet in Juneau around September 21-25. Had that meeting been held, resolution might have been achieved and the Pacific War avoided.

Ambassador Nomura followed established diplomatic procedures by initiating communications with the secretary of state of his host country. Unfortunately, this placed the crucially important relationship in the hands of a person whose previous experience left him woefully unqualified to deal with it. Roosevelt might have preferred that the contact be made with Sumner Welles, but Nomura had correctly approached Hull, and Welles' relationship with Hull was problematic because of Roosevelt's obvious preference for him on previous occasions. Admiral

Leahy, who was a highly valued advisor to Roosevelt and who would later return, was still in Vichy. Nomura's approach left the matter in Hull's hands. The Japanese cabinet had moved from the belligerent confrontation of the Matsuoka period to the quest for accommodation that followed Matsuoka's departure and the report of the Total War Research Institute. Hull, overwhelmed with the trappings of his office, including his staff, and by the influence of the other pro-China War Council members, failed to understand the shift in Japanese policy.

One of the curious aspects of Roosevelt's long tenure in office was his leaving persons in high appointive office for long periods regardless of the reasons for their initial appointments. Cabinet secretaries appointed in 1933 following Roosevelt's first inauguration, such as Cordell Hull at State, Harold Ickes at Interior, and Frances Perkins at Labor, served right through to the end of Roosevelt's presidency in 1945. Henry Morgenthau, appointed treasury secretary in 1934, also served until 1945. Although Hull was useful in the 1932 election, his reward—appointment as Secretary of State—had long since been satisfied and was hardly relevant in 1941. Meanwhile, he was still there, and would be fundamental to the decisions that determined whether there would be war or peace in the Pacific.

Roosevelt enjoyed a cocktail hour in the afternoons with a group of friendly compatriots that included Cordell Hull, Henry Stimson, Frank Knox, Harold Ickes, sometimes Harry Hopkins, and occasionally others. It was a time for jokes and quips. Roosevelt mixed the drinks, and when there was a particularly good joke or pithy remark, Roosevelt typically would laugh and wave his cigarette holder, making rejoinders such as, "I love it!" Stimson was arguably the senior member of this group, not just in age but in having begun his long career in public service in 1911. Whether by happenstance or design, the pro-war elements, including Stimson and Knox, were heavily represented in the afternoon cocktail group. How much the views of the afternoon cocktail group affected the outcome of world events is one of the imponderables of history.

The armed forces leaders, such as Admiral Stark and General Marshall, were not part of the afternoon cocktail group. They were seen when invited to formal meetings of the War Council. They counseled that the country was not ready for war with Japan and the focus should be on the greatest threat, Nazi Germany. This position was, in effect, a qualified endorsement of the Delay policy, but unlike the civilian members of the War Council they were adamantly opposed to war with Japan.

For Prince Konoe to achieve a diplomatic solution was complicated. Even an attempt to achieve a unified position exposed the contradictions and rivalries in the Japanese government. There was a rivalry between the civilian and military sectors of the government, as shown by the power of the military to bring down a government if the civilians took actions contrary to their views. There was a bitter rivalry within the armed forces between the army and the navy, which had at its core a battle for power in the government. This showed itself in a debate over the allocation of resources—primarily steel and oil. Further, within each armed service there were moderates, who saw the need for diplomacy to avoid a war with the United States, and hardliners, who believed the power of the samurai fighting spirit would overcome any material and resource imbalance. Within the latter group were those who would rather fight and die in a glorious defeat than succumb to the humiliation of slow strangulation from an embargo. Finally, there were contradictions within individuals, who in large meetings boisterously and confidently advocated aggressive actions, and later privately admitted to close confidants their concerns about Japan's ability to win a war with the United States. The public bravado was most evident when important decisions were made in large or important group meetings, such as Imperial Conferences. These decisions were then difficult to reverse or even modify as circumstances or opinions changed because of the Imperial Mandate attached to such decisions.

To arrive at a policy that could satisfy these diverse and constantly changing positions within the government was very difficult. Konoe made a huge effort to bypass all these conflicting elements by doing everything he could to have a one-on-one summit meeting with Roosevelt. Having been rebuffed by Hull, Konoe and his advisers struggled to reply to Hull's demands with points that would be approved by the armed forces. The position that was approved on August 29 provided that Japan would withdraw from China, without specifying a timetable, that it would not revoke the Tripartite Pact—a point insisted upon by the army—but it clarified the pact so that Japan would not be committed to a war with the United States if the United States became involved in a war with Germany.[96]

Staying in the Tripartite Pact was an unfortunate situation for Japan. The assault on Russia had changed the basis of the pact, but the army would not agree to a revocation. The Russian assault marked the time when Germany and Japan took different courses. However, Hull viewed the pact that Japan had with Adolf Hitler—the most hateful aggressor on the planet—in a very negative light and was highly inflexible in discussions with Nomura because of it.

On September 3 Nomura received an invitation to meet at the White House with Roosevelt and Hull to receive the official US response to his August 8 request for a meeting between the president and the prime minister. Roosevelt's War Council had persuaded him that Prince Konoe lacked the power to effect an agreement. In the official reply to Prince Konoe, Roosevelt said:

> At this particular moment I cannot avoid taking cognizance
> of indications of the existence in some quarters in Japan of
> concepts which, if widely entertained, would seem capable of
> raising obstacles to successful collaboration between you and
> me along the line which I am sure we both earnestly desire to
> follow. Under these circumstances I feel constrained to suggest

---

96   Hotta, *Japan 1941*, 162-63.

that . . . [we] enter immediately upon preliminary discussions
of the fundamental and essential questions . . .[97]

The substance of discussion had gone, yet again, from agenda points to be agreed at a summit meeting of leaders, followed by detailed resolutions in meetings of the respective junior diplomats, to negotiations by the junior diplomats who then would present their agreements for ratification by the leaders. The latter procedure in this circumstance would accomplish nothing.

In addition to the formal reply, an oral statement to Nomura referred to the Four Principles to maintain peace that the Secretary of State had put forward on April 16, and to which he insisted Japan should agree: respect for the territorial integrity and sovereignty of each and all nations, support for the principle of noninterference in the internal affairs of other countries, support for the principle of equality, including equality of commercial opportunity, and non-disturbance of the status quo in the Pacific, except as the status quo may be altered by peaceful means. In addition, Hull referred to other items contained in a document dated June 21, all of which required resolution before productive negotiations could take place. In Hull's Memorandum of Conversation of the meeting, he stated that, in addition to all the above, it would be necessary to discuss the matter fully with the British, the Chinese, and the Dutch.

The overture from Konoe requested a one-on-one meeting with Roosevelt. It did not suggest including the heads of other countries. For Hull to state the need to consult with the British, Chinese, and Dutch was an unnecessary complication and was just an argument used to dissuade Roosevelt from moving forward with the meeting. Hull's excessive preoccupation with the British, Chinese, and Dutch in

---

97   "President Roosevelt's Reply to the Japanese Prime Minister (Prince Konoye), Handed to the Japanese Ambassador (Nomura) on September 3, 1941," Papers Relating to the Foreign Relations of the United States, Japan, 1931-1941, Volume II, Document 329, Department of State, Office of the Historian, accessed Jun 8, 2022, https://history.state.gov/historicaldocuments/frus1931-41v02/d329.

virtually every decision that had any connection with them, however remote, throughout this difficult period characterized his diplomacy with the Japanese. He carried this view to such an extreme that he became a virtual prisoner of the countries he considered allies.

Hull assumed the motives of these other countries were the same as those of the United States, but they decidedly were not. The British wanted the United States in the European war and, short of that, a guarantee that the United States would join an Asian war if Japan attacked British interests in the Far East. Such an involvement, by one means or another, could then spread to US involvement in the European war. The Chinese simply wanted the United States in the war against Japan to add US manpower and armaments to their own defense. The Dutch, while fearful of a Japanese attack on their Pacific colonies, wanted to retain rights to their colonies and were in favor of policies they thought would support them.

Nomura's subsequent reply to Hull's objections was recorded in Hull's September 3 Memorandum of Conversation:

> [A] meeting between the President and the Prime Minister would enable Japan to overcome these disagreements at home and that the opposition would gradually get in line with the Government.

Such a meeting would involve a discussion of:

> [T]he complete evacuation of Japanese troops from China, the question of nondiscrimination in commerce . . . and the Tripartite Pact."

Despite Nomura's further attempts at clarification, the request for a summit meeting between Roosevelt and Konoe was rejected.[98] By this action, Hull, acting for the administration, was raising the issues of

---

98   Cordell Hull, Memorandum of Conversation, Document 90, Papers as President: President's Secretary's files.

internal Japanese politics, repeating issues of supplementary demands and the need to counsel with allies, all in a strategy of Delay. He tolerated Acheson's asset freeze and, whether by active support or by default, it became the policy of the government of the United States.

A day after the September 3 meeting, Ambassador Grew sent a telegram reflecting a conversation he had just had with Foreign Minister Toyoda about the urgent need for a meeting between the prime minister and the president. Grew communicated:

> [T]he desire of the Prime Minister and himself [Toyoda] to make every effort to bring about the proposed early meeting between the heads of the two governments and to make that meeting successful because if it should fail in achieving its fundamental object he feared that further efforts would be futile.[99]

The message continued with a series of issues that constituted an agenda for discussion by the two heads of government, including an interpretation of an article of the Tripartite Pact other than that placed upon it by Matsuoka, no further advance of Japanese armed forces beyond French Indochina, conditions for a withdrawal of armed forces from China, and the United States discontinuing the freezing order and withdrawing the prohibition on the use of the Panama Canal by Japanese ships.

The telegram concluded with a statement that the foreign minister understood Ambassador Nomura had seen the president again the previous day but that the ambassador's report of the conversation had not yet been received. Ambassador Grew added that he also was without information on that conversation. Whether an earlier meeting in Tokyo, followed by a report as above to Hull, could have made a difference is

---

99   Telegram from Ambassador Grew to Secretary Hull, September 4, 1941, Document 91, Papers as President: President's Secretary's Files.

left to sad speculation. The minds of Hull and the civilian War Council were clearly made up, and if Grew's message had changed their views they could have revised the September 3 statement. This was not done.

Impelled by the oil embargo and mindful of the huge naval mobilization in the United States that began in 1940 and was now gaining significant strength, the Japanese armed forces leaders were moving steadily toward war. They made a strong argument that time was not on their side, that the oil embargo was making them weaker, and the US mobilization was making the United States stronger. A deadline had to be established, and if diplomacy had not succeeded by a certain date, war would be launched. This was the lashing out, even if it proved to be suicidal, that Ambassador Grew had warned about.

The Japanese finance officials, having been denied the use of their funds deposited in US financial institutions or the sale of gold for dollars, finally devised an extensive barter proposal. They proposed a trade of a huge basket of commodities, primarily silk, for a list of items they desired from the United States, primarily oil. This proposal had a strong logic, as it built on the high volume of trade between Japan and the United States over many previous decades. The heavy volume of oil from the United States had been matched by the equally heavy export of Japanese silk. Silk was highly desired in the United States for hosiery and other uses. The Japanese finance officials held a series of discussions with Secretary Hull, who turned the matter over to the official least likely to approve it, Dean Acheson. Discussions continued until mid-September, when Acheson told Hull that such a transaction would be harmful to US foreign policy. Wallace declined to intervene, and Acheson informed the Japanese representatives that the United States had no interest in barter transactions. That was the final attempt by the Japanese to acquire oil from the United States.[100]

---

100   Miller, 212.

Now the Japanese were desperate; they had to get oil. Stockpiles in Japan would be drawn down, and everything that depended on oil in the domestic economy, as well as the army and navy, would stop. Japan was backed into a corner; they had to negotiate access to oil, or they would wage war to get it. The problem with the dual-track approach—diplomacy or war—was that the diplomatic option was necessarily a bilateral or even multilateral process. The war option was unilateral. If Japan decided to go to war, no agreement with any other party was required. If the armed forces were ordered to attack, they would do so. On the other side, the Acheson asset freeze/oil embargo also was unilateral. Acheson was unwilling to budge on the complete oil embargo, and no more senior person overruled him. Roosevelt had said early on that he wanted Japan brought to its senses, but hard-driving lawyer Acheson had spent twenty years bringing opponents to their knees, and to do otherwise was alien to his training and instincts.

In Tokyo no action was taken to avoid confrontation, and Emperor Hirohito realized he had been kept in the dark on the plans of the armed forces. Konoe suggested he call in his armed forces chiefs. In a meeting of these leaders with Konoe present, the forty-year-old emperor, in a rare show of incisiveness, asked General Sugiyama how long he estimated their planned war in the south would last:

> Sugiyama: Sir, we intend to complete [our mission] in the South Seas in three months.

> Hirohito: When the China Incident broke out you were our army minister. I remember you telling me then the conflict would be over in about a month. But after four long years, it hasn't ended.

> Sugiyama: China has a huge hinterland. That was why we couldn't carry out our plans as we had originally envisioned.

Hirohito: If you say that China has a huge hinterland, the Pacific Ocean is even bigger. On what basis are you telling me three months?

Sugiyama, deeply embarrassed, was at a loss for words.[101]

As the pro-war faction in the cabinet began to sense the withering of their power, they ironically became more assertive with their diplomatic demands in cabinet meetings. Following a September 20 liaison meeting, Toyoda sent a message to Nomura, perhaps motivated by the discussions in the meeting, that insisted the United States broker a peace between the puppet government of Wang Jingwei, which governed the Japanese-controlled areas of China, and Chiang Kai-shek. This was an unfortunate, unintelligent, and futile proposal. Chiang hated Wang, and the United States would never agree to broker a peace between the two.[102]

On September 27, Toyoda met with Ambassador Grew. He knew of Grew's close relationship with Roosevelt, and asked the ambassador to make a personal request for a summit meeting between Roosevelt and Konoe. There was the opportunity in such a communication from Grew to imply that Konoe was constricted by holdover staff from the Matsuoka period and would be able to make much more explicit proposals when meeting directly with Roosevelt. Unstated but implicit was the opportunity for the two leaders to form an understanding outside the approval process imposed by the Japanese armed forces.[103] Once an agreement was reached, the pressure would be on the armed forces to concede. Grew complied, and on September 29 sent a lengthy communication to that effect through official channels. In a paraphrase of the original text prepared by the State Department, Grew said:

---

101   Hotta, 174.
102   Hotta, 185.
103   Hotta, 189.

Germany's attack on the Soviet Union upset the basis of the Tripartite Pact . . . the Japanese Government, though refusing . . . that it will overtly renounce its alliance membership, actually has shown a readiness to reduce its adherence to a dead letter.

[W]hen the Konoye-Toyoda government began last July, American diplomacy obtained a very active new lease on life . . . United States policy has helped to discredit [previous] Japanese leadership, notably that of former Foreign Minister Matsuoka.

American policy of forbearance, patient augmentation, and efforts at persuasion. . . may bring about . . . a complete readjustment of relations between Japan and the United States.[104]

Grew also explained that explicit public statements from Prince Konoe could arouse violent opposition from hardline elements on the fringes of power:

Should the United States expect or await . . . clear cut commitments . . . the conversations will drag along indefinitely . . . until the Konoye cabinet . . . will come to the conclusion . . . that the United States Government is only playing for time . . . The logical outcome of this will be the downfall of the Konoye government.

Japan's future objectives [as stated] . . . are so abstract and equivocal . . . that they create confusion . . . Prince Konoye is in a position in direct negotiations with President Roosevelt to offer him assurances which . . . will not fail to satisfy the United States.

---

104   Joseph C. Grew, *Ten Years In Japan* (Simon and Schuster, New York, 1944), 436-442.

Ambassador Grew's lengthy and very carefully considered communication, more than four pages, on September 29 had no effect on Hull. Instead, in a meeting with Nomura on October 2, Hull repeated the Four Principles he insisted Japan recognize. In addition, he wanted to know the status of Japan's withdrawal from Indochina and China and, most important, clarify its position regarding other Axis powers— meaning the other members of the Tripartite Pact. Following normal protocol, a communication from an ambassador must go through the Secretary of State. It is unfortunate that in this single case Grew did not make an exception and, building on his personal relationship with Roosevelt going back to Groton and Harvard, had not written directly to Roosevelt in a message "for your eyes only." This was a major lost opportunity, and there would not be another one.

On October 6 Ambassador Grew sent a lengthy report to Secretary Hull that showed a significant contraction in the Japanese economy:

> *Various reports point toward [a] progressive decline [in] industrial production chiefly due to scarcity [of] supplies . . . freezing orders have isolated Japan from practically all foreign markets . . . iron fences around government and large business quarters have disappeared . . . [silkworm] cocoon production down twenty-seven percent . . . [as a result of] decreased acreage of mulberry farms caused by conversion into cereal production.[105]*

It takes little imagination to realize that the asset freeze was taking a heavy toll on the Japanese economy, on the life of Japanese citizens, and ultimately on the armed forces. How long the Japanese leadership would tolerate this, and what actions they would take, are matters Hull and his advisers might have considered but clearly did not.

---

105   Message from Grew to Hull, October 6, 1941. Document 101, Papers of Henry Morgenthau, Jr.

To understand Ambassador Grew's views on the crucial importance of the proposed summit meeting, it is necessary to look ahead to
a document dated August 14, 1942.[106] It is a thirteen-page letter from
Grew to President Roosevelt, composed as a cover letter to Grew's
final State Department report. Grew wrote the letter while aboard *S.S.
Gripsholm*, a Swedish passenger vessel chartered by the US government
to effect an exchange of diplomats who were held in countries that had
become adversaries. The letter is among the papers of Ambassador
Grew that he donated to Harvard University and which are located in
Harvard's Houghton Library. A notation at the bottom of the first page
indicates that the letter possibly was composed as of February 19, 1942,
but not finalized until later. A small handwritten notation in pencil at
the top of the first page states, "not sent."

The letter is addressed, "Dear Mr. President." It refers to an appended
report, Grew's "final political report from Tokyo, covering the period
immediately prior to the outbreak of war." The letter itself discusses whether
the war with Japan could have been avoided. Central to this question is
Grew's anguished disappointment regarding the failure to agree to Prince
Konoe's plea for a summit meeting with President Roosevelt:

> *Japan during the summer and autumn of 1941 found herself in
> an increasingly precarious position . . . Prince Konoe was the
> only Japanese statesman capable of reversing the engine, and
> this he did his best to accomplish.*

> *Prince Konoe chose to follow a program of peace. He was
> supported not only by the Emperor, but also by the highest
> responsible officers of the military and naval commands. With
> this support Prince Konoe was convinced, and I so informed
> our government, that the military hot-heads and other
> extremists in the country could and would be controlled if he*

---

106   Joseph C. Grew Papers, Houghton Library, Harvard University.

could come to an agreement with the United States at that moment, before the opposition of those extremist elements . . . had sufficiently organized to overturn his Government and torpedo the conversations. Time was of the essence.
Prince Konoe was pinning all his faith on this proposed meeting with you in Alaska and he had told me with unquestionable sincerity that he was prepared at that meeting to accept the American terms whatever they might be. In the opinion of former Prime Minister Hirota [Koki] and other influential Japanese at that time, "he could and would carry the entire Japanese nation."

On returning from Juneau, Prince Konoe would have been able to announce to the Japanese people that he had succeeded in assuring to them, without further force of arms . . . a prosperous future. It was clearly understood and admitted in Japan that the proposed agreement would inevitably entail the withdrawal of all Japanese troops from French Indochina and China . . . Japan's adherence to the Axis . . . would automatically become a dead letter.

The sort of agreement that was visualized would not have resulted in "selling China down the river," but on the contrary would have resulted in the greatest possible benefit to China.

Ambassador Grew recounted the chronology of events, raising some troubling questions:

On August 28 . . . you informed Admiral Nomura . . . "that you looked forward with real interest to the possibility of conferring for several days with the Japanese Prime Minister," with tentative dates set for September 21-23. Yet from that moment [there is] no further indication of any encouragement whatsoever to Prince Konoe with regard to the proposed meeting . . . It is my belief that the United States had everything to gain and nothing to lose by accepting Prince Konoe's

unqualified assurances that he would and could bring his
country to meet whatever requirements you might lay down . . .
and [move to] assured channels of peace instead of war . . .

The Japanese people had never been directly told of the great
advantages to them which would accrue from an agreement
with the United States. Instead, the oil embargo and Axis
propaganda has created the impression of US motivation to be
one of greed and control.

The failure of the United States to move ahead with the
meeting with Prince Konoe inevitably conveyed to him and his
associates the unfortunate impression that our Government
was merely playing for time and had no real intention to come
to an agreement with Japan. It was this impression which
finally brought about the fall of Prince Konoye's cabinet.

Following a final paragraph, the document closes, "I am, my dear Mr. President, Respectfully yours," and below is the handwritten signature "Joseph C. Grew."

For almost two weeks in early October, meetings of the Japanese cabinet took place with no change in the confusing and convoluted arguments. There were still the divisions between those advocating diplomacy and those advocating war, with shifting positions from day to day, from open meetings to private discussions, and from confidence in war to misgivings about it.

Konoe and Tojo continued their private conferences. In a particularly telling exchange, Tojo, again asserting that the September 6 Imperial Resolution for war was sacrosanct, said, "One must conjure up enough courage, close one's eyes, and jump off the platform of Kiyomizu," referring to the 300-year-old Kyoto temple of Kiyomizu-dera, built against a steep slope with a forty-foot drop on one side. Konoe replied,

[J]umping into the abyss was all well and good if one were talking only about oneself, but if I think of the national polity that has lasted twenty-six hundred years and of the hundred million Japanese belonging to this nation, I, as a person in the position of great responsibility, cannot do such a thing.[107]

Finally, on October 14, Konoe met with Tojo prior to a cabinet meeting and tried to persuade him to accept a troop withdrawal:

I suggest that we now concede to the US withdrawal formula and avoid opening fire between Japan and the US. We really need to end the China Incident. Japan's future growth is doubtless desirable, but in order to make a great leap we must sometimes concede to greater forces so that we can preserve and nurture our national strength.[108]

Tojo asserted that, in the aftermath of Konoe's failure to secure a meeting with President Roosevelt, the cabinet had lost faith in Konoe's leadership. The United States was seen as merely playing for time, and Konoe was gullible by tolerating it. He pushed for Konoe's resignation.

Whatever Konoe's personal preferences had been, the war in China had begun while his government was in power and had been going on for four years. Konoe had been prime minister for three of those years. The army had suffered huge casualties in China and was looking for a way out. Relationships with the western powers had reached a difficult stage, and the army's invasion of southern Indochina had made those relationships worse. His appointment of Matsuoka as foreign minister had been a disastrous decision, and his plea for a meeting with President Roosevelt had failed. Konoe may have decided that his association with the war in China made resolution of that issue impossible, and Japan's

---

best hope now for avoiding war with the United States was for him to get out of the way.

On October 16, 1941, the Konoe cabinet resigned, and on the next day, October 17, the emperor appointed General Tojo as prime minister. At that very time President Roosevelt had just drafted a personal letter to the emperor expressing his disappointment that a meeting had not taken place with the prime minister and warned against further Japanese movements of its armed forces. Because of the change in government from Prince Konoe to General Tojo, the letter was never sent, and that avenue of communications was never opened.[109]

Tojo, now in power, underwent a dramatic transformation. Possibly recalling the sessions with the Total War Research Institute, the previously inflexible, doctrinaire general and army minister, who had asserted the sanctity of the July 6 Imperial Resolution mandating the invasion of Indochina, now suddenly became the one who was reevaluating the entire situation facing Japan. Tojo appointed a seasoned diplomat, Togo Shigenori, as foreign minister, replacing Admiral Toyoda. Kaya Okinori was the new finance minister, and both he and Togo were committed to avoiding a war. Not only was the September 6 resolution to be reconsidered, but the readiness of the army and navy was evaluated, the supply of materials in case of war was calculated, and other aspects of diplomacy versus war were considered.

The role of the army and navy continued to be complicated and constantly in a state of flux. Tojo's discussions with Sugiyama still revealed interservice rivalry even at this critical stage. Sugiyama stated that the army had concerns over the navy's uncertainty about waging war, and, trying to push the responsibility onto the navy, said that if the navy was uncertain the army also would have to admit to uncertainty.[110] Navy Minister Oikawa Koshiro had previously stated that he did not have

---

109   Cordell Hull, Memorandum for the President, Document 104, Papers as President: President's Secretary's Files.

110   Hotta, 210.

confidence in victory, and if the war continued for a few years he could not predict the outcome.[111] While these constantly shifting arguments continued, always in the background was the unspoken rivalry over resource allocation. If a minister or service chief was uncertain about being resolved for war, allotment of resources to that service became subject to question. Such an argument showed the weakness of having military officers, current and former, in the government cabinet— particularly when their resignation, followed by the military's refusal to appoint a successor, would cause the government to fail. There was insufficient power in the office of the prime minister to resolve such matters as resource allocation or to force the two services to coordinate and implement an overall strategy.

The pro-war elements in the Roosevelt inner circle—primarily Stimson and Knox, along with a slightly more moderate Hull—were convinced that Konoe's replacement by Tojo made war inevitable. Stimson, having been in favor of war all along, now focused on "making sure Japan was put in the wrong and made the first bad move."[112]

In the closing months of 1941, Stimson overcame his earlier scruples about reading other gentlemen's mail. The US government had built very sophisticated MAGIC decoding machines, and these were so successful at reading the supposedly secret Japanese diplomatic communications that the messages might as well have been sent in the clear. Stimson delved into reading continually about Japanese naval movements in the south Pacific, and he and the others in the War Council jumped to the conclusion that they were seeing all the movements of the Japanese armed forces. As a result, they assumed that if the Japanese were going to attack, it would be somewhere in the south Pacific. If Stimson had observed his earlier scruple about not reading other gentlemen's mail, but instead paid more attention to other sources, such as the information

---

111   Hotta, 199.

112   Kaiser, 304.

coming from Ambassador Grew, he and other War Council members would have had a broader view and considered other options.

The War Council was unable to devise a strategy to avoid war with Japan other than forcing a Japanese capitulation. They had consistently ignored important information from Ambassador Grew, who reported sensitive observations on the internal workings of the Japanese cabinet and their probable courses of action. In April he, along with Ambassador Leahy, had gleaned information about the possible invasion of the southern portion of Indochina. He recommended, instead of responding to such an event after it occurred, that Secretary Hull communicate privately with the Japanese government and inform them the United States was likely to impose sanctions if Japan invaded.

Unfortunately, much of the important information Ambassador Grew sent to Washington was largely overlooked or ignored, and dialogue between Washington and Tokyo was strained. This state of affairs is indicated by Grew's cable on July 10, 1941, in which he pointed out that he had to go to the British ambassador in Tokyo, Sir Robert Craigie, to find out about discussions between the State Department and the Japanese ambassador in Washington.[113] This occurred because the State Department kept the British ambassador in Washington abreast of events, who promptly informed the foreign secretary in London, who in turn informed their ambassador in Tokyo. Sir Robert then kindly passed the information to Ambassador Grew.

---

113   Wohlstetter, 129.

CHAPTER 10

Escalating Tensions

While the discordant discussions in the Japanese cabinet were taking place over the last two weeks of October, on October 20 Admiral Yamamoto presented his Pearl Harbor attack plan to the naval general staff for approval. An attack carried out undetected across 3,700 miles of the north Pacific Ocean and then executed successfully was considered an extremely difficult and risky operation.

Opposition to the plan focused on several arguments. It committed the entire Striking Force of six carriers to the 3,700-mile eastward movement and drew power away from the primary southward amphibious operations against Malaya, the Dutch East Indies, and the Philippines. It would require underway replenishment in severe storms and heavy seas—predictable conditions in the north Pacific at that time of year. Once at Pearl Harbor, the execution of the plan against heavy defenses could lead to the loss of one or more carriers in an all-out battle with US land-based and carrier forces.

Yamamoto had been working on the plan for nearly a year and refused to budge. He believed the best chance, and perhaps the only chance, to win a war with the United States was on the first day. This would be accomplished by a massive surprise attack at Pearl Harbor that would destroy the US Pacific Fleet and push any remnants back to the West Coast. He was so immensely powerful in the navy that he was able to force approval of his plan. He understood the risks, and he worked to bring the Striking Force to a peak of readiness. What began as a planning exercise by Yamamoto in January 1941 became a finely tuned and powerful attack plan by October.-

In a rare spirit of compromise, the Japanese army and navy agreed on a comprehensive plan to invade the Malay Peninsula on December 8 (Tokyo time), together with a first attack on the Philippines and Guam. Further rapid expansion would follow into the Dutch East Indies, other Pacific islands, and ultimately Singapore. The Pearl Harbor attack to destroy the US Pacific Fleet forces would protect the flank of the invasions.

If Japan invaded any Pacific islands, Yamamoto was resigned to the United States entering the war. The desired goal, therefore, was a fast attack in which a powerful Japanese navy and a destroyed Pacific Fleet would lead to a negotiated settlement giving Japan access to the oil and other resources embargoed by the US asset freeze. If the United States became involved in the European war, there would be even greater incentive for the United States to come to an agreement with Japan. However, because Japan was committing all its amphibious forces to the south Pacific, the Pearl Harbor attack plan was limited to carriers, other surface units as necessary, and submarines. It would be a raid, not an invasion.

The Pearl Harbor attack plan was developed over several months in early 1941, followed by comprehensive training in early September. Carrier operations were practiced intensely. Air crews were trained on a remote northern island in the tactics of target recognition, pinpoint accuracy in dive-bombing, and effective high-altitude bombing. Knowing that the water depth of Pearl Harbor was only forty feet, just enough to allow passage of the largest ships, special fins were adapted for the aerial torpedoes so they would stay at a shallow depth and not dive to their usual 100 feet before finding their set running depth. Special bombs to penetrate armored hulls and turrets were developed for the planes used as level bombers by attaching fins to sixteen-inch armor-piercing battleship projectiles. The final approval for the mission was given on November 3 by the navy chief, Admiral Nagano Osami. The projected attack date was set for December 8, Tokyo time, or in Hawaii, December 7.

In both the US and Japanese navies, almost all senior officers, commissioned before the growth of naval aviation, had built their careers in surface commands. U.S. Navy Admirals King and Halsey, however, had become qualified for flight operations in mid-career. In the Imperial Japanese Navy, both Yamamoto and Vice Admiral Ozawa Jisaburo had qualified for flight operations. Ozawa, a highly capable, skilled commander and strong advocate of carrier operations, was given command of the operation considered most critical: the powerful Malayan invasion force. This force consisted of transports carrying thousands of troops supported by battleships, cruisers, and light carriers. Vice Admiral Nagumo Chuichi was given command of the Striking Force to execute the flanking move against Pearl Harbor. Nagumo was a battleship and cruiser officer of the old school who believed in guns and torpedoes. His skills were better suited to the Malayan operation, and Ozawa's to commanding the Striking Force. However, when the Imperial Navy central command considered overall competence versus specific skills, it gave command of the mission it considered more important to Ozawa. As a result, the Striking Force of six carriers ended up with a commander inexperienced in carrier operations. The wisdom of those decisions would be tested over the next six months.

Nagumo had opposed the attack plan because of serious doubts about its chances for success. However, he had solid staff backing from Commanders Genda Minoru and Fuchida Mitsuo, both highly experienced fliers and air group commanders. Commander Genda was a brilliant tactician and strategist of carrier warfare who, under Yamamoto, had helped plan the Pearl Harbor attack from its inception. Commander Fuchida thought the Pearl Harbor plan was inadequate, that it should have included not only the complete destruction of the Pacific Fleet but also an invasion of the Hawaiian Islands to push the United States completely out of the central Pacific.[114] That evaluation should have been taken more seriously by senior Japanese officers.

---

114   Nelson, 145.

In the translated diary of Admiral Ugaki Matomi, chief of staff to Admiral Yamamoto:

> *If [Nagumo] and chief of staff [Kusaka] stoutly oppose the operation, and feel they cannot carry it out, they should resign their posts. I expressed this to the commander-in-chief [Yamamoto] and he also said he thought so . . . the Navy has no other adequate candidate [to replace Nagumo]. I hope he performs his mission well.*[115]

The Japanese cabinet knew that invading the south Pacific islands was risky because of the possibility of war with the United States. They also should have known, because of their alliance with Germany, that they would be impacted by the outcome of the German war in Russia. Just as Matsuoka had failed to reevaluate Hitler's circumstances prior to Japan's signing the Tripartite Pact in late September 1940, by November 1941 it should have been clear to Japanese leadership that the German blitzkrieg into Russia had stalled. None of the targets of the original three-pronged attacks on Moscow, Leningrad, and the Caucasus had been captured, and the brutal Russian winter had already enveloped the German army. It also was becoming clear that the German forces were bogged down in a two-front war. With most of the German army stuck in Russia over the winter, the plan for another attempt to invade Great Britain in 1942 already was starting to look doubtful. Hitler's assurances that he would support Japan in a war with the United States were sounding increasingly hollow. The Japanese army had not wanted to revoke the Tripartite Pact when the initial invasion of Russia looked like another win for Hitler. But with the German army failing to roll to another victory the risks inherent in taking actions that could result in war with the United States had grown significantly. In these drastically changed circumstances, Japan

---

115   Ugaki, Matome, *Fading Victory* (Naval Institute Press, 1991), 13.

should have reconsidered their position and withdrawn from the pact, but the army still refused to consider it.

Further negotiations took place in the cabinet over October 29-30. The army was opposed to withdrawing troops from any territory it occupied, but Tojo was tougher about this issue than Konoe, who had had great difficulty standing up to the army. At an all-day meeting on November 1, a further plan was offered by Foreign Minister Togo: a unilateral withdrawal from southern Indochina as a way to break the deadlock and get the asset freeze revoked. The army reacted furiously against this, but despite their adamant assertions, the prospect of victory in a war with the United States was uncertain. Finance Minister Kaya, citing the Total War Research Institute, reminded them that the industrial capacity of the United States was overwhelmingly greater than Japan's. He again asserted that they could not win a protracted war against the United States.

Togo supported Kaya and insisted that no decision be made at that time, for or against war, that would constrict his diplomatic efforts. The pro-war faction of the army opposed him, arguing that, because of the oil embargo and the US buildup of forces, November 30 was absolutely the last day for diplomacy.[116] By that time amphibious forces would be underway, heading for the south Pacific, as would the Striking Force for Pearl Harbor. If diplomacy succeeded, these forces could be called back. If not, messages would be sent to proceed with their attacks. The previously agreed message that would be sent to the Striking Force commander to proceed with the attack on Pearl Harbor was "Climb Mount Niitaka."

As Pacific tensions continued to escalate and war became a real possibility, the wide disparity in outcomes for Japan should have been considered but were not. If Japan won a war, the best they could hope for was control of islands in the central and southern Pacific, along with

---

116   Nelson, 130.

portions of Malaysia. The mainland of the United States was not even considered. If they lost, the entire empire they had built up over the previous fifty years—Taiwan, Korea, Manchuria and the Pacific island mandates—would be lost and Japan itself would be threatened with defeat and occupation.

After the long conference of October 31-November 1, Foreign Minister Togo realized the situation was building to a climax. Searching for a way to add experience and expertise to his Washington delegation, he reached out to a retired but highly experienced diplomat, Kurusu Saburo. Their efforts in Washington were not getting results, and time to achieve a diplomatic solution and avoid war was becoming critical. To improve their negotiations with Secretary of State Hull and President Roosevelt, Togo requested that Kurusu go to Washington immediately to supplement the efforts of Ambassador Nomura.

Kurusu, unlike Nomura, had spent his career in Japan's Foreign Ministry. Also, unlike Nomura, he was completely fluent in English, and the need to define matters carefully and accurately in the diplomatic world was beyond Nomura's more limited English skills. Kurusu in his long career had experienced the usual postings in Japanese embassies around the world. He was considered to have been particularly successful in the Philippines, and his penultimate assignment, as ambassador to Belgium from 1936 to 1939, was marked by his attempts, through the offices of the Belgian and French governments, to mediate a settlement of the conflict between Japan and China. His final posting was to Berlin where, even though he was opposed to Japan's participation in the Tripartite Pact and made strong arguments to Konoe and Matsuoka against it, he was required to sign the pact on behalf of Japan and be photographed standing next to Hitler.[117] Meanwhile, Togo was sending a series of urgent messages to Ambassador Nomura emphasizing the need for a resolution with the US government. It must have been painfully obvious to Togo that

---

117   Hotta, 245.

the German army was frozen in the Russian winter and no help would be forthcoming from Hitler. Unknown to Togo, these messages were immediately decrypted by the MAGIC system and read by Roosevelt's War Council. On November 2 Togo wrote:

> *The Government has for a number of days since the forming of the new Cabinet been holding meetings with the Imperial headquarters . . . This will be our last effort to improve diplomatic relations . . . the situation makes it urgent that we reach a decision at once . . . no longer is procrastination possible . . . we have decided to gamble once more on the continuance of the parleys, but this is our last effort . . . when it comes to our existence and our honor, when the time comes we will defend them without recking the cost.[118]*

On the same date, Togo also communicated to Ambassador Grew the urgency of a resolution with the United States. Togo was backing away from the adamant demands made on August 6 but was still wrestling with the China problem. He was reluctant to give up on the possibility of using a resolution with the United States to achieve a favorable exit from China.

The Roosevelt War Council, even with the MAGIC decryption of Togo's increasingly desperate messages to Nomura, failed to realize that a massive shift had occurred in Tokyo. The increasing bite of the Acheson total oil embargo was creating a crisis, and the Japanese army was even more adamant that the time for war was now. In addition, the comprehensive conclusions of the Total War Research Institute were having a profound effect on Togo and Tojo. They now realized a diplomatic solution was necessary, and if war was to be avoided, their diplomatic efforts needed to produce results.

---

118   Wohlstetter, 192-193.

Secretary Hull continued to play for time so the US could build up its forces. He did not seem to realize that the Japanese had figured out what he was doing, and they were not going to play along and get backed into a steadily weakening position. His advisers, led by Hornbeck, were firmly in the China camp, and any interpretations that favored that country were preferred. Hornbeck had a staff of international experts that included Alger Hiss. Stimson and Ickes had been consistently pro-war primarily because of the threat from Nazi Germany and were less concerned with how and where the United States entered the war. Roosevelt, in addition to all the other considerations of his office, was focused on the European situation. All this endorsed the strategy of Delay, but Delay was not going to avoid war.

Kurusu visited Ambassador Grew prior to his departure so that Washington would be aware of his trip and have some background about him. Grew was able to delay the scheduled departure of the next eastbound Pan American Clipper across the Pacific so that Kurusu could make the flight and be in the United States in the shortest possible time. Following Kurusu's departure, on November 4, in a repeat of his telegram of November 3, Ambassador Grew again attempted to communicate important background for the impending discussions in Washington:

> *Japan cannot tolerate perceived humiliation . . . If war should occur . . . Japan may go all-out in a do-or-die effort to render herself invulnerable to foreign economic pressure, even to the extent of committing national hara-kiri . . . this is not only possible but probable . . . Japan's standards of logic or reason cannot be gauged by any Western measuring rod . . . It would be hazardous to base our national policy . . . [on our assumption] that our economic pressure will not drive Japan to war . . . We would be lacking in perspicacity if we were to disregard or underestimate Japan's preparations for war merely*

as a bluff . . . War between Japan and the United States may
*come **with dangerous and dramatic suddenness.**[119]*

Regarding Ambassador Grew, Hull "was more inclined to listen
to Stanley Hornbeck, his Far East adviser in the State Department, a
staunch believer in using a stick rather than a carrot as far as Tokyo was
concerned."[120] Hornbeck regarded Grew as old-fashioned, honorable
but gullible. His comments about Grew stand in contrast to the remarks
of others about Hornbeck, who was considered by many to be arrogant,
highly opinionated, and dictatorial. As for the armed forces, "Hornbeck's
opinions were viewed with horror and alarm by the Joint Board of the
Army and Navy."[121] As a result of that highly conflicted situation, Grew's
messages received limited consideration in the State Department. Hull's
attitude when dealing with the Japanese diplomats was further shaped
by his failure to realize the full economic and human effects of the oil
embargo on Japan. From November 2-26 there was a continuous flow of
at least nineteen messages—almost one per day—from Togo to Nomura
stressing the urgency of achieving a settlement with the United States.
All were decrypted and available to Hull. Typical of these were:

November 5: Time is becoming exceedingly short and the
situation is becoming very critical . . . Absolutely no delay can
be permitted.

November 11: [I]t is absolutely impossible that there be
any further delays . . . cooperate in bringing about an early
agreement.

November 13: The United States is apparently still assuming
that the [talks] are of a preliminary nature. We pleaded with

---

119   Grew, Joseph C., Cable to Secretary of State, Nov. 4, 1941, *Ten Years in Japan*, Lightning Source
UK Ltd. (paperback), 406.

120   Hotta, 252.

121   Wohlstetter, 265.

the US Ambassador again on the 12th to try and see the
seriousness of the situation. [122]

November 15: [C]ooperate with him in an unsparing effort to
guide the negotiations to an early agreement.

The combination of Grew's warnings and the decrypted Togo messages should have created an accurate picture of the situation in Tokyo, but all of this was carelessly overlooked in Washington.

The War and Navy Departments, solidly backed by their War Plans Divisions, expressed a clearly defined position. Admiral Stark and General Marshall, not privy to the State Department communications, sounded the plea for more time, more men, and more equipment. Their memos to the president were all directed at soft-pedaling any State Department efforts toward a 'firm stand' with Japan."[123] This was advocating for the strategy of Delay, but for Delay to succeed, the crisis as perceived by the Japanese had to be mitigated.

Roosevelt "was so deeply interested in the European situation that he left Far Eastern matters almost entirely to Secretary Hull," [124] but

[B]y November, Hull was—more than anything else—weary.
Again and again the private accounts from government
circles describe him with this adjective. He could only use his
remaining energy . . . to not be so severe [with Japan] as to
cause a break in relations and not so kind as to offend China or
Britain or the Netherlands. [125]

We are left to ponder why such a high priority was placed on avoiding any possible offense to three countries that had varied interests in Asia, to the possible detriment of the United States.

---

122   Wohlstetter, 195.
123   Wohlstetter, 231.
124   Wohlstetter, 230.
125   Wohlstetter, 231.

Against this tense and deteriorating background, and considering the distance of Kurusu's trip and the time involved, Nomura continued his discussions with Hull. Togo had constructed a primary negotiation plan, known as Plan A, and if that failed the fallback plan, Plan B, would be submitted. On November 7 Nomura presented Plan A, the primary point of which was a timed withdrawal of Japanese armed forces from China. Hull said he would consider it. In fact, Hull was already aware of both A and B plans because the diplomatic messages to Nomura had been decrypted as soon as they arrived.

On November 10 Nomura met with both Hull and Roosevelt. Roosevelt did not discuss the specifics of Plan A, but rather raised the idea of a "modus vivendi," or temporary stand-still. Nomura understood this to be a three-month accommodation between the two countries, during which no important initiatives, including movements of armed forces, would occur. This would provide time to reach a more permanent agreement. Of course, it was also consistent with the strategy of Delay until US armed forces, particularly B-17s, could be built up, even if a three-month modus vivendi would restrain their immediate deployment to the Philippines.

The problem with the proposal was the drastically different time frames of the two parties. The Japanese were constricted by the asset freeze, and the pro-war elements in the government, aware of the massive naval construction in US shipyards, continued to argue that Japan's best opportunity to win a war against the US was to launch an attack immediately. They perceived the Americans as wishing to appear oblivious to the effects of the asset freeze on the Japanese economy, and were carrying out the Delay strategy: proceed in a slow manner in accordance with dignified diplomatic procedures while their forces were building. Nomura had been unable to convince US diplomats of the urgency of the situation.

General Marshall had given a date in March 1942 when, without any restraint, he expected to have seventy B-17s and associated fighters on the ground in the Philippines. The strategy of Delay was a gamble that Japan could be "babied along." But did anyone think the Japanese would sit idly by while their intelligence sources were informing them of the US buildup of heavy air power? Their spies at Honolulu, for example, were reporting flights of B-17s arriving from California and then departing to the west.

An example of the failure to resolve outstanding issues between Japan and the United States is shown by the records of a November 15 meeting with Hull in his Washington apartment, attended by Ambassador Nomura and Minister Wakasugi Kaname, one of Nomura's advisers at the embassy. Not only was this a discussion of old, stalled points—nondiscrimination in trade, revocation of the Tripartite Pact, and Japanese troops in China—but Hull also made it clear that it was only an exploratory conversation. It was not a negotiation, as that would involve British, Dutch, and Chinese diplomats. However, bringing in Allied diplomats could not occur before "the attitudes between Japan and the United States are such as to afford a basis for negotiation." It would then be necessary to include allies, Hull said, "otherwise they might read in the newspapers that he was negotiating with Japan on matters affecting them without their being consulted."[126] Such was the hopeless state of play. The asset freeze continued, and the deadline in Tokyo for the end of diplomacy was two weeks away.

On November 17 Kurusu, having arrived and acclimated, was ready for a meeting with Hull and Roosevelt. He came burdened by complicated instructions from Togo, including the staging of various concessions and culminating in an offer for the immediate withdrawal of troops from southern Indochina to the northern portion of that territory. Togo was trying to micromanage the proceedings by telegraph from Tokyo with diplomats who did not have cabinet standing, as they attempted

---

126   Hotta, *Japan 1941*, 248.

to negotiate with the Secretary of State and President Roosevelt. He should have made the trip to Washington himself.

Kurusu introduced himself to Roosevelt in perfect English, stating that he was there to assist in the discussions, and asked that Roosevelt see things from the Japanese "frame of mind." Roosevelt, in his most charming manner, said, "There is no last word between friends." This phrase echoed a statement made three decades earlier by Secretary of State William Jennings Bryan to Japanese Ambassador Chinda Sutemi during difficult discussions on the immigration rights of Japanese. Chinda had brought dozens of cherry trees to be planted on the banks of the Potomac and around the Lincoln and Jefferson memorials.[127] Kurusu brought up the subject of US assistance in bringing about a settlement of the war in China and was able to secure Roosevelt's willingness to "introduce" Chinese and Japanese diplomats.

Kurusu also attempted to achieve an understanding regarding Japan's commitment to the Tripartite Pact. He pointed out that the terms of the pact were restricted to situations in which one of the parties to the pact was attacked by a third party. To illustrate the limitations of Japan's obligations under the pact, Japan had no desire or obligation to participate in Germany's invasion of Russia, and did not do so. He stated that a formal renunciation of the pact would be difficult, but that an agreement with the US would "outshine" the pact. There were statements from both sides of a mutual desire for a peaceful Pacific area, and the Japanese came away from the meeting with the impression they had made progress.

Following the discussions, an undated, handwritten note from President Roosevelt to Secretary Hull gave his ideas about the outlines of an agreement:

---

127   Hotta, 250.

President Roosevelt to the Secretary of State [52]

undated

6 months

1. *U. S. to resume economic relations—some oil and rice now—more later.*

2. *Japan to send no more troops to Indo-China or Manchurian border or any place South—(Dutch, Brit, or Siam).*

3. *Japan to agree not to invoke tripartite pact even if U. S. gets into European war.*

4. *U. S. to introduce Japs to Chinese to talk things over but U. S. to take no part in their conversations.*

Later on Pacific agreements. [128]

The Japanese diplomats did not appreciate that the Tripartite Pact was an immovable sticking point with Hull, and he was not going to move away from it. The fact that Kurusu had signed the pact in the presence of Hitler did not help matters.[129] Hull, in his Memorandum of Conversation of the meeting, wrote:

> *Ambassador Kurusu made some "specious" attempt to explain away the Tripartite Pact . . . I made it clear that any kind of peaceful settlement for the Pacific area, with Japan still clinging to her Tripartite Pact with Germany, would cause the President and myself to be denounced.* [130]

---

128   Foreign Relations of the United States Diplomatic Papers, 1941, The Far East, Vol. IV, Chapter VI, Document 460.

129   Hotta, *Japan 1941*, 245.

130   Cordell Hull, Memorandum of Conversation, Document 119, President's Secretary's Files, November 17, 1941.

Hull's negative attitude was unchanged from several months earlier when Konoe was attempting to schedule a summit meeting with Roosevelt. Kurusu's involvement with the Tripartite Pact was another reason Togo should have been the one to make the trip to Washington.

Also on November 17, Hull received a telegram from Ambassador Grew "emphasizing [the] need for guarding against sudden military or naval actions by Japan in areas not at present involved in the China conflict." Grew added that security had become so tight in Japan that "military and naval observation is almost literally restricted to what can be seen with our own eyes, which is negligible."[131] Supported by Acheson and his asset freeze, and despite Grew's warnings, Hull still thought that the Japanese would back down.[132]

Hitler had avoided war with the United States for a year despite serious confrontations in the North Atlantic. If war came with Japan without Hitler getting involved, it would commit the United States to the less important Pacific theater, confronting the powerful Japanese navy in the vast expanse of the Pacific Ocean. An all-out war with Japan then could take precedence over the larger and more dangerous European theater, drawing off US forces from Europe. Roosevelt had stated earlier that such precedence would not be allowed, and a war with Japan would be taken as a war with all the parties of the Tripartite Pact. Because of the weaker state of the US armed forces at that time, expanding a war to all parties of the pact would involve the United States in a two-ocean war for which it was not prepared. In the light of grim reality, Roosevelt's commitment to expand the war beyond Japan to Germany and Italy might not be feasible.

If a war were to be waged at some point, time was not on the side of the Japanese. The US was building naval strength as quickly as possible. Even more quickly, the B-17s moving to the Philippines could bomb Formosa

---

131   Ambassador Grew telegram to Secretary and Under Secretary, November 17, 1941.

132   Nelson, 136.

and Shanghai, and an advanced model could reach the southern islands of Japan. This was the essence of the Delay strategy, and the reason the pro-war elements in Japan wanted to wage war immediately.

Hull had no way of knowing that Nomura and Kurusu, while informed of the deadline for negotiations with the US, were uninformed about the movement of the Striking Force, which was to be underway and headed east across the north Pacific on November 26. If the code message "Climb Mount Niitaka" was not received by an agreed deadline, the Striking Force would reverse course and return to Japan. If a diplomatic agreement had not been reached, however, the code message would be sent, and Vice Admiral Nagumo would proceed with the attack.

In view of the slow progress of the talks, on November 18 Nomura played Japan's trump card: a proposal that the military would withdraw from southern Indochina and revert to the status that had existed in July, before the asset freeze.[133] Hull said he would consider it. Kurusu sent a message to Togo summarizing the discussion, noting some positive response from the US, but added that Japan's participation in the Tripartite Pact was a major impediment. (The hangover from Matsuoka's tenure as foreign minister was still showing itself.) Kurusu emphasized that, because the deadline was now just days away, it was better to pursue the simpler strategy instead of adding more conditions, especially the more complicated and difficult terms involving China. Nomura and Kurusu met again with Hull on November 19, and the atmosphere was cordial and optimistic. Informal discussions with persons close to the administration indicated that Hull was favorably disposed toward Nomura's proposal. He said he would discuss it with the British and Dutch governments.[134] It appeared that the offer to withdraw from southern Indochina had taken precedence in Hull's

---

133   Hotta, 257.
134   Hotta, 258.

mind over Japan's continuing affiliation with Germany through the Tripartite Pact. At that point, an agreement, or at least a modus vivendi, seemed possible.

However, on November 20, a message was received from Togo stating strongly that Nomura had stepped outside the parameters of his assignment, and that in view of this an amended proposal was to be made. Plan B was modified to include five main points, and Nomura was instructed to submit this to Hull the same day:

1. *Both the governments of Japan and the United States undertake not to make any armed advancement into any of the regions in Southeastern Asia and the southern Pacific area excepting the part of French Indo-China where the Japanese are stationed.*

2. *The Japanese Government undertakes to withdraw its troops now stationed in French Indo-China upon either the restoration of peace between Japan and China or the establishment of an equitable peace in the Pacific area.*

    *In the meantime the Government of Japan declares that it is prepared to remove its troops now stationed in the southern part of French Indo-China to the northern part of the said territory upon the conclusion of the present arrangement which shall **later** [emphasis added, indicating Japan's willingness to begin withdrawal immediately] be embodied in the final agreement.*

3. *The Government of Japan and the United States shall cooperate with a view to securing the acquisition of those goods and commodities which the two countries need in the Netherlands East Indies.*

4. *The Governments of Japan and the United States mutually undertake to restore their commercial relations to those prevailing prior to the freezing of the assets.*

*The Government of the United States shall supply Japan a
required quantity of oil.*

5. *The government of the United States undertakes to refrain
    from such measures and actions as will be prejudicial to
    the endeavors for the restoration of general peace between
    Japan and China.*[135]

Togo's November 20 proposal showed that the army had shifted
from its previous adamant position, and Togo was able to include in
the proposal an immediate withdrawal from southern Indochina. Togo
also had instructed the Japanese diplomats to avoid disclosing the
possibility of Japan acting independently regarding any provisions of
the Tripartite Pact. His reasoning was that, in the event negotiations fell
through, the United States could then use such a disclosure to weaken
any enforcement by the other parties to the Pact.

On November 21, while awaiting the US response to the amended
Plan B proposal, Kurusu realized that negotiations were at a climax.
Togo's mandate about not making any disclosures about the Tripartite
Pact was less important than setting any impediments aside to secure
an agreement with the United States. He arranged a meeting with
Hull to deal with the question of the Tripartite Pact. With a written
statement in hand to present to Hull, Kurusu repeated the points in oral
statements. He first acknowledged that as ambassador to Germany, on
instructions from his government, he was required to sign the Tripartite
Pact. He stated that the treaty did not infringe on the rights of Japan as a
sovereign state, that Japan was not obligated to become "a collaborator
or cooperator" in any aggression by another power, and that it would
accept warfare only as an "ultimate, inescapable necessity for the preservation of national life." Specifically, "Japan would act independently of
its Tripartite Pact partners in the event the US went to war in Europe."

---

135   Wohlstetter, 233-4.

This statement was bolstered by Japan's refusal to enter Germany's war against Russia.

Upon reading the statement, Hull asked if he could keep it to show to someone else. Kurusu asked if that person was the president, or if he wanted to present it at a cabinet meeting. Hull said "No" to both, and Kurusu agreed that he could keep the note. The meeting concluded with small talk about their careers, and it seemed to Kurusu that Hull appreciated the efforts he and Nomura were making to achieve a diplomatic solution. Kurusu noticed that Hull was apparently ill and wished him a speedy recovery.[136]

Hull's memorandum of the discussion tells a different story. He said he looked at the paper, did not think it would be of any particular help, and dismissed it. It is not clear, therefore, why he wanted to show the paper to someone else if he did not think it would be of any particular help. Hull had a discussion with Secretary Ickes later that day, and his forecast of the probable sequence of events if war broke out with Japan is shown by an entry in Ickes' diary, in which he quoted Hull, dated November 23, 1941:

> *I felt that by going to war with Japan now we would soon be in a position where a large part of our Navy, as well as of the British Navy, and of the Dutch East Indian Navy, could be released for service in the Atlantic.*[137]

This statement in Ickes' diary is reinforced in the record of a conversation Hull had several days later. On December 1, in a conversation with an assistant, Hull said he:

> *felt that by going to war with Japan now, we would soon be in a position where a large part of our Navy, as well as of the British*

---

136   Hotta, 261-262.

137   Ickes, Harold L., *The Secret Diary of Harold L. Ickes, Volume III (Simon and Schuster, 1954),* 649-650.

*Navy, and of the Dutch East Indies Navy, could be released for
service in the Atlantic."*[138]

This statement, virtually word-for-word identical to the one in the
Ickes diary, clearly represented the prevailing view of Hull and the
civilian members of the War Council.

At about the same time, Navy Secretary Knox was interviewed by
Collier's magazine in an article called "The Navy Is Ready." In the article
he was quoted,

> *[I]f it came to war . . . the Navy would need no more than six
> months to knock Japan out of the water.*

A similar, even more strident article was printed in *The American
Magazine.* Referring to the U.S. Navy, Knox stated,

> *[T]he biggest, toughest, hardest-hitting, straightest-shooting
> navy in the world is primed and ready to write 'finis' to
> aggressors . . . Let 'em come . . .*[139]

All this communicates that Hull, Stimson, Knox and Ickes thought
that if the United States and Japan went to war there would be a short
naval campaign in the southern Pacific resulting in a Japanese navy so
reduced and defeated that in several months US naval forces could be
transferred to the Atlantic theater, where the more serious European
threat could be addressed. This belief shaped the negotiations with the
Japanese diplomats but was directly contrary to the views of the armed
forces chiefs, General Marshall and Admiral Stark. It showed a massive
communications gap at the highest levels of the government of the
United States.

Hull apparently was unaware at the time of these discussions that
the Imperial Japanese Navy had been building its fleet of battleships

---

138   Nelson, 162.

139   Ian W. Toll, *Pacific Crucible* (New York: W.W. Norton, 2012), 45.

and aircraft carriers since the naval treaties were abandoned, and in 1941 was the most powerful navy in the world. The U.S. Navy had been conducting fleet exercises every year for the past twenty years against a potential conflict with the Japanese navy and had regular intelligence on its composition and the movements of its ships. How the State Department, and specifically Hull, was not aware of this information is incredible.

Considering the potent air, naval, and amphibious power Japan would unleash over the ensuing four years, all of which could have been foreseen with better communications with the chiefs of the armed forces, the Hull, Ickes and Knox statements were terrible absurdities. This woeful ignorance in the United States cabinet regarding the Japanese navy, and the influence this ignorance had on the decisions that led to Pearl Harbor, is staggering. A five-minute conversation with Admiral Stark could have corrected this huge misconception, but that conversation never took place.

The question emerges: why was Hull operating under such erroneous assumptions? The War Council included both Stark and Marshall, but the core group around Roosevelt was Stimson, Hull, Knox, Ickes, and sometimes Harry Hopkins. It was not just the civilian control over the armed forces that mattered, but the easy camaraderie that Hull, Ickes, and Hopkins had built with Roosevelt over eight years, which Stimson and Knox seamlessly slipped into. Stark and Marshall were new by comparison. In formal meetings, the uniformed officers spoke when spoken to, and answered questions when they were posed. Very little was volunteered. Roosevelt's old friend Admiral Leahy, unfortunately, was still in Vichy, and that opportunity to bridge the massive gap in communications and information was never realized.

CHAPTER 11

Final Negotiations

The Japanese were waiting for a reply to their modified Plan B. On the US side, two documents had been prepared by November 21. The first was a draft modus vivendi, or temporary agreement. The second, drafted by Harry Dexter White, an assistant to Treasury Secretary Morgenthau, was a statement of longer-term goals that would involve a more comprehensive agreement amongst all interested countries in the Far East—the United States, Britain, China, Japan, the Netherlands, Russia, and Thailand. The longer-term goals would be considered after there was an agreement and initial execution of the modus vivendi. The Japanese referred to the modus vivendi as the "present arrangement." Implementing the modus vivendi would allow time for the more comprehensive agreement to be negotiated.

The first document, to be submitted to the Japanese diplomats on November 22:

Draft of Modus Vivendi by the United States[140]

[Washington,] November 22, 1941.

Outline of Proposed Basis for Agreement Between
the United States and Japan

---

140 "Draft of Proposed 'Modus Vivendi' with Japan," Foreign Relations of the United States Diplomatic Papers, 1941, The Far East, Volume IV, Document 467, Department of State, Office of the Historian, accessed June 8, 2022, https://history.state.gov/historicaldocuments/frus1941v04/d467.

Modus Vivendi

1. *The Government of the United States and the Government of Japan, both being solicitous for the peace of the Pacific, affirm that their national policies are directed toward lasting and extensive peace throughout the Pacific area and that they have no territorial designs therein. They undertake reciprocally not to make by force or threat of force, unless they are attacked, any advancement, from points at which they have military establishments, across any international border in the Pacific area.*

2. *The Japanese Government undertakes forthwith to withdraw its armed forces now stationed in southern French Indochina, not to engage in any further military activities there, including the construction of military facilities, and to limit Japanese military forces in northern French Indochina to the number there on July 26, 1941, which number in any case would not exceed 25,000 and which number would not be subject to replacement.*

3. *The Government of the United States undertakes forthwith to remove the freezing restrictions which were placed on Japanese assets in the United States on July 26 and the Japanese Government agrees simultaneously to remove the freezing measures which it imposed in regard to American assets in Japan. Exports from each country would thereafter remain subject to the respective export control measures which each country may have in effect for reasons of national defense.*

4. *The Government of the United States undertakes forthwith to approach the British and the Dutch Governments with a view to those Governments' taking, on a basis of reciprocity*

with Japan, measures similar to those provided for in paragraph three above.

5. *The Government of the United States would not look with disfavor upon the inauguration of conversations between the Government of China and the Government of Japan directed toward a peaceful settlement of their differences nor would the Government of the United States look with disfavor upon an armistice during the period of any such discussions. The fundamental interest of the Government of the United States in reference to any such discussions is simply that they be based upon and exemplify the fundamental principles of peace which constitute the central spirit of the current conversations between the Government of Japan and the Government of the United States.*

   In case any such discussions are entered into between the Government of Japan and the Government of China, the Government of the United States is agreeable to such discussions taking place in the Philippine Islands, if so desired by both China and Japan.

6. *It is understood that this modus vivendi is of a temporary nature and shall not remain in effect for a period longer than three months unless renewed by common agreement.*

[Annex]

Strictly Confidential,
Tentative and Without
Commitment

On November 21 Secretary Hull showed a preliminary version of the modus vivendi to Admiral Stark and General Leonard Gerow of the Army War Plans staff, General Marshall being away. General Gerow sent back a comment on behalf of both officers, again stressing the importance of avoiding war with Japan:

> *The adoption of its provisions would attain one of our present major objectives—the avoidance of war with Japan . . . War Plans Division wishes to emphasize it is of grave importance to the success of our war effort in Europe that we reach a modus vivendi with Japan.*[141]

To keep discussions going while waiting for the US reply to the amended Plan B, Ambassador Nomura and Kurusu Saburo at their request held a meeting on November 22 with Secretary Hull and Joseph W. Ballantine, special assistant to the secretary. Hull had recovered from the illness Kurusu had noticed during their discussions on the previous day. He stated that he had communicated with representatives of the British, Dutch, and Chinese governments and was awaiting their replies. Hull questioned why there was not more support from the Japanese Diet for the negotiations. Kurusu replied that it was unfortunate that a current special session of the Diet had brought out the difficulties suffered from the oil embargo, but it was significant that the army had agreed to withdraw the troops from southern Indochina.

The secretary pointed out the difficulty of "injecting the Chinese matter into the proposal." He also asked whether "the Japanese proposal was intended as a temporary step . . . and that it was looking to the conclusion of a comprehensive agreement." Kurusu said, "Yes." Hull said that even if Japan moved its troops out of south Indochina, it could return them "overnight," and that "this would not relieve the apprehensions of neighboring countries." Kurusu replied that it would not be possible to move troops overnight and that Japan "desired the troops in northern Indochina in order to bring about a settlement with China." Hull said "he was obliged to confer again with representatives of the

---

141   Wohlstetter, 237.

other governments concerned after they had had an opportunity to consult with their governments." Nomura "said that the Japanese had in mind negotiating a bilateral agreement with [the United States], to which other powers could subsequently give their adherence." There was no further reference to the draft modus vivendi, which at that time Hull was circulating to the British, Dutch, and Chinese. On that note, the meeting concluded.[142]

On the same day, Togo informed Nomura and Kurusu that the deadline had been extended to November 29, that there would be no more extensions beyond that date, and that after that events would progress "in an automatic fashion."[143] Upon seeing the decrypted note, the War Cabinet was uncertain but apprehensive about the meaning of events proceeding "in an automatic fashion." Hull continued to work on the final draft of the modus vivendi to ensure the support of allies. The earlier version had been modified by adding more detail, and restricting oil shipments to only the quantity required for civilian needs:

Final Modus – November 25, 1941[144]

Outline of Proposed Basis for Agreement Between the United States and Japan

Modus Vivendi

1. *The Government of the United States and the Government of Japan, both being solicitous for the peace of the Pacific, affirm that their national policies are directed toward lasting and extensive peace throughout the Pacific area and that they have no territorial designs therein.*

---

142   Joseph Ballantine, Special Advisor to the Secretary, Memorandum of Conversation. Papers as President. President's Secretary's Files, Document 126.

143   Hotta, 265.

144   Foreign Relations of the United States Diplomatic Papers, 1941, The Far East, Vol. IV, Chapter VI, Doc. 483.

2. *They undertake reciprocally not to make from regions in which they have military establishments any advance by force or threat of force into any areas in Southeastern or Northeastern Asia or in the southern or the northern Pacific area.*

3. *The Japanese Government undertakes forthwith to withdraw its armed forces now stationed in southern French Indochina and not to replace those forces; to reduce the total of its forces in French Indochina to the number there on July 26, 1941; and not to send additional naval, land or air forces to Indochina for replacements or otherwise.*

   The provisions of the foregoing paragraph are without prejudice to the position of the Government of the United States with regard to the presence of foreign troops in that area.

4. *The Government of the United States undertakes forthwith to modify the application of its existing freezing and export restrictions to the extent necessary to permit the following resumption of trade between the United States and Japan in articles for the use and needs of their peoples:*

   (a)

   Imports from Japan to be freely permitted and the proceeds of the sale thereof to be paid into a clearing account to be used for the purchase of the exports from the United States listed below, and at Japan's option for the payment of interest and principal of Japanese obligations within the United States, provided that at least two-thirds in value of such imports per month consist of raw silk. It is understood that all American-owned goods now in Japan the movement of which in transit to the United States has been interrupted following the adoption of freezing measures shall be forwarded forthwith to the United States.

(b)

Exports from the United States to Japan to be permitted as follows:

(i)

Bunkers and supplies for vessels engaged in the trade here provided for and for such other vessels engaged in other trades as the two Governments may agree.

(ii)

Food and food products from the United States subject to such limitations as the appropriate authorities may prescribe in respect of commodities in short supply in the United States.

(iii)

Raw cotton from the United States to the extent of $600,000 in value per month.

(iv)

Medical and pharmaceutical supplies subject to such limitations as the appropriate authorities may prescribe in respect of commodities in short supply in the United States.

(v)

Petroleum. The United States will permit the export to Japan of petroleum, within the categories permitted [for] general export, upon a monthly basis for civilian needs. The proportionate amount of petroleum to be exported from the United States for such needs will be

*determined after consultation with the British and the
Dutch Governments. It is understood that by civilian
needs in Japan is meant such purposes as the operation
of the fishing industry, the transport system, lighting,
heating, industrial and agricultural uses, and other
civilian uses.*

(vi)

*The above stated amounts of exports may be increased
and additional commodities added by agreement
between the two governments as it may appear to them
that the operation of this agreement is furthering the
peaceful and equitable solution of outstanding problems
in the Pacific area.*

5. *The Government of Japan undertakes forthwith to
    modify the application of its existing freezing and
    export restrictions to the extent necessary to permit the
    resumption of trade between Japan and the United States
    as provided for in paragraph four above.*

    *The Government of the United States undertakes
    forthwith to approach the Australian, British and Dutch
    Governments with a view to those Governments' taking
    measures similar to those provided for in paragraph
    Four above.*

6. *With reference to the current hostilities between Japan
    and China, the fundamental interest of the Government
    of the United States in reference to any discussions which
    may be entered into between the Japanese and the Chinese
    Governments is simply that these discussions and any
    settlement reached as a result thereof be based upon and
    exemplify the fundamental principles of peace, law, order
    and justice, which constitute the central spirit of the current*

> *conversations between the Government of Japan and the*
> *Government of the United States and which are applicable*
> *uniformly throughout the Pacific area.*

7. *This modus vivendi shall remain in force for a period of*
   three months with the understanding that the two parties
   shall confer at the instance of either to ascertain whether
   the prospects of reaching a peaceful settlement covering
   the entire Pacific area justify an extension of the modus
   vivendi for a further period.

Strictly Confidential,
Tentative and Without
Commitment

Roosevelt, after reading the November 25 draft, added a handwritten addendum to Hull, to be transmitted to Churchill:

"[T]his seems to us a fair proposition for the Japanese but its acceptance or rejection is really a matter of internal Japanese politics. I am not very hopeful but we must all be prepared for real trouble, possibly soon."[145]

The clause restricting oil exports to the level needed for civilian uses made Roosevelt pessimistic about reaching an agreement. Had he been informed of the increasingly desperate messages from Togo to his diplomats in Washington over the previous several weeks that had been deciphered by MAGIC, he might have been more optimistic about a positive response. In addition, Japan had sufficient petroleum stockpiled to carry on if it received, as an interim agreement, just the civilian allotment pending further developments.

On the morning of November 25, following their usual weekly custom, War Council members Cordell Hull, Henry Stimson, and Frank Knox met to discuss outstanding items. Stimson was pessimistic about

---

145   Document 129, Papers as President: President's Secretary's Files, November 24, 1941.

the Japanese accepting the US changes to their proposal because the United States was asking Japan to forgo any military action against any of her neighbors in exchange for trade in sufficient quantities only for their civilian population.[146] However, the Japanese landings on southern Indochina had resulted in a crippling oil embargo, the resulting diplomatic crisis, and tedious negotiations with the United States. In view of the forceful response to the Japanese actions in Indochina, it was not clear why Stimson thought they would be contemplating further military action.

At noon the three met with Roosevelt, Marshall, and Stark at the White House, where the latest decoded Japanese diplomatic message was reviewed. The most startling point in the message was the statement by the Japanese foreign minister that unless an agreement was reached by November 29, "things are automatically going to happen." Suddenly, it looked as if war was going to break out. The presumption in the War Council was that the Japanese attack would fall on Siam, Malaya, or the Dutch East Indies rather than the Philippines. Stimson recorded in his diary, "The question was how we are going to maneuver them into firing the first shot without allowing too much danger to ourselves."[147] Instead of redoubling his efforts to achieve an immediate diplomatic resolution, Stimson was accepting war as inevitable.

Later the same day, Stimson received an Army intelligence report that a large convoy of Japanese amphibious force transports had left Shanghai headed south. This information was from British sources and was several days old. He reported that information to Hull and, instead of picking up the telephone, wrote a memorandum to Roosevelt.

After the noon War Council meeting, the reactions to the November 22 draft modus vivendi from the other governments started coming in to Hull. Lord Halifax, the British ambassador in Washington, called on

---

146   Wohlstetter, 239.
147   Wohlstetter, 240.

Hull in person to deliver a memorandum in response to the first draft modus vivendi from "the Former Naval Person," the private form of address between Roosevelt and Churchill. The memorandum stated that "the Japanese proposal is clearly unacceptable, and the only question appears to be whether to reject it, [and] leave it to the Japanese to make a better offer or make a counter proposal." He added, "[T]he Japanese will try to force a hurried decision by magnifying the dangers of delay." The memorandum further suggested:

> [T]hat any counter proposal should stipulate for the total
> withdrawal from [all of] Indo China not merely of the
> Japanese "troops" as in the Japanese proposal but of Japanese
> naval military and air forces with their equipment, and for
> the suspension of further military advances in China; . . . the
> quid pro quo being legitimate relaxation of existing economic
> measures . . . so as to allow the export of limited quantities of
> goods of direct importance to the war potential, in particular
> oil . . . These relaxations would of course only become effective
> as and when withdrawal of Japanese armed forces took place.[148]

The British clearly were not in favor of the modus vivendi. In the discussion between the ambassador and the secretary, as recorded in the Memorandum of Conversation, Lord Halifax opined that 25,000 troops in northern Indochina were still a threat to Kunming in China. General Marshall, on the other hand, had assured Hull that a force of that size could not threaten Kunming, which was a significant distance to the west of Indochina over difficult terrain. Secretary Hull took the position that he had to appeal to Lord Halifax and expressed the "impossibility of not letting the Japanese have some oil for strictly civilian use, if we, in turn, are to secure the tremendously valuable commitment by the

---

148   Cordell Hull, Memorandum of Conversation with the British Ambassador, Lord Halifax,
President's Secretary's Files, Document 130, November 25, 1941.

Japanese not to move on any aggressive course outside of China proper during the next three months." [149]

Generalissimo Chiang Kai-shek received a copy of the first draft modus vivendi and sent a telegram dated November 25 that was delivered to Secretary Stimson by the brother of Madame Chiang, Dr. T. V. Soong. Soong had spent years building strong diplomatic relationships in Washington that gave him significant power in the US government. He asked Stimson to "see me to discuss the message or otherwise let me know if you have any reply." Stimson then forwarded the message to Hull. The core issues of the message were the following:

> *If . . . there is any relaxation of the embargo or freezing regulations, or if a belief of that gains ground, then the Chinese people would consider that China has been completely sacrificed by the United States. The morale of the entire people will collapse and every Asiatic nation will lose faith, and indeed suffer such a shock in their faith in democracy that a most tragic epoch in the world will be opened. The Chinese army will collapse, and the Japanese will be enabled to carry through their plans, so that even if in the future America would come to our rescue the situation would be already hopeless. Such a loss would not be to China alone.[150]*

Prior to this telegram being delivered, Chiang and Madame Chiang sent telegrams to every official in Washington they thought could influence the actions of the Roosevelt administration, as well as to Churchill in London. These found their way into the hands of the press, causing the media to voice concerns about the administration's possible appeasement of Japan. "Appeasement" at that time smacked of Neville

---

149   Cordell Hull, Memorandum of Conversation, Papers as President: President's Secretary's Files, Document 130.

150   Foreign Relations of the United States Diplomatic Papers, 1941, The Far East, Vol. IV, Chapter VI, Document 482.

Chamberlain's disastrous Munich agreement with Hitler. It was unclear how an agreement between Japan and the United States to avoid war would cause a shock in every Asiatic nation's faith in democracy when democracies in Asia at that time were hard to find. The Chiangs simply wanted US armed forces in the war to support China.

Another message from London, this time directly from Churchill to Roosevelt, was delivered to John Winant, US ambassador to the United Kingdom, on November 26, who forwarded it to Secretary Hull. The telegrams from the Chiangs clearly were having an effect:

London, November 26—6 am.

(Received November 26 – 12:55 a.m.)

For the President from the Former Naval Person.

Your message about Japan received tonight. Also full accounts from Lord Halifax of discussions and your counter project to Japan on which Foreign Secretary has sent some comments. Of course, it is for you to handle this business and we certainly do not want an additional war. There is only one point that disquiets us. What about Chiang Kai Shek? Is he not having a very thin diet? Our anxiety is about China. If they collapse, our joint dangers would enormously increase. We are sure that the regard of the United States for the Chinese cause will govern your action. We feel that the Japanese are most unsure of themselves.

Winant[151]

Sent to President Roosevelt on November 26 at 9:05 a.m. and forwarded to Hull.

---

151   Foreign Relations of the United States Diplomatic Papers, 1941, The Far East, Vol. IV, Chapter VI, Document 484.

Hull sat at his desk in a quandary. He was concerned by the British opposition to the modus vivendi but could understand their apprehension about any possible lessening of US support for their interests in the Far East. However, he was completely shaken by the intense, adamant opposition by the Chinese, including the mobilization of their powerful influence in the government and the Washington press. He was staggered by the power of the Chinese effort in Washington that was pulling out every possible ploy and leverage to prevent a settlement between the United States and Japan. Hull felt stuck to the commitment to them as allies, even though their interests were very different from those of the United States.

For anyone to think that war between the United States and Japan was inevitable, the strong doubts expressed by the British and the strident efforts of the Chinese leadership to prevent an agreement are proof that it was not inevitable. In fact, Hull had been about to avoid war by submitting the final modus vivendi to the Japanese diplomats. Togo and the Japanese government, as evidenced by their plaintive and desperate pleas for an agreement, surely would have embraced it. But Hull was not capable of taking that step because he allowed himself to be controlled by opposition from governments he thought he dared not oppose, whatever the results for the United States. In this situation of massive, world-shaking importance, the United States had a Secretary of State who was unable to maintain a policy that was critically important for the United States but questioned by the British and violently opposed by the Chinese. In failing to maintain that policy, he failed in his duty as Secretary of State and failed in his loyalty to the United States. After his ineptitude was later realized, he would be described by Roosevelt as "that old fool, Hull."[152]

Hull was staggered by the heavily weighted arguments of the British and the strident demands of the Chinese. He also was operating under

---

152   Welles, 345.

the mistaken belief that in a war with Japan US forces would prevail in a few months. Taking five minutes to talk with Admiral Stark on the power of the Japanese navy never occurred to him. The southward movement of the amphibious force through the South China Sea was a small indication of their total capabilities. A war with Japan would not be over in a few months, but on the contrary would be long and bloody. Hull's failure showed a massive gap in communication and coordination between the armed forces and the State Department—two departments of the federal government that should have integrated their resources to avoid disasters and achieve positive results for the United States.

About this time Harold Ickes found out that the State Department and Japanese diplomats were in negotiations on an agreement to avoid war. He wrote in his diary:

> *The strong opposition of China and Britain caused the appeasers of the State Department to pause . . . If this negotiation with Japan had been consummated, I would have promptly resigned from the Cabinet with a ringing statement attacking the arrangement and raising hell generally with the State Department and its policy of appeasement.*[153]

Hull felt he must abandon the modus vivendi. What could he give the Japanese in its place? The other document, already prepared, was the long-term proposal that articulated the eventual goals to be achieved in the Pacific, the Ten Point Note.[154] Hull's way out was to deliver the Ten Point Note to the Japanese diplomats. That note would become known from that day forward as the Hull Note of November 26. It was a turning point in the history of the United States and the countries of Asia.

---

153   Ickes, 655.

154   Wohlstetter, *Pearl Harbor*, 244.

The text of the Ten Point Note follows:[155]

1. *The Government of the United States and the Government of Japan will endeavor to conclude a multilateral non-aggression pact among the British Empire, China, Japan, the Netherlands, the Soviet Union, Thailand and the United States.*

2. *Both Governments will endeavor to conclude among the American, British, Chinese, Japanese, the Netherlands and Thai Governments an agreement whereunder each of the Governments would pledge itself to respect the territorial integrity of French Indochina and, in the event there should develop a threat to the territorial integrity of Indochina, to enter into immediate consultation with a view to taking such measures as may be deemed necessary and advisable to meet the threat in question. Such agreement would provide also that each of the Governments party to the agreement would not seek or accept preferential treatment in its trade or economic relations with Indochina and would use its influence to obtain for each of the signatories equality of treatment in trade and commerce with French Indochina.*

3. *The Government of Japan will withdraw all military, naval, air and police forces from China and from Indochina.*

4. *The Government of the United States and the Government of Japan will not support—militarily, politically, economically—any government or regime in China other than the National Government of the Republic of China with capital temporarily at Chungking.*

---

155   Foreign Relations of the United States: Japan, 1931-1941, Vol II, 769f.

5. *Both Governments will give up all extraterritorial rights in China, including rights and interests in and with regard to international settlements and concessions, and rights under the Boxer Protocol of 1901.*

   Both Governments will endeavor to obtain the agreement of the British and other governments to give up extraterritorial rights in China, including rights in international settlements and in concessions and under the Boxer Protocol of 1901.

6. *The Government of the United States and the Government of Japan will enter into negotiations for the conclusion between the United States and Japan of a trade agreement, based upon the reciprocal most-favored nation treatment and reduction of trade barriers by both countries, including an undertaking by the United States to bind raw silk on the free list.*

7. *The Government of the United States and the Government of Japan will, respectively, remove the freezing restrictions on Japanese funds in the United States and on American funds in Japan.*

8. *Both Governments will agree upon a plan for the stabilization of the dollar-yen rate, with the allocation of funds adequate for this purpose, half to be supplied by Japan and half by the United States.*

9. *Both Governments will agree that no agreement which either has concluded with any third power or powers shall be interpreted by it in such a way as to conflict with the fundamental purpose of this agreement, the establishment and preservation of peace throughout the Pacific area.*

> *10. Both Governments will use their influence to cause other governments to adhere to and to give practical application to the basic political and economic principles set forth in this agreement.*

The Ten Point Note differed significantly from the three-month modus vivendi. It stipulated that the agreement must be multilateral and include the designated seven countries, an impossibility to achieve before the deadline. It also stipulated that Japanese forces withdraw completely from Indochina and China. Whether Manchuria was included in "China" was unclear. Japan was required to recognize Chiang Kai-shek's government as the only legitimate government of China and must withdraw from the Tripartite Pact. There was no statement specifically ending the oil embargo.

There is no indication that Hull talked to any other member of the War Council during the daylight hours of November 26. The chiefs of the armed forces, who surely would have counseled against any actions that could provoke a war, were not consulted. However, Hull knew he could not change the diplomatic documents without Roosevelt's approval, since Roosevelt had been involved in the preparation of the modus vivendi.

Hull's staff prepared a one-page memorandum for him to take to President Roosevelt. It included two bland and misleading descriptions of the two documents. A convoluted, 143-word sentence followed, occupying about one-third of the page, that referred to the opposition of the Chinese, British, Dutch, and Australian governments to the modus vivendi. It ended with a recommendation that the "broad basic peaceful settlement" (the Ten Point Note) be handed to the Japanese diplomats instead of the modified modus vivendi. It was an effort to "slide it by" Roosevelt:

The Secretary of State to President Roosevelt
Washington, November 26, 1941.[156]

With reference to our two proposals prepared for submission to
the Japanese Government, namely:

1. *A proposal in the way of a draft agreement for a broad*
   basic peaceful settlement for the Pacific area, which is
   henceforth to be made a part of the general conversations
   now going on and to be carried on, if agreeable to both
   Governments, with a view to a general agreement on
   this subject.

2. *The second proposal is really closely connected with the*
   conversations looking toward a general agreement, which
   is in the nature of a modus vivendi intended to make more
   feasible the continuance of the conversations.

   In view of the opposition of the Chinese Government and
   either the half-hearted support or the actual opposition
   of the British, the Netherlands and the Australian
   Governments, and in view of the wide publicity of the
   opposition and of the additional opposition that will
   naturally follow through utter lack of an understanding
   of the vast importance and value otherwise of the modus
   vivendi, without in any way departing from my views
   about the wisdom and the benefit of this step to all
   of the countries opposed to the aggressor nations
   who are interested in the Pacific area, I desire very
   earnestly to recommend that at this time I call in the
   Japanese Ambassadors and hand to them a copy of the
   comprehensive basic proposal for a general peaceful

---

156   "The Secretary of State to President Roosevelt," Foreign Relations of the United States Diplomatic Papers, 1941, The Far East, Volume IV, Document 485, Department of State, Office of the Historian, accessed June 8, 2022, https://history.state.gov/historicaldocuments/frus1941v04/d485.

settlement, and at the same time withhold the modus
vivendi proposal.

Cordell Hull

Penciled notation on the file copy of the Secretary of State:
"Delivered orally & agreed to by the President—Hull"

"Delivered orally" suggests that the president may not have even read the memorandum. It could have been read to him in a brief visit by Hull to the White House, or over the telephone. Whether Roosevelt read the one-page memorandum himself or not, "Delivered orally and agreed to" means that after hearing what Hull had to say, Roosevelt gave him approval to use the "broad basic peaceful settlement," or the Ten Point Note. The convoluted sentence that followed the descriptions of the two draft notes is written in the long, complicated style frequently used by Stanley Hornbeck. Roosevelt was misled by the one-page memorandum and accepted the recommendation from Hull without a comprehensive analysis of the situation. He clearly did not understand that matters with Japan had progressed to such a critical stage.

In normal legal and business practice on important matters, staff persons prepare a memorandum that includes copies of relevant documents, analyses and comparisons of major points in the documents, background information including a summary of previous discussions and events, alternative courses of action with the implications of each, and final recommendations citing substantiating facts. Copies of such a memorandum should have been prepared and hand-delivered as soon as possible to the members of the War Council, including Admiral Stark and General Marshall, for a meeting with the president.

In such a conference, it would have become apparent that to introduce the Ten Point Note at this point was to initiate a radically different basis for negotiation. The War Council and the armed forces chiefs would have considered the many implications and possible courses of action that would follow, and one of them would have been war. The misconceptions held by Hull and other civilian War Council members about the supposed weakness of the Japanese navy would have been disabused immediately and emphatically by Marshall and Stark. The importance of avoiding war with Japan while the European situation was at such a difficult stage and the US buildup was continuing would have become a prime focus of such a conference. Roosevelt, a trained lawyer, would have dug into the situation with penetrating questions and not been put off with insipid generalities. Had such a conference occurred, the outcome surely would have been different than the one that followed.

The obvious question is: why was such a conference, at such a crucial moment, not convened? Did Hull think he could pacify Churchill and Chiang by shelving the modus vivendi and get away with the Ten Point Note? Was he so tired and sick that he just wanted to get the whole matter out of the way so he could go home and rest? Was he convinced by Hornbeck, who in turn was influenced by Alger Hiss, that it was time to stop babying Japan and start using a stick and not a carrot? We may never know.

The position that should have been taken, in the interests of the United States and Japan, to avoid war was the final draft modus vivendi of November 25. At the eleventh hour, the final modus vivendi, with Kurusu and Nomura's endorsement, would have easily persuaded Togo and Tojo to agree, as shown by the many earlier (decrypted) messages from Togo. If the governments in Washington and Tokyo agreed, it would have headed off war. It was not to be.

Late in the afternoon of November 26, Nomura and Kurusu were summoned to the State Department to receive the Ten Point Note. This was the reply they had been waiting for since they delivered Plan B on November 20. After reading the note, the shocked Japanese diplomats attempted to discuss modifications to the document, but Hull rebuffed them at every turn. In view of the list of new and impossible demands, particularly in such a short time frame, the Japanese requested a meeting with Roosevelt. The next day, November 27, the meeting took place in the Oval Office.

Shortly before the meeting, Stimson called Roosevelt to ask if the president had seen his memorandum from the day before about the large Japanese amphibious fleet that had been seen heading south, clearly on its way to invade somewhere in the south Pacific. Roosevelt had not seen it, but he now perceived this fleet movement as another Japanese aggression. He was furious at the thought that the Japanese diplomats had been discussing peace initiatives in Washington, while at the same time their armed forces were underway for another attack. This apparent betrayal, after many months of discussions, was intolerable to him.

When Kurusu and Nomura were shown into the Oval Office, the president confronted them with this information. He stated that the continuing movement of the Japanese armed forces had an effect contrary to the assertions of the Japanese diplomats in Washington, and this raised a serious question of diplomatic credibility. The charming personality for which he was famous could turn into arrogant belligerence when he was angry. There was no flexibility in his position. He warned that if Japan continued its aggressions, it would be "the ultimate loser."[157] The Japanese, unaware of the fleet movements, were taken aback. There was never any discussion of the Ten Point Note. The Japanese diplomats were dismissed from the Oval Office meeting and returned to their embassy, where they sent the Ten Point Note to Tokyo.

Roosevelt's enormous confidence in his ability to make decisions was built on a simple model: information flowed in, and decisions flowed out. This was viable provided the information he received was truthful and comprehensive, and Roosevelt had time to consider it. Even with an assistant trailing behind his wheelchair handing him papers, with so many situations facing the federal government he could not cover

---

157   Hotta, *Japan 1941*, 271-72.

everything adequately himself. On the international scene, he was most preoccupied with Europe. With Japan, he would take the occasional meeting with Japanese diplomats but relied primarily on Secretary Hull. His verbal approval of Hull's one-page memorandum allowed the Ten Point Note to be delivered to the Japanese and, when they came the next day to protest, the news of Japanese amphibious movements in the South China Sea convinced Roosevelt that they were misleading him. From Stimson's diary entry for November 27:

> *I called up Hull to find out what his finale had been with the Japanese . . . He told me now that he had broken the whole matter off. As he put it, "I have washed my hands of it and it is now in the hands of you and Knox—the Army and the Navy."*[158]

If it was up to the Army and the Navy, that meant just one thing: Hull had given up and was now willing to accept war.

Stanley Hornbeck took it upon himself to add a personal memorandum after the Hull Note was delivered:

> *In the opinion of the undersigned, the Japanese Government does not desire or intend or expect to have forthwith armed conflict with the United States. Were it a matter of placing bets, the undersigned would give odds of five to one that Japan and the United States will not be at "war" on or before March 1 (a date more than 90 days from now, and after the period during which it has been estimated by our strategists that it would be to our advantage for us to have "time" for further preparation and disposals.)*[159]

Hornbeck had advocated a stand against Japan based on his conviction that it could be coerced into concessions, and "if Japan did fight the

---

158   Henry L. Stimson Diary, November 27, 1941, as quoted in Wohlstetter, 258.

159   Wohlstetter, 264-5.

war would be short and would end in a complete and easy victory for the United States."[160] The many decrypted messages from Togo to his diplomats desperate for an agreement to avoid war were ignored. It was another example of the disastrous advice Hull had received all along from Stanley Hornbeck—with the help of Hiss. Hiss may have calculated that a war between Japan and the United States would benefit Russia, and if that was his intention he waited until this moment to pour the poison of his influence into Hornbeck's ear.

In a war between Japan and the United States, the winner, after years of brutal fighting and millions dead, would be the United States—as the Total War Research Institute had predicted. Japan would be forced to give up its empire and be beaten back to its home islands, leaving a power vacuum in the western Pacific. None of the US diplomats realized that the ultimate winner after a war between Japan and the United States would not be Russia, but China.

November 26 was the day the Striking Force departed from Hitokappu Bay, north of the main islands of Japan. They steamed east, awaiting the prearranged message "Climb Mount Niitaka." If the message was received, they would proceed with the Pearl Harbor attack. If the message was not received, it would mean that a diplomatic solution had been achieved, and the Striking Force would reverse course, abort the mission, and return to Japan.

The reaction of the Japanese government in Tokyo following the receipt of the Ten Point Note was shocked surprise. In the end, the discussion within the government was a replay of previous ones. The pro-war chauvinists finally saw their way clear to wage war, and their opposite numbers were looking for a way to avoid a war they were convinced they would lose. Prince Konoe, now out of power but attending as a senior statesman in an assemblage of former prime ministers, tried to establish a middle position. There was uncertainty

---

160   Wohlstetter, 264.

about whether Manchuria was to be the part of China that was to be evacuated. He proposed that the best course of action was to maintain the status quo in the short run, postpone the Pearl Harbor attack, and look for a more reasonable solution.

Showing how desperate the Japanese government was for an agreement, they gave serious consideration to accepting the terms of the Ten Point Note if Manchuria was not included. It also showed how readily the November 25 modus vivendi would have been accepted. But, in the face of the uncertainty about Manchuria and the arrogance they perceived in the Ten Point Note, both that and Prince Konoe's proposal were rejected.

On December 1, Emperor Hirohito convened another Imperial Conference. The discussions referred to the November 5 decision to go to war with the United States, Britain, and the Netherlands unless a diplomatic solution was achieved. The Imperial Conference determined that a diplomatic solution had not been achieved by the deadline. On December 2 the signal flashed out to the six-carrier Striking Force, by this time nearly halfway across the north Pacific Ocean: "Climb Mount Niitaka."

Generalissimo Chiang Kai-shek
Photo National Archives

State Dept. Adviser Stanley Hornbeck
Photo Public Domain, wikpedia.org

CHAPTER 12

Pearl Harbor: The Attack

Beginning on November 10, elements of the Striking Force, one by one, had departed from the naval base at Kure in the Inland Sea, bound for the small, nearly deserted Tankan Bay on the island of Etorofu in the Kurile Island chain north of Hokkaido. Security was tight, and radio silence was strictly observed onboard the ships. Because individual "fists," or styles of wireless transmission, were as recognizable as handwriting by other experienced operators, the regular wireless operators were left behind at Kure and new operators were transferred to the ships of the Striking Force. The operators left behind kept up a regular chatter, giving the impression to anyone listening that the ships themselves were still anchored at the Kure naval base. Pacific Fleet analysts reported, "Some tactical traffic from carriers intercepted . . . Carriers still located in home waters."[161]

The Striking Force of six fleet carriers of the Imperial Japanese Navy carried a total of 426 planes, and the attack itself would involve 353 planes. Combat air patrol (CAP), the defending fighters flying over the fleet while the major portion of the air group was carrying out the attack, would require thirty Zero fighters, and forty-three planes were to be held in reserve.[162] Because only about half of a carrier's aircraft

---

161 Center for Cryptologic History, Series IV: World War II, Volume 6, Appendix C, Entry for 27 Dec., 72.

162 Morison, 85.

complement could be spotted on the flight deck at one time, the Pearl Harbor attack would be sent in two waves. After the first wave was launched and underway, the second, already armed and fueled below on the hangar deck, would be brought up on elevators and quickly spotted into position. The second wave would be launched within a half hour of the first and would be over Pearl Harbor as the first wave completed its attack. In the event the Striking Force was discovered just prior to the attack and Pacific Fleet had time to *sortie* from the harbor, the long-range planes of the Striking Force could search many miles beyond Pearl Harbor to find and attack the ships.

Out in front in a screen were seven of the nine destroyers of Destroyer Squadron 1. The 6 carriers followed in two lines abreast. Vice Admiral Nagumo Chuichi was embarked on *Akagi* as Striking Force commander and commander of Carrier Division 1. Carrier Division 2, including carriers *Hiryu* and *Soryu*, was commanded by Rear Admiral Yamaguchi Tamon embarked on *Hiryu*. Yamaguchi was one of the most capable officers in the Imperial Japanese Navy and generally considered to be the eventual successor to Yamamoto. Graduating first in his class at the Imperial Japanese Naval Academy in 1912, he had shipboard assignments in destroyers and cruisers and finally was given command of the battleship *Ise*. As a young officer he attended Princeton University, was a member of the delegation to the London Naval Conference of 1930, and was naval attaché in Washington—all prestigious assignments. He commanded the First Combined Air Group in China before assuming command of Carrier Division 2.

Carrier Division 5, including the newest and largest carriers, *Zuikaku* and *Shokaku*, was commanded by Rear Admiral Hara Chuichi embarked on *Zuikaku*. Also a graduate of the Imperial Japanese Naval Academy, Hara was first assigned to surface ships, becoming a torpedo expert. As a captain he was assigned as a naval attaché in Washington. Returning to take command of the fast cruiser *Tatsuta* with its triple-mount torpedo launchers, he later was promoted to carrier division command.

Behind the carriers were two battleships, *Hiei* and *Kirishima*. Two destroyers were on the left flank, three submarines were on the right, and two heavy cruisers, *Tone* and *Chikuma*, were several miles away on either flank. The two cruisers were redesigned for reconnaissance operations by having the after part of each ship reconfigured to catapult up to five floatplanes. Eight oilers filled with fuel trailed the formation.

The Japanese attack on Pearl Harbor also included twenty-seven mostly I-type submarines that departed earlier and would remain outside the harbor at distances between 8.5 to 100 miles to transmit any intelligence data they could gather. They also would be ready to attack any ships that sortied from Pearl Harbor after the beginning of the carrier attack. The I-type submarines, 320 feet in length and 1,955 tons on the surface, had a range of 14,000 miles and a surface speed of 14 knots. Eleven carried small reconnaissance-type aircraft in airtight capsules on deck, and five others carried battery-powered midget submarines. These midgets, with a crew of two and two torpedoes each, would be released outside the harbor entrance. They would attempt to gain entry to the inner harbor and fire torpedoes at targets of opportunity.[163] Following the attack, the submarines would patrol between the Hawaiian Islands and the US West Coast to sink any US ships they encountered.

Admiral Yamamoto issued the order on November 25 to sortie and "attack the main force of the United States Fleet at Pearl Harbor." But there was a proviso: "Should the negotiations with the United States prove successful, the task force will hold itself in readiness forthwith to return or reassemble." Yamamoto also ordered the Striking Force to reverse course and return if discovered prior to December 6 (Tokyo time, one day ahead of US time). If discovered on December 7, the force commander would use his judgment. On December 8 they were committed to the attack regardless of discovery. In an ironic coincidence, the Striking Force sortied from Tankan Bay on November 26, the very day Cordell Hull

---

163   Morison, 95.

delivered the infamous Ten Point Note that precipitated war between Japan and the United States.

Progressing east from Tankan Bay, the fast carriers, cruisers, and destroyers were held to only thirteen knots by the sluggish oilers and surfaced submarines, but the slower speed conserved fuel. The weather, as expected, was stormy with high winds, rain, and fog. These conditions were ideal for avoiding detection as the force progressed, but underway refueling and navigation were difficult. In the heavy seas, the battleships, cruisers, and destroyers took not just spray but "green water" over their decks. Refueling hoses from the tankers broke as the ships pitched and rolled, leaking oil over the decks. Sailors attempted to keep the decks clean of the slippery oil and, to gain traction, tied straw rope around their shoes. This was of limited help, and a few sailors were swept overboard and lost.[164]

The plan for the Pearl Harbor attack, as developed by Yamamoto staff officer Commander Genda Minoru, was to sink the Pacific Fleet and devastate Pearl Harbor as an operating base. That meant sinking the ships in the harbor, destroying the repair facilities, igniting the fuel tanks, devastating the dry docks—including the largest one in the Pacific— together with any ships in them, and demolishing the submarine base and any submarines there. Whatever Pacific Fleet ships were left would be withdrawn to West Coast ports, leaving Japan in control of the central and western Pacific Ocean.

The Genda plan drew on the tactics of the samurai. In Western societies swordsmanship was parry and thrust, back and forth, until the opponent leaves an opening for a winning thrust. The samurai strategy was different. With his heavy, two-handed steel sword sharpened to a razor-like edge, the samurai warrior confronts his enemy, jockeys for position, and then in an instant makes a single, powerful, lightning slash

---

164   Morison, 92.

that kills the enemy with a single stroke. Yamamoto's father had been a samurai warrior, and the young Isoroku learned the fighting style.

Like a samurai battle, Pearl Harbor was not going to be just the beginning of the war; it was going to be the beginning and the end. The war was to be won on the first day—or over the next two days, as the carriers, having destroyed the US aircraft on Oahu on the first day, stayed on station off Oahu and continued their attacks. The battleships might come in close for shore bombardment. Yamamoto said the preemptive strike was Japan's only chance to win the war. It was a samurai principle: "Win first and fight later." As Admiral Togo had devastated the Russians at Tsushima in 1905, Yamamoto would do the same to the Americans at Pearl Harbor.

On December 2, Vice Admiral Nagumo received the "Climb Mount Niitaka" message. Now resolved on its mission, the force continued eastward before turning to the southeast on December 3, arriving at a point 490 miles directly north of Pearl Harbor by sundown on Saturday, December 6, Hawaii time. A spy attached to the Japanese consulate in Honolulu transmitted the latest intelligence to Yamamoto's flagship for relay to Nagumo: nine battleships in Pearl Harbor, but no carriers.

On *Akagi* all available hands went to the flight deck as the actual "Z" flag that had flown from Admiral Togo's flagship at Tsushima Strait in 1905 was hoisted to the masthead. Flight leaders, shouting over the wind, made motivational speeches to cheering sailors.[165] The course was changed to 180 degrees, straight south. Speed increased to 26 knots, leaving the oilers behind. Surging through heavy seas in the early hours of Sunday, December 7, Hawaii time, the Striking Force closed on Pearl Harbor. Far ahead, the cruisers went to flank speed of 35 knots to get in position to launch their floatplanes for a last reconnaissance over the target. In the predawn darkness, sailors braced against the heavy wind

---

165   Morison, Vol. 3, 93.

on the flight deck as they struggled to get the fueled and armed planes into position for takeoff.

Meanwhile, thousands of miles to the west, the Japanese invasions of the Pacific islands were underway. The Third Fleet invasion force of nearly 100 ships under Vice Admiral Takahashi Kakuichi was headed for landing sites in the northern Philippines, the Fourth Fleet invasion force under Vice Admiral Inoue Shigeyoshi was underway for Guam, and Vice Admiral Kondo Nobutake's powerful Second Fleet of nineteen transports, two battleships, and two heavy cruisers was heading toward Malaya under Vice Admiral Ozawa Jisaburo.[166] It was one of the most amazing series of conquests in world history. These territories, plus Singapore, would be captured in a matter of weeks. By contrast, the "China Incident," the army's land war in China, had been going on for four years and was a hopeless quagmire with heavy casualties.

Over a period of many months, the U.S. Navy command in Washington had sent the commanders of US military forces on Hawaii continuous and repetitious warnings of war. In fact, there had been so many they had lost their effect. Admiral Husband E. Kimmel, the commander-in-chief of the Pacific Fleet, and General Walter Short, the Army commander on Hawaii, were planning a golf game for the morning of Sunday, December 7.

In the final days of November and early December, intelligence information showed significant Japanese naval movements in the western Pacific. The latest estimates sent to Kimmel from Washington stated that if war came, it probably would be in the western Pacific area. Kimmel had requested torpedo nets to protect ships in the harbor, including those on Battleship Row, the line of battleships moored at Ford Island, but the nets had not been delivered. As for General Short, he believed the primary threat to the Army Air Force planes was from sabotage by the Japanese-American community in Honolulu and elsewhere on Oahu. He ordered

---

166   Nelson, 165.

the planes to be formed up in lines, wingtip to wingtip, on the edges of the runways so they could be guarded more easily by sentries and other patrols around the airfields.

Kimmel had ordered Pacific Fleet carriers to deliver fighters to defend the US islands in the Pacific. On December 2, the carrier *Enterprise*, with Vice Admiral William F. Halsey embarked, delivered Marine Corps Fighter Squadron 211, consisting of twelve F4F-3s, to Wake Island. Several hundred miles farther east, the carrier *Lexington* was approaching Midway Island to deliver a squadron of Marine aircraft.

Enterprise, returning from Wake, was scheduled to arrive in Pearl Harbor on Saturday afternoon, December 6, but a fouled propeller shaft on one of the escorting destroyers had caused a delay, and it would not be back before Sunday afternoon. Some of the officers on board were disappointed about missing a party at the Officer's Club on Saturday evening, but there would be other times. The delay would turn out to be very fortunate for *Enterprise*, Admiral Halsey, and the more than 2,000 officers and crew of *Enterprise*.

At 0342 Hawaii time on December 7, the officer of the deck of a minesweeper, USS *Condor*, two miles outside the harbor entrance buoy, spotted a midget submarine heading toward the harbor. Not having anti-submarine weaponry, *Condor* blink-lighted the contact information to the duty patrolling destroyer, USS *Ward*. Believing it necessary to verify the contact before taking it to higher authority, *Ward* hunted unsuccessfully for the midget submarine for more than two hours. While *Ward* searched, the anti-torpedo net at the harbor entrance was left open because two minesweepers entered the harbor at 0458 and another ship was to pass through the entrance about three hours later. The net was open that entire time.[167] Because of that derelict attention to security, at least two midget submarines gained entrance to the inner harbor.

---

167   Morison, 97.

Before the first streaks of light at dawn, 275 miles north of Oahu, the six carriers of the Striking Force turned into the southeast wind. Pounding into heavy swells at high speed, the carriers pitched severely with thunderous impact. The wind, surging seas, and roar of warming aircraft engines made communications possible only by hand signals and handheld signal lamps. Salt spray reached the high flight decks, and Commander Fuchida, the group leader, was very concerned about the conditions for launching planes. If this had been a training exercise, the launch might have been delayed until conditions improved. However, this was not an exercise, and there would be no delay.

Fuchida boarded his plane, and with wheel chocks and brakes holding it fast, he brought his engine to full throttle. With the sky still dark and the horizon not yet visible, the signal officer, waving a green lamp, timed the launch of Fuchida's plane so it would reach the end of the flight deck as the bow of the ship was thrusting upward. With the restraints released, Fuchida accelerated, left the flight deck, and clawed his way into the gloom. The second plane was already in position to catch another upward pitch of the ship. The same maneuvers were taking place on the five other carriers. Carrier operations had been practiced to a peak of efficiency and speed, and in a matter of twenty minutes the first wave of 189 planes was launched from six carriers: 50 high-altitude horizontal bombers, 40 torpedo bombers, 54 dive-bombers, and 45 Zero fighters formed up and headed south for Pearl Harbor. As the first wave roared away, the second wave, fueled and armed, was quickly hoisted to the flight decks. The first faint light of dawn was now visible on the eastern horizon.[168]

The tactical plan had two scenarios. If surprise was achieved and there was no opposition, the torpedo planes would attack first because they had to fly low over the harbor to drop their torpedoes before air defenses were mobilized. The Zeros and bombers would attack the

---

168   Nelson, 190.

airfields to destroy U.S. fighters on the ground as well as antiaircraft defenses. If surprise was not achieved and there were defensive fighters and antiaircraft batteries waiting for the attacking planes, the vulnerable torpedo planes would hang back and the Zeros would engage defending fighters, while high-level bombers and dive-bombers carried out the destruction of airfields and antiaircraft batteries. After defenses had been neutralized, the torpedo planes would carry out their attacks, together with level bombers, on the ships of the Pacific Fleet.

At 0633, with dawn breaking over Pearl Harbor, the flight crew of a Navy PBY flying over the area outside the harbor spotted a midget submarine near the harbor entrance. It might or might not have been the same one seen by *Condor* more than two hours earlier. The PBY crew dropped a smoke pot to guide *Ward* to the location. Sighting the submarine, at 0645 *Ward* attacked and sank it with a combination of gunfire and depth charges. These were the first shots fired in the Pacific War.

A new radar outpost had been installed in late November by the U.S. Army high up at remote Kahuku Point, on Oahu's north coast. Although there were six such outposts on the island, on the morning of December 7 the Kahuku unit was the only one operating. The radar equipment could detect aircraft at a distance of up to 150 miles, but the entire concept of using radar in active warfare was new, and the radar crews had received no training with this technology. They were to secure their watch at 0700, but the pickup truck that was to take them back to their base was delayed. To pass the time, one of the men explored the different controls on the radar set. Suddenly a huge blip appeared on the screen moving south toward Oahu, and fast. Wondering whether the blip was a sign that the equipment had malfunctioned, which happened frequently, the operators called the information center. After a delay, they were told at 0654 a flight of B-17s was due to arrive from California in about an hour, and the blip the operator saw was no doubt the arriving B-17s.[169]

---

169   Nelson, 203.

Also at 0654, destroyer *Ward* transmitted, in code, a message to the office of the Commandant of the 14th Naval District in Pearl Harbor stating that the ship had attacked a submarine with gunfire and depth charges. Decoding the message took until 0712—almost 20 minutes. Relaying the information from the naval district office to the CINCPAC (Commander-in-Chief, Pacific Fleet) duty officer occurred between 0720 and 0725. The duty officer attempted to reach Admiral Kimmel at his quarters, but telephone switchboard congestion delayed the call. The admiral got the report at about 0740 and said he would leave for his headquarters immediately.[170]

As Admiral Kimmel was being driven to his headquarters, the Japanese first wave was closing in on Pearl Harbor. As it approached, Commander Fuchida saw the white surf breaking against the northern shore of Oahu, then the green mountains and the sun-dappled green fields. Beyond that lay Pearl Harbor and the battle line of the Pacific Fleet. Ford Island was in the middle of the harbor, and the battleships were moored along its southeast shore, mostly in pairs, starboard sides to the quays with bows facing the harbor entrance. It was all unfolding according to plan. There it was, all quiet, hardly a sign of life, let alone any defenders. The Striking Force had moved undetected across 3700 miles of Pacific Ocean and launched its planes, which now closed on Pearl Harbor, undetected and unopposed.

Battleships were named after states, and Fuchida could pick out the ships just as they had been described a day earlier by the spy in Honolulu. Approaching the harbor from the north, he could pick out *California* by itself, closest to the harbor entrance. Next was *Neosho*, a tanker. After that was a pair tied up together: *Maryland* inboard next to the quay, and *Oklahoma* outboard. Then came another pair: *Tennessee* next to the quay and *West Virginia* outboard. Then it was *Arizona* with *Vestal*, an old repair ship tied up outboard. Finally, *Nevada* was easternmost

170   Morison, 97.

by itself and last in line. The spy had said there were nine battleships, and Fuchida counted only seven, but that was because *Pennsylvania*, flagship of the Pacific Fleet, was in a dry dock for minor repairs and not readily visible. The final battleship was the ancient *Utah*, moored on the far side of Ford Island where the carriers usually tied up. *Utah* was used just for gunnery practice and was covered with lumber. There were no carriers in the harbor, just as the spy had reported earlier.

Fuchida had his radio operator send the message TO RA TO RA TO RA back to Nagumo. "TO" was the first syllable of *totsugeki,* meaning "attack." "RA" was the first syllable of *raigeki,* meaning "torpedo." Because the torpedo planes were being sent in first, the message meant that surprise had been achieved and the attack, led by torpedo planes, was underway. On board *Akagi*, the news was greeted with cheers of great joy and relief that the risky attack plan had worked.[171] The message was relayed to Admiral Yamamoto onboard his flagship *Nagato*, at anchor in the Inland Sea of Japan, who soberly accepted that Japan and the United States were now to be at war.

Fuchida then signaled the order to execute the surprise scenario by firing his flare gun: one flare if surprise had been achieved and two flares if they would have to contend with defenders. At 0740 he fired his flare gun once. The various air squadrons moved away to take up positions for their attacks, which included the torpedo planes dropping down low for their torpedo runs. After firing, Fuchida then noticed that the fighter group had not prepared for the attack. He concluded that the group commander had not seen his flare, so he fired again to alert the fighter group commander. The second flare, however, was interpreted by the dive-bomber commander as an order to execute the non-sur-prise scenario, which required some of the dive-bombers to first take out the air defenses on nearby airfields at Ford Island and Hickam Field. Because smoke from bomb blasts on Ford Island could obscure the

---

171   Nelson, 208.

torpedo runs, the torpedo planes were ordered to execute their attacks as quickly as possible. The result was that, after all the detailed planning and training, the ordered execution of the entire attack was abandoned, and all the planes executed their attacks at the same time.

Onboard the ships of the Pacific Fleet in Pearl Harbor, sailors in summer whites were standing by the jack staffs and flagstaffs with the blue jacks and the forty-eight-star Stars and Stripes ready to execute "Colors" at 0800. Onboard the battleships, the ship bands were topside, ready to play the national anthem. A plane from the northeast flew low over Ford Island and dropped a bomb before turning and flying up the channel outboard of the row of battleships tied up at the island. All could see the bright red disc on the side of the plane. It was Japanese, and it signaled an attack on Pearl Harbor. At 0758 Rear Admiral Patrick Bellinger, from his position on Ford Island, transmitted a message that shook the American government and nation like no other in decades: "Air Raid, Pearl Harbor—This Is No Drill." The klaxon sounds of the call to general quarters echoed throughout the harbor. As quickly as possible some machine guns were mobilized, and even a few five-inch antiaircraft guns started firing, but reaction was scattered at best.[172]

The Japanese had prepared well for this moment, and the confusion over the flare gun signals did not have any appreciable effect. Twelve torpedo planes roared across Merry Point and the submarine base at treetop level, over Southeast Loch, and then out over the harbor toward Battleship Row. The first group of planes flew so low the pilots had to take notice to avoid the masts of several cruisers at piers in the Navy Yard before dropping their torpedoes. Three planes followed, skimming the water as they dropped their torpedoes. Then a single plane, perhaps a straggler, piled on, all targeting the battleships. The specially altered torpedoes sped toward their targets. There were no anti-torpedo nets around the battleships, just as the spy had reported. Battleships that

---

172   Morison, 101.

were inboard in paired moorings next to the quays were protected from torpedoes by those outboard and exposed to the open harbor. But bombers dropped armor-piercing bombs on the inboard battleships that penetrated the ships' steel decks and exploded inside.

The most devastating casualty was *Arizona*, flagship of Battleship Division One. Hit first by a torpedo before the call to general quarters, which would set Condition Zed and close all watertight hatches, one of the sixteen-inch naval projectile bombs penetrated through several decks before exploding in the forward magazine.[173] The hit caused an enormous explosion, and flames shot 500 feet into the air. Flaming debris from the explosion fell on other ships. Several more bombs hit *Arizona*, and within minutes the ship was a sunken wreck. Oil released from the ship floated on the surface of the harbor, caught fire, and drifted toward other ships. More than 1,000 men were aboard *Arizona*, and the ship settled so fast there was no chance to order Abandon Ship. Almost all those aboard were either incinerated, suffocated, or drowned. The commanding officer of *Arizona*, Captain Frederick Van Valkenburgh and Rear Admiral Isaac Kidd, commander of Battleship Division One, were among those killed in the attack.[174]

Oklahoma, moored outboard of *Maryland*, went to general quarters immediately after the first bomb exploded on Ford Island. Almost simultaneously, three torpedoes hit *Oklahoma* below the waterline, blasting huge holes in the portside hull. Too late to counterflood, *Oklahoma* rolled to port as two more torpedoes hit. The executive officer ordered the crew to abandon ship, and sailors scrambled over the starboard side. Many swam to shore on Ford Island, and others went aboard *Maryland* to assist with the wounded and help man antiaircraft batteries. *Oklahoma* stopped rolling when her masts struck the harbor bottom.[175] A portion of the ship's keel showed above water level. Many

---

173 Morison, 108.

174 Morison, 108.

175 Morison, 111.

sailors were trapped inside the capsized hull, and rescuers later would cut holes in the bottom for rescue, saving many lives. Even so, twenty officers and 395 crew members were lost.

Aboard *West Virginia*, the in-port officer of the deck, a young ensign, saw the bomb hit on Ford Island directly behind *California* and, thinking it was an explosion on *California* itself, called away the Fire and Rescue Party. This prompt action brought many sailors topside and saved many lives. *West Virginia* took several torpedo hits on its port side that blasted huge holes in the hull. Commanding Officer Captain Mervyn S. Bennion went to the bridge and almost immediately was mortally wounded by shrapnel from a bomb hit on *Tennessee*, inboard from *West Virginia*.[176] Junior officers and senior petty officers trained in damage control quickly ordered counterflooding and probably saved the ship from capsizing. For two hours sailors manned antiaircraft guns in open gun mounts even as they were bombed and strafed. Other sailors were blown over the side by bomb blasts, and those who swam toward shore were endangered by burning oil on the surface drifting toward them. Although general quarters had been called at the earliest possible moment, there was no way to prevent *West Virginia* from sinking. At 1005, the ship was on the bottom of Pearl Harbor with fire engulfing the superstructure above the surface. The crew was ordered to abandon ship. Two officers and 103 crew were lost on *West Virginia*.

California was spared torpedo hits in the first few minutes of the attack, but its crew did not react quickly to events going on around it. General quarters, setting Condition Zed, did not sound until after two torpedoes hit the ship at 0805. An alert junior officer ordered counterflooding, which prevented capsizing as the ship continued to take on water.[177] By 0810 electric power was lost, but sailors kept up an anti-aircraft barrage by hoisting ammunition man-to-man to the gun mounts.

176   Morison, 106.
177   Morison, *Rising Sun*, Vol. 3, 112.

A burning oil patch then surrounded the ship's stern, confusing damage control efforts. Power was restored, but despite pumping efforts, which were assisted by two minesweepers that came alongside, *California* settled into the mud of Pearl Harbor. Six officers and ninety-two crew were lost.

On *Nevada*, gun mounts were manned and ammunition was loaded immediately after the attack began. Antiaircraft fire from its five-inch battery on the port side shot down one and perhaps two attacking torpedo planes. Fifty-caliber machine guns kept up a steady defense and were probably responsible for another plane that crashed into the harbor off the ship's port quarter. The antiaircraft defenses no doubt resulted in *Nevada* avoiding more disastrous damage in the early minutes of the attack, but one torpedo plane pilot was able to make a hit near the port bow. A huge hole was made in the forward hull, but the engineering spaces were not damaged. Under ferocious bombing attack, two or three bombs hit *Nevada*.

Unencumbered by another ship at its quay, the senior officer aboard *Nevada* at the time, Lieutenant Commander Francis J. Thomas, was determined to head for the open ocean despite serious damage to the ship. Sailors under strafing attack cast off lines and *Nevada* was underway, moving down Battleship Row past other stricken and sinking battleships. Planes that had been ready to attack *Pennsylvania* in dry dock, seeing a ship underway, diverted their attack to *Nevada*. The ship's anti-aircraft batteries kept up a steady fire, and the bombing assault of hits and near misses enveloped the ship in a huge cloud of spray and debris from explosions that virtually concealed it from view. After taking more bomb hits that disabled the ship, Rear Admiral W. R. Furlong, aboard minelayer *Oglala*, who was senior officer present afloat (SOPA) in Pearl Harbor at the time, ordered tugs to beach *Nevada* at Waipio Point, a small projection of land west of Ford Island. *Nevada* had taken at least five bomb hits in addition to the torpedo, and beaching the ship prevented it from blocking the channel entrance if it sank. Three officers and forty-seven crew were killed and many more were wounded.[178]

Of the battleships nested in pairs, the inboard ships *Maryland* and *Tennessee* received relatively less damage, but not without loss of life. *Maryland*, inboard from *Oklahoma*, was hit by one of the sixteen-inch armor-piercing projectiles and a fragmentation bomb that did relatively little damage. The ship was repaired without the need for dry-docking and returned to service within two months. Two officers and two crew were killed. *Tennessee* was hit by two bombs that did minor damage, but one exploded with the flying shrapnel that killed the commanding officer of *West Virginia*.[179] Flaming debris and burning oil from *Arizona*, moored just astern, caused more damage than the two bombs. Five *Tennessee* sailors were killed.[180]

Pacific Fleet flagship *Pennsylvania*, in a dry dock shared with two destroyers, *Cassin* and *Downes*, was targeted by dive-bombers in the early stages of the attack, but the bombs mostly missed *Pennsylvania*. An incendiary bomb hit a dock between the two destroyers, resulting in an oil fire that spread to both ships. The destroyers had to be abandoned, and shortly afterward the fires spread to magazines and torpedo warheads, which then exploded. *Cassin* rolled onto *Downes*, and both ships were lost. *Nevada* became a more attractive target than *Pennsylvania*, but one dive-bomber pilot, not to be deterred, hit *Pennsylvania* with a bomb that caused modest damage to the ship, killed two officers and sixteen crew, and wounded thirty more. One bomb hit destroyer *Shaw* in a nearby floating dry dock, penetrated to a magazine, and destroyed the bow section of the ship in a huge explosion.

Another torpedo attack, coming in from the northwest over East Loch and Pearl City, approached the other side of Ford Island from Battleship Row. The Japanese pilots saw the old battleship *Utah* moored

---

178   Morison, 109-110.

179   Morison, 107.

180   Morison, 107.

where carriers would have been had they been in port, and possibly mistook the lumber on deck for a flight deck. *Utah*, hit by two torpedoes, capsized and sank. Other ships in the line of moorings northwest of Ford Island took action against the attacking planes. Seaplane tender *Tangier* was responsible for downing a dive-bomber and diverting others. Light cruiser *Raleigh* at the berth next to *Utah* took a torpedo hit, but counter-flooding prevented capsizing. The ship was able to continue fighting and was credited with assists on several downed planes. Later in the battle, a bomber hit *Raleigh* with an armor-piercing bomb that went completely through the thin armor and exploded against the harbor bottom.[181]

Monagham, the designated ready destroyer, had been ordered to support *Ward* when *Ward* encountered the midget submarine at the harbor entrance. Detaching itself from a nest of four destroyers in East Loch north of Ford Island, *Monagham* was underway west of Ford Island when it encountered *Curtis*, a tender showing a flag hoist that signaled the presence of an enemy submarine. The submarine, one of the midgets that had gained entrance to the harbor earlier, was under fire from *Curtis* and the repair ship *Medusa*. It fired a torpedo at *Curtis* that missed and exploded against a dock at Pearl City. *Monagham* charged onto the scene and attempted to ram the midget while the midget fired a torpedo at it. The torpedo missed *Monagham* and exploded against the shore. *Monagham* rammed the submarine and dropped depth charges, eliminating that threat. The destroyer then stood out to sea to assist *Ward*.[182]

Curtis resumed antiaircraft fire against attacking planes, shot down a dive-bomber, and hit another that crashed into the ship, starting a fire. *Curtis* then was the target of several bombing attacks, one of which scored a hit that started more fires. All fires were brought under control within half an hour. Twenty sailors were killed and another fifty-eight

---

181   Morison, 114.
182   Morison, 115.

wounded. Destroyers and other ships in East Loch and Middle Loch kept up anti-aircraft fire against the attacking planes.

At the Navy Yard itself, across the main channel from Battleship Row, the light cruiser *Helena* at Pier 1010 received a torpedo hit even though it was inboard from the shallower-draft minelayer *Oglala*, a tribute to the depth settings of the Japanese aerial torpedoes. Prompt damage control prevented *Helena* from sinking. Farther into Southeast Loch, many ships were under repair and not in an alert status. These ships were in ideal positions to fire at the torpedo planes as they flew overhead toward Battleship Row, but they could not react in time. Minor damage was incurred by some ships there.

Light cruiser *St. Louis* got underway at 0931 and stood out to sea. At the channel entrance a midget submarine attacked the ship with two torpedoes, but the torpedoes missed and exploded against the shoreline. *St. Louis* attacked the submarine with gunfire. The submarine was not seen again and was presumed sunk.[183] Destroyer *Blue* got underway soon after the attack began, and its five-inch main battery downed an attacking plane. *Blue's* gunners also spotted a midget submarine in the harbor and sank it with gunfire.[184]

The Hawaiian Department of the US Army was responsible for land and aerial defense of the Hawaiian Islands. There were four Army Air Force airfields with planes that could have fought the attackers: Wheeler Field, in the center of the island; Hickam Field, south and almost adjoining Pearl Harbor; Bellows Field, in the eastern part of the island; and the small Haleiwa Field on the northern shore. The Marine Corps had a base at Ewa, two miles west of Pearl Harbor at Barbers Point, which had thirty-two patrol bombers and a squadron of F4F-3s, all lined up in anti-sabotage rows. The Navy stationed thirty-six PBY Catalina patrol craft at Kaneohe Bay on the east coast of the island.

---

183   Morison, 120.
184   Stinnett, 245.

Thorough planning by the Japanese, combined with the disposition of the American planes in anticipation of sabotage, resulted in a nearly complete elimination of Oahu's aerial defenses early in the battle. The Japanese plan was to take out the enemy's planes on airfields in the first minutes of the battle to remove any threat of counterattack. The dive-bombers bombed and strafed the planes in their neatly parked rows, and the Zeroes, not needed to defend the bombers and torpedo planes, also came in low to strafe the planes. The task was much easier than expected because the planes were tightly packed together in rows as a defense against sabotage. Of the thirty-six Catalinas at Kaneohe Bay, three were on patrol. The remaining thirty-three were shot up, burned, sunk, or otherwise destroyed. The Army Air Corps had several squadrons of P-40 fighters at their airfields, but few if any at the three largest fields got off the ground, and most were destroyed by the dive-bombers and Zeros. The same was true of the Marine patrol bombers and F4F-3s at Ewa. Some ground personnel at the airfields valiantly wrenched machine guns off destroyed planes or otherwise attempted to improvise firing stations, and there were reports of one or two possible hits. Only at Haleiwa, the small field on the north coast that the Japanese did not think would be used, did four P-40s and one P-36 get into the air. There were no Zeros assigned to attack that field, and the oversight resulted in the loss of seven Japanese planes, while the P-40s lost one of their own.

The Navy air facility on Ford Island did not play a role in defending against the attack but suffered losses later in the day when several planes from *Enterprise* were shot down by friendly fire. The Hawaiian Department of the Army had 60,000 troops on Oahu, but they were deployed to prevent an amphibious invasion. The Hawaiian Department also had deployed approximately a dozen antiaircraft batteries at various locations around Pearl Harbor, but only a few were manned at the time of the attack, and those had no ready ammunition. In contrast to the calls to general quarters and rapid manning of guns aboard many of the ships in the harbor, there was no antiaircraft fire from the Hawaiian Department of the Army.

By 1000 the second wave had completed its attack. The Striking Force planes assembled around the north shore of Oahu and headed north, back to their carriers. Commander Fuchida, herding the last of his planes back, flew the last plane to land on *Akagi*. On the *Akagi* hangar deck, and on the hangar decks of the other five carriers, plane crews were refueling and rearming the planes for the next strike. Going straight to the bridge to report, Fuchida approached Admiral Nagumo, who was reading the reports coming in from the other carriers. It was clear the first strike had sunk or heavily damaged all the battleships in the harbor Almost all the Navy, Marine Corps, and Army planes located on the island were destroyed.

In the Inland Sea of Japan, Admiral Yamamoto was in the operations room aboard *Nagato*. The *Akagi*'s powerful low-frequency radio equipment had transmitted the reports of the first strike back to Yamamoto almost simultaneously with the reports Nagumo was reading. It was clear the first strike had accomplished all its goals. In one fell swoop the battle line of the US Pacific Fleet had been destroyed. It was not a partial result; it was a complete success.

The mock battle scenarios had indicated that one or possibly two Japanese carriers would be lost in the attack as the US forces retaliated. But there was no retaliation. Virtually all the US air power on Oahu had been destroyed in the first minutes by the surprise attack and the brilliant tactics of the Japanese carrier pilots. The next attack, set for the early afternoon, would sink cruisers, destroyers, submarines, and the Pacific Fleet carriers, if they showed up to defend the harbor. Probably the next day they would go on to the shore facilities, fuel tanks, and dry docks. There were sixteen-inch guns in open, unfortified emplacements near the harbor entrance.[185] If the dive-bombers and level bombers

---

185   Williford and McGovern, *Defenses of Pearl Harbor and Oahu 1907-50 (Osprey Publishing, 2003)*, 30, 39, 59.

could make them inoperable, the two battleships could move in for shore bombardment of the entire harbor.

Yamamoto sensed a feeling of culmination about the huge success of the first strike, and the same incisive intuition that guided his brilliant moves at the gaming tables told him what the next move on the bridge of *Akagi* would be. In Nagumo he knew his man. Nagumo had never been committed to the Pearl Harbor mission. He had not been Yamamoto's choice to command the Striking Force; his assignment was the decision of the Navy Ministry in Tokyo, based on seniority. It perhaps would have been better if one or two battleships in Pearl Harbor had escaped the first attack because it might have spurred him to further action. While the exultation of the officers and sailors on his staff swirled around him, Yamamoto sat quietly. Finally, he fixed a steely gaze on his chief of staff, and in a low, intense voice: "Admiral Nagumo is going to withdraw."[186]

North of Pearl Harbor, the planes of the first wave were being spotted on all six flight decks for another launch. The second wave was on the hangar decks being fueled and rearmed. Nagumo considered the reports of the sinking ships at Pearl Harbor. There were almost no attack aircraft left undamaged on Oahu, and no capability for any meaningful attack on the Striking Force. There were still many ships and important targets left in the harbor. A nervous Nagumo may have thought US carriers might make an appearance while the Striking Force was launching or recovering planes. Unknown to Nagumo, *Enterprise* was close to the harbor and *Lexington* was a day away. In a prospective carrier battle, Striking Force would have a six-to-one or six-to-two advantage against Pacific Fleet pilots with no combat experience.

Nagumo had done the minimum that was expected of him. His navy career had been on surface ships, and he was uncertain about carrier operations. He was relieved that all six carriers were still intact. He was safe and had no taste for further action. After a review with his chief of staff,

186   Lord, 181.

Nagumo pronounced that the anticipated results had been achieved. The cruisers, destroyers, submarines, shore facilities, fuel tanks, and possible carriers near Pearl Harbor would have to wait for another time—a time that would never come.

After a final pause and reflection, Nagumo gave the order to withdraw. The young officers on the *Akagi* bridge looked at each other in disbelief. They would associate Nagumo with an old Japanese aphorism: he was like a small dog that takes one bite and runs. But there was no debate. The order went out to the five other carriers. The planes on the flight decks of all six carriers were lowered to the hangar decks, and the carrier fleet turned to a northwest course, away from Pearl Harbor and back to Japan.

First torpedo hit at Pearl Harbor
Photo National Archives

CHAPTER 13

Pearl Harbor: The Aftermath

At about 1:30 in the afternoon on December 7, 1941, the Washington office of Secretary of the Navy Frank Knox received a message from the Pacific Fleet commander in Hawaii: "Air Raid, Pearl Harbor – This is no drill." Knox's immediate reaction was, "My God! This can't be true! This must mean the Philippines!" Knox immediately called the president, first getting Harry Hopkins. Hopkins, shocked, also thought the report had to be wrong, that if an American facility was being attacked it must be in the Philippines. Roosevelt was surprised but realized it probably was true, perhaps remembering Ambassador Grew's warnings. Emergency telephone searches went out to government officials, urgently summoning them to the White House. Reports later described Roosevelt wheeling himself into the Oval Office in a state of high agitation. He contacted Secretary Hull at his State Department office just before 2:00 p.m., who at that moment was about to receive the two Japanese envoys, Nomura and Kurusu. The envoys were delivering the last part of the fourteen-part message terminating further discussions. The appointment had been scheduled for 1:00 p.m., or 7:30 a.m. in Hawaii, a half hour before the Striking Force planes were to hit Pearl Harbor. However, delayed decoding and preparing the message in the Japanese embassy made the envoys late.[187]

---

187   Nelson, 277.

Because the envoys were late arriving at Hull's office, the Japanese plan for a thirty-minute notice of a declaration of war did not occur, and the attack on Pearl Harbor thereafter was considered a sneak attack. The message itself was softened from an earlier draft, so that the final edition, after listing a series of complaints about the way the United States had conducted negotiations, stated that it was impossible to reach an agreement through further negotiations. While this was a stiff statement, it was not exactly a declaration of war. In fact, it was not so different from other aggressive messages from the Japanese foreign office, going back to the Matsuoka days.

US cryptographers, having already broken the Japanese diplomatic code, had produced a typed copy of the fourteenth part of the Japanese ultimatum even earlier than the staff at the Japanese embassy. As a result, Hull had read a copy of that part of the message before the diplomats arrived and was prepared by the news from Pearl Harbor. If Hull had thought that it was a declaration of war, he presumably would have attempted to alert the armed forces to immediately contact all commands, but he did not do so. However, he had time to prepare for the arrival of the Japanese. History records Hull's reaction to the fourteenth part to the envoys: "I've never seen a document that was more crowded with infamous falsehoods . . . on a scale so huge that I never imagined until today that any government on this planet was capable of uttering them."[188] The Japanese envoys, having been kept in the dark by their own government, were shocked by this turn of events. They departed for their own embassy, which gave them diplomatic protection.

Just before 2:30 p.m. on the East Coast, the radio networks were broadcasting the Pearl Harbor news. By 3:00 p.m., several senior officials and advisers were in the upstairs Oval Study—Stimson, Knox, Hopkins, Hull, Admiral Stark, and General Marshall. Roosevelt was furious and couldn't understand how his Navy had been caught so unprepared.

---

188   Nelson, 278.

Hopkins noted that the tone of the meeting, particularly with Stimson and Knox, was less horrified than resolved that the United States was finally in the war. At that point it was only a war with Japan, and the greater danger, Germany, was not involved. Thinking about further attacks, Roosevelt had a fundamental concern about the Panama Canal, because an attack making the canal inoperative would make it much more difficult to move ships from one ocean to the other.[189] Roosevelt also wanted to censor the full extent of the losses at Pearl Harbor to avoid panic in the general public.

It was still late morning at Pearl Harbor and the surrounding Pacific Ocean. *Nevada* was beached on the Waipaio Peninsula near the harbor entrance. *West Virginia* was sunk, and the superstructure above water was burning. *Arizona* had exploded, and was a sunken hulk, its burning oil still spread on the harbor surface. *Oklahoma* had capsized, and its huge bottom stuck out of the water. *California* was sunk. Fires on various ships would continue for three days before finally being extinguished.[190]

Hundreds of sailors on stricken ships were killed outright, and others were wounded or blown over the sides of their ships. On Ford Island, seriously wounded sailors crawled ashore with shattered limbs, heavy bleeding, or other serious injuries. One badly burned sailor managed to get to shelter covered in oil from swimming through an oil slick that was not on fire. The oil covered his burned flesh, and his blue eyes were stark against the black oil on his face.[191] Such medical personnel as were available did the best they could to cope with severe injuries.

There were great feats of heroism and brave actions beyond the call of duty. Onboard *California*, Gunner's Mate Jackson Pharris initiated counterflooding that prevented the ship from capsizing and then organized work parties to manually haul ammunition from the magazines to the guns. Pharris would be awarded the Medal of Honor for his heroism that

---

189   Nelson, 320.
190   Nelson, 298-301.
191   Nelson, 303-4.

day. Also on *California*, Machinist's Mate Robert Scott refused to abandon ship, even as the ship was sinking, so he could continue to run the forward air compressor whose power was needed for the anti-aircraft batteries. He also would be awarded the Medal of Honor—posthumously.[192] Sailors in a whaleboat made repeated trips to the edge of the flaming oil on the harbor surface to try to prevent the oil from spreading to other ships. When their whaleboat caught fire, they would back off to extinguish the fire and then move in again.

Meanwhile, on Ford Island, Lieutenant Commander Logan Ramsey, the same Ramsey who had reported a PBY sighting a submarine earlier, was trying to find out where the Japanese attack had come from. The Opana radar station was out of communication. All the PBYs at Kaneohe Point had been bombed or strafed. There was an intact squadron of antique Sikorsky parasol-winged amphibians used for mail deliveries and target towing, and these made a circle around Oahu, finding nothing. Contact with the Opana station was restored, and that station and B-17s still in the air indicated the Japanese force was north of Oahu. Kimmel's office broadcast the report of Japanese ships north of Oahu. A radio message was picked up giving a bearing, but the 1930s equipment produced a streak across the instrument screen so that an operator could not tell if the signal came from the north or south.

Some unidentified person said he had seen enemy ships thirty miles southwest of Barber's Point, south of Oahu. Kimmel's office ordered *Minneapolis* to catapult its search planes. The "enemy ships" turned out to be the *Minneapolis* and its escorts, so the search planes were looking for their own ships.[193] To make matters worse, a message stating "no" enemy ships were found was transcribed erroneously as "two" enemy ships found. Dauntless SBDs from *Enterprise* that had landed on Ford Island earlier were ordered back into the air to search the Barber's Point

---

192   Nelson, 296.

193   Nelson, 305.

area. They conducted a broad search south of Oahu and found nothing except *Minneapolis*.

At about 1100 two Seagull biplane scouts patrolling 100 miles north of Kauai were attacked by two Zeros. Staying virtually at wave-top height above the water, they survived the attack by executing slow-speed sharp turns. After inflicting some minor hits, the Zero pilots gave up, and the Seagulls made it back to Ford Island, more than 200 miles away. This encounter provided no actionable information because the pilots made no report of it until they landed, and the slow speed of the Seagulls made their eventual report useless.[194]

Several blatant gaps in operating procedures at Pearl Harbor became apparent. General Arnold, inspecting Hawaiian air defenses in September 1939, had noted the failure to integrate Air Force, Navy, and Army commands on Hawaii.[195] In the last months of 1941, the army had viewed Pearl Harbor primarily as a way station for ferrying B-17s to the Philippines. The Pacific Fleet commanders considered the water depth of Pearl Harbor too shallow for aerial torpedoes and consequently delayed installing torpedo nets. The ships tracking a midget submarine outside the harbor entrance could have provided several hours' notice of the attack had they sent an immediate, emergency, uncoded message. Better training of radar operations on Oahu could have provided an hour's notice prior to the attack. The army's antiaircraft batteries were unready. The squadron of thirty-six PBYs on Oahu had only three planes patrolling on the morning of December 7. To improve early warning capabilities, picket boats might have been stationed 600 miles north and west of Oahu to provide continuous coverage of the approaches to Pearl Harbor, instead of single reports from patrol planes as they reached the outer limits of their search patterns. The Japanese stationed picket boats 600 to 700 miles east

---

194   Nelson, 306.
195   Hamilton, 63.

of Tokyo, which, several months later, caused the Doolittle fliers to launch prematurely from *Hornet*.

The military heads in Washington, Admiral Stark and General Marshall, had thought a Japanese attack would come in the western or southern Pacific. They had issued war warnings to all Pacific commands continually over the months prior to the Pearl Harbor attack. The news from Pearl Harbor was as much of a surprise to them as it was to Kimmel and Short. It was also a surprise to those most responsible for Navy intelligence, Rear Admirals Richmond Kelly Turner, head of Navy War Plans, and Theodore Wilkinson, Director of Naval Intelligence. The latter received important information from MAGIC decoding and other sources that was not given to Admiral Kimmel.[196]

Roosevelt was so disappointed with his service chiefs that he considered firing them immediately. Almost everything they had done to prepare US forces for war in the Pacific had failed. Secretaries Stimson and Knox had not done any better. Roosevelt questioned both on their versions of what had happened and what they could do to repair the situation. Neither had immediate answers.[197] As for Secretary Hull, he blamed Stimson and Knox. As he "told his staff at the State Department, 'time after time' in recent months he had 'warned our military and naval men' with all the vigor at his command 'that there was constant danger of attack from Japan,' and how 'deeply' he regretted his 'warnings had not been taken more seriously.'"[198]

Across the Atlantic it was 9:00 p.m. in the UK, and Prime Minister Winston Churchill was outside London at Chequers, his country house. He had just finished dinner with his guests, US Ambassador Gil Winant and Mr. and Mrs. Averell Harriman, and turned on his new radio to stay abreast of the news. The Japanese strike at Pearl Harbor was a surprise and a shock. An aide made a call that went straight through

---

196   Paul Stillwell, *Air Raid: Pearl Harbor!* (Naval Institute Press, 1981), 87.

197   Hamilton, 65.

198   Hamilton, 69.

to the White House and Roosevelt. Churchill grabbed the phone. "Mr. President, what's this about Japan?" "It's true," Roosevelt replied. "They've attacked us at Pearl Harbor. We're all in the same boat now." As Churchill recorded later, he went to bed and "slept the sleep of the saved and thankful."[199] In Chunking, Chiang Kai-shek, a convert to Christianity, sang "Ave Maria."[200]

Back in Washington, alone in the late afternoon of December 7, a chastened Franklin Roosevelt considered the situation. He had dealt with his shocked and uncertain cabinet advisers after the immediate news of the Pearl Harbor attack, and they had now departed. Eight years earlier, Roosevelt had rallied a despairing and depressed country over the financial and economic collapse with an inaugural speech that assured the country "we have nothing to fear but fear itself." Now he had to again communicate a message of confidence and resolution.

Roosevelt gathered his thoughts. He may have wondered how things had gone so terribly wrong, how many were dead, and how many more would die. But what might have been was now hindsight—the United States was at war and was in it to win. He spoke quietly to his secretary, Grace Tully. "Sit down, Grace. I'm going before Congress tomorrow. I'd like to dictate my message. It will be short." Taking his time, he began dictating the message that would again mobilize the nation. It began, "Yesterday, December seventh, 1941, a date which will live in world history, the United States was suddenly and deliberately attacked by naval and air forces of the Empire of Japan."

He continued for about 500 words, citing deceitful diplomacy and the massive, preplanned attacks that, even as he spoke, were still occurring throughout the western and southern Pacific. He concluded, "No matter how long it may take us to overcome this premeditated invasion, the American people in their righteous might will win through to absolute

---

199   Nelson, 322.
200   Hotta, 9.

victory." Tully typed the dictation, and when she brought it back, he crossed out "world history" in the first line and wrote "infamy."

Later in the evening the cabinet and congressional leaders gathered around the president again. A message arrived that the Japanese had struck the army airfield in the Philippines and destroyed the B-17s on the ground. More messages of simultaneous attacks by Japanese forces were coming in from Hong Kong, Thailand, the East Indies, Guam, and Wake Island. It was a staggering execution of air, naval, and amphibious power carried out with precise timing and skill. Roosevelt reviewed the message he had dictated to Grace Tully earlier in the day with the cabinet. Hull and Stimson, having regained their composure, advised that he should make a longer address citing the numerous transgressions of the Japanese. Roosevelt brushed these comments aside.

Just 24 hours after the Pearl Harbor attack, President Roosevelt, grim and determined, appeared before a joint session of Congress and began his speech: "Yesterday, December seventh, 1941—a date which will live in infamy . . ." He continued, interrupted by thunderous applause from the representatives and senators throughout the speech and even more at the end. A motion to declare war on Japan passed both houses of Congress almost unanimously. The United States and Japan were at war.

As a result of the total surprise and apparent unpreparedness at Pearl Harbor, there were public demands to assign blame. The most horrendous losses at Pearl Harbor had been suffered by the Navy, and the person in Washington most directly responsible for the Navy was the Secretary of the Navy, Frank Knox. Both Roosevelt and Knox realized he had to avoid the immediate hard questions, get out of Washington, and be seen getting control of the situation. That meant an immediate flying trip to inspect the damage at Pearl Harbor. The fury and lust for vengeance that swept the country focused on the destruction and losses suffered primarily by the Navy. In the new determination to wage war the actions of cabinet members and other civilian officials leading up to the war were largely unknown outside a select few officials, and were overlooked.

Admiral Stark communicated with Admiral Kimmel again the day after the Pearl Harbor attack. Anticipating that the Striking Force was still in the area, possibly replenishing at bases in the Marshall Islands, Stark said he expected another attack on the Pearl Harbor shore installations and anticipated attempts to occupy Midway, the big island of Hawaii, and Maui. He hoped that the islands of Johnston, Palmyra, and Samoa might be held.[201] Kimmel replied, acknowledging the damage, but also emphasized that the Pacific Fleet carriers were intact, the shore facilities and fuel storage tanks were untouched, and the morale of officers and men was resolute. Anticipating the arrival of Secretary Knox on December 11, he prepared an operating program for his forces going forward. Acknowledging that the loss of battleships limited his offensive options, he stressed that the Pacific Fleet still had a powerful force of carriers, cruisers, destroyers, and submarines. Specifically, he anticipated employing three carrier strike groups, with two at sea at all times and one in port for replenishment. He would have the remaining cruisers and destroyers organized for convoy work maintaining communications with the West Coast, employ submarines offensively against Japan in the western Pacific, and support army buildup of pursuit and patrol planes and bomber strength.[202]

Roosevelt had realized some months earlier that the United States would have to join the war against Hitler. However, he faced several problems. Prior to Pearl Harbor, the United States had not been attacked by either Germany or Japan, and Roosevelt was adamant that the United States would not initiate hostilities. Before Pearl Harbor, the isolationist movement was powerful, but after Pearl Harbor it collapsed. The Armed Forces were only now rearming and were still not ready for a wider war. The United States was in the war, but there was no way for the army to land on any territory controlled by Japan or deploy a force

---

201   Morison, 219.
202   Morison, 222.

against Germany. The only armed service that could take any effective action anywhere for the foreseeable months was the United States Navy.

On December 9, two days after the attack, Roosevelt broadcast a Fireside Chat to the nation. He stated what had happened at Pearl Harbor and what the country was going to do in response:[203]

> *My fellow Americans:*
>
> *The sudden criminal acts perpetrated by the Japanese in the Pacific provide the climax of a decade of international immorality. Powerful and resourceful gangsters have banded together to make war upon the whole human race . . .*
> *The Congress and the people of the United States have accepted that challenge . . . We are now in this war, and we are in it—all the way.*

Roosevelt went on to say that the government would make public all pertinent facts as soon as they were verified. He warned against spreading rumors, identifying this as "an old trick of propaganda . . . to spread fear and confusion among us." Regarding newspapers and radio stations,

> *You have a most grave responsibility to the nation now . . . you have no right in the ethics of patriotism to deal out unconfirmed reports in such a way as to make people believe that they are gospel truth . . . Every citizen, in every walk of life, shares this same responsibility.*

Then Roosevelt turned to the specific plans for the war:

> *It will not only be a long war, it will be a hard war . . . Production will be increased by working on a seven day week basis in every war industry, and by building more new plants, by adding to old plants, and by using the many smaller plants for war needs.*

---

203   Roosevelt, 99-104.

He spoke on sacrifice:

The United States does not consider it a sacrifice to do all one can, to give one's best to our nation, when the nation is fighting for its existence and its future life.

And he explained the final goal:

I repeat that the United States can accept no result save victory, final and complete. Not only must the shame of Japanese treachery be wiped out, but the sources of international brutality, wherever they exist, must be absolutely and finally broken . . . The true goal we seek is far above and beyond the ugly field of battle . . . [W]e are determined that this force shall be directed toward ultimate good as well as against immediate evil . . . We are now in the midst of a war, not for conquest, not for vengeance, but for a world in which this nation, and all that this nation represents, will be safe for our children . . . So we are going to win the war and we are going to win the peace that follows.

Navy Secretary Knox returned to Washington from his flying inspection visit to Pearl Harbor and Pacific Fleet headquarters. To quell public outcry it was necessary that someone be identified and held responsible for the disaster, and the most readily available targets were the admiral in command of the Pacific Fleet and the Army general at Oahu. After Knox returned to Washington, on December 17 Admiral Kimmel and General Short were relieved, and Kimmel was reduced to the permanent rank of two stars. It showed once again that every officer, from ensign to admiral, serves at the pleasure of the president. Abrupt removals have little recourse.

The following day, December 18, a commission was appointed by executive order "to ascertain and report the facts relating to the attack made by Japanese armed forces upon the Territory of Hawaii on December

7, 1941."[204] The members of the commission were Supreme Court Justice Owen Roberts, Admiral W. H. Standley, Admiral J. M. Reeves, General Frank R. McCoy, and General Joseph T. McNarney. It would be known as the Roberts Commission. The commission held 30 meetings between December 18, 1941, and January 23, 1942, both in Washington and in Oahu. A total of 127 people were interviewed under oath. These included cabinet officers, Armed Forces officers including Admiral Kimmel and General Short, and civilians who were involved with the Japanese attack. More than 3,000 pages of documents were examined. The report to Congress was made on January 28, 1942.

The Roberts Commission concluded that the Secretary of State, the Secretary of War, the Secretary of the Navy, the Army Chief of Staff, and the Chief of Naval Operations had fulfilled their obligations and command responsibilities. The commission also found that Admiral Kimmel and General Short were derelict in "failure to confer with respect to warnings" and failure to execute "the distant reconnaissance of the Navy, and the inshore air patrol of the Army." In its concluding paragraph, the commission stated, "The Japanese attack was a complete surprise to the commanders and they failed to make suitable dispositions to meet such an attack . . . These errors of judgment were the effective causes for the success of the attack."[205]

Admiral Kimmel retired from the Navy later in 1942 and took measures to mitigate his liability for the attack. In September 1945, pursuant to an executive order, a congressional Joint Committee on the Investigation of the Pearl Harbor Attack was formed. The committee heard forty-four witnesses, including Admiral Kimmel, General Short, Ambassador Grew, and former Secretary of State Hull. The hearing transcript came to over 5,000 pages and was supplemented by 14,000 pages of printed exhibits. The Joint Committee, in its final report on

---

204   Presidential Order of December 18, 1941.

205   Roberts Commission, Conclusions, Para. 18.

June 20, 1946, concluded that "[t]he Hawaiian commands . . . made errors of judgment and not derelictions of duty."[206]

Despite the Joint Committee report softening the criticism of the Roberts Commission, Admiral Kimmel continued in his attempts to clear his reputation. He referenced a series of critical messages (the MAGIC intercepts) between the United States and Japanese governments immediately prior to the Pearl Harbor attack that were never sent to him. Decrypted spy reports, updated daily, that disclosed detailed positions of the ships in Pearl Harbor prior to the attack were never passed to him. Months earlier, he had specifically requested of Admiral Stark that he be copied on all relevant information and was assured this would be done. He noted and considered it remiss that MAGIC codebreaking capabilities were given to the small Asiatic Fleet and to the British government in London but not to the Pacific Fleet command. He later discovered that some parts of the US government assumed he was receiving MAGIC intelligence when in fact he was not, adding further to his contention that he was disciplined unjustly. He maintained that had he received relevant and timely information, he would have taken greater actions to protect the Pacific Fleet, to have taken the fleet to sea when the attack was imminent, and to have mobilized his forces at sea against the attacking Japanese carrier force.

Admiral Kimmel died in 1968 at the age of eighty-six, and family members continued efforts to clear his reputation. In 1999 a bill to restore his four-star rank passed through Congress but was never signed into law. Despite this, the granite memorial on his grave in the Naval Academy cemetery at Annapolis is engraved with four stars.

---

206   Joint Committee on the Pearl Harbor Attack, June 20, 1946, Process, Second Paragraph.

Roosevelt address to Congress
Photo Public Domian, wikpedia.org

CHAPTER 14

The Battle for Wake Island

Roosevelt spent a lot of time on matters concerning the Navy. He was actively involved in flag officer assignments—and the resulting promotions. Rear Admiral Chester W. Nimitz was chief of the Bureau of Navigation, which, despite the misleading title, had primary responsibility for non-flag assignments and had influence on fleet commands. Roosevelt's interest in these matters would have drawn him into regular contact with Nimitz, and he was impressed with the admiral's ability and judgment. On the same day Admiral Kimmel was relieved, Roosevelt appointed Nimitz commander-in-chief of the Pacific Fleet. The promotion from two stars directly to four stars skipped over the third star and fifty-six other, more senior admirals. Roosevelt's message to Nimitz was simple and straightforward: "Get out to Pearl Harbor and don't come back until the war is won." His confidence in Nimitz was confirmed throughout the war.

Chester W. Nimitz was born in Fredericksburg, Texas in 1885 and graduated near the top of his class at the US Naval Academy in 1905. His early career was in ships of the Asiatic Fleet. His assignments to submarines built his expertise in that class of vessel when submarines themselves were primitive and hazardous. He also became an innovator in the use and design of diesel engines. He was executive officer of the battleship *South Carolina* and commanding officer of the cruisers *Chicago* and *Augusta*. Assignments ashore involved two tours in the Bureau of Navigation, interspersed with command of Battleship Division

One. Seeing how a navy had to operate in the vast expanses of the Pacific Ocean, he innovated techniques in underway replenishment.

Dealing quickly with his affairs in Washington, Nimitz turned over his responsibilities at the Bureau of Navigation and prepared for his new assignment at Pearl Harbor. His devoted wife of many years, thinking of the warm weather in Hawaii, pinned the four-star insignias of rank to the collars of a tan summer uniform shirt. Rolling across the United States by train, he would not reach Pearl Harbor for another week after his appointment.

Vice Admiral William S. Pye, commander of the Pacific Fleet Battle Force in Pearl Harbor, was appointed interim commander of the Pacific Fleet pending Nimitz's arrival. Pye brought many of his Battle Force staff to Pacific Fleet headquarters. He also brought aboard Rear Admiral Milo Draemel, commander of the destroyer flotilla at Pearl Harbor, as his chief of staff. Draemel brought several of his officers with him as well. Pye's plan was to integrate all these officers with the existing Pacific Fleet staff while awaiting Nimitz's arrival. However, the Imperial Japanese Navy had no intention of waiting for Nimitz's arrival, and the fight for Wake Island was already underway.

Wake Island, 2300 miles west of Pearl Harbor, consisted of three islands that formed a rough rectangle enclosing a lagoon. The largest island, a V-shaped landmass at the south, east and north was Wake, to the west was the small Wilkes Island, and to the north was Peale Island. The entirety of Wake was annexed as a territory by the United States in 1899, and a 4,500-foot airstrip was built in January 1941. Wake had been a stopover point for the amphibious Pan American Clippers since the mid-1930s. The Clipper carrying Ambassador Kurusu had stopped there several weeks earlier as he was making his hasty trip to Washington.

Of the 1,738 persons on Wake at the time of the Pearl Harbor attack, 449 were Marines under the command of Major James P. S. Devereux, 68 were Navy personnel under the command of Commander Winfield Scott Cunningham, and five Army personnel manned a small communications unit. Commander Cunningham, as the senior line officer, was the island commander. The civilians consisted of approximately seventy Pan American employees and 1,146 employees of the Morrison-Knudsen Company, there under an agreement to complete aircraft servicing facilities and various buildings.[207]

Admiral Kimmel had realized months before the Pearl Harbor attack that desolate Wake was strategically important to both the United States and Japan in the event of war. In a letter to Admiral Stark dated April 18, 1941, he recommended that Marine ground forces, fighter planes, and Pacific Fleet carriers be assigned to support the defense of Wake. These forces would be capable of repelling up to a medium-sized force if the Japanese attempted to invade. The alternate plan was to evacuate the island and remove all personnel—both armed forces and civilians.

The Marine buildup occurred over several months, beginning in August. Major Devereaux arrived in October with another detachment of Marines and took command of the entire Marine force on the island. Major Devereaux also brought three batteries of twin five-inch naval guns, twelve three-inch antiaircraft guns, and thirty machine guns. The five-inch guns were set up at Peacock Point on the southeast corner of Wake, on the western tip of Wilkes, and on the western tip of Peale.[208]

Major Devereaux believed it would be impossible to hold the island against a major attack, and he discussed this with officers of the Marine and Pacific Fleet commands before he left Pearl Harbor. The transfer of the recommended air unit for Wake was delayed, and Squadron 211, consisting of twelve F4F-3 fighters, was finally transferred by the carrier *Enterprise* only four days before the Pearl Harbor attack.[209] In a fortunate turn of events, that delivery resulted in *Enterprise* being away from Pearl Harbor at the time of the attack.

---

207 Morison, 228-229.
208 Morison, Vol. 3, 229.
209 Morison, *Rising Sun*, Vol. 3, 228.

December 7 in Pearl Harbor was December 8 on Wake Island and all other territories west of the international date line, which runs north-south on the Pacific Ocean just east of Midway and well to the east of Wake. Within minutes of the attack on Pearl Harbor, a force of thirty-four Japanese G3M medium bombers took off from airfields in the Marshall Islands and were over Wake by noon. There was no radar on Wake, and there were no sounds above the pounding surf as the planes glided in out of the clouds from 1,500 feet. The one lookout posted atop an oil tank had only seconds to sound an alarm before bombs were exploding on the runway, and eight of the twelve F4F-3s delivered by *Enterprise* only four days earlier were destroyed on the ground. Ground crews on the runway and around the planes were cut down by bombs, exploding planes, and strafing, and in the first few minutes of the attack more than half of the ground crew was either killed or injured. Ten Pan American employees were killed, and the ground facilities were extensively damaged. The remaining four F4F-3s of the squadron were patrolling at 12,000 feet, but the cloud layer far below prevented them from seeing the attack. Similar attacks were carried out on following days. One of the F4F-3s damaged in the first attack was reconstructed by cannibalizing parts from other destroyed planes, and the defenders then had five operational fighters.

Dependents and civilians had been evacuated from Guam in October 1941 in response to the increasingly tense situation in the Pacific. Civilians on Wake remained. The question for the Navy command now was whether to reinforce the Marine garrison on Wake or evacuate all Armed Forces and civilian personnel. Despite Admiral Kimmel's letter of April 18, no advance plan had been made. Admiral Pye and the Pacific Fleet staff were uncertain whether the afloat forces could move promptly enough to the area of Wake, and once there ensure air control over the island while carrying out either option.

It also was unclear to Admiral Pye how much power the Japanese had on the Marshalls to employ against Wake. Naval Intelligence had picked up information leading it to believe there was a significant assignment of submarines in the Marshalls, possibly indicating a major deployment of forces. It also was possible that the Japanese carrier Striking Force had moved westward after the attack on Pearl Harbor and would now appear at Wake to support an invasion. Judging from the number of planes the Japanese had used in the Pearl Harbor attack, Naval Intelligence estimated that at least four and as many as six carriers had taken part. However, a decision to execute either plan—reinforcement or evacuation—was deferred pending further developments. Meanwhile, on Wake, the Japanese attacked each day with medium bombers from the Marshalls, and the continuous pounding was taking a toll on men and equipment. It was clear the Japanese planned an invasion, and time was of the essence. The Marine pilots flew with skill and courage against huge odds, but daily air combat was taking a toll.

Just before 0300 on December 11, Major Devereaux was awakened by a lookout who reported faint lights on the horizon. He immediately ordered his bugler to sound the call to arms, and Marines, scrambling to their gun positions, could see by moonlight a column of ships headed by three light cruisers approaching the island. The lead ship was *Yubari*, flagship of Cruiser Division 18 under the command of Rear Admiral Kajioka Sadamichi, together with two additional light cruisers, *Tatsuta* and *Tenryu*.[210] Other ships in the column were the six destroyers of Destroyer Divisions 29 and 30, two transports containing garrison troops, and two converted destroyers equipped for disembarking the No. 2 Maizuru Special Naval Landing Force.

The column dispersed. At first light *Yubari* and the other two light cruisers took firing lines parallel to the Wake southern shore and began shore bombardment of the island. Major Devereaux ordered the artillery positions to hold fire until he gave the order. Three destroyers came in close to the southern shore to support the landing parties, and three

---

210   Morison, 231.

others took a course to the western shore to deliver enfilade fire. The Special Naval Landing Force were preparing to disembark into landing craft. *Yubari* continued to close its firing line from 8,000 yards to 4,500 yards, and at that point Devereaux gave the order to commence firing. After several straddles of the five-inch battery on Wake, *Yubari* was hit.[211] The five-inch battery on Wilkes sank destroyer *Hayate*, and also hit a troop transport and cruiser *Tenryu*. The third five-inch battery on Peale, which was out of range for the attack off the south shore, opened up on the three destroyers off the west shore, hitting one.

The entire invasion force turned south and retreated behind smoke screens. The flyable F4Fs, jury-rigged with hundred-pound bombs, took off from the airstrip to pursue the retreating force. F4Fs are fighters, not attack planes, and are not designed for or normally equipped with ordnance. Hundred-pound bombs were all that could be loaded onto those planes and still allow them to fly. The effort paid off. One bomb hit a rack of depth charges on destroyer *Kisaragi*, causing a huge explosion that blew off the stern and sank the ship.[212] Admiral Inoue had underestimated the strength and tenacity of the defenses on Wake. It was a great victory for the U.S. Marines.[213]

To deal with the situation on Wake, the Pacific Fleet carriers were organized into three Task Forces:

Task Force 14, including carrier *Saratoga* with Rear Admiral Aubrey Fitch, was underway on December 8 from California. *Saratoga* was bringing Marine Corps Fighter Squadron 221, a force of eighteen Brewster Buffalo fighters. Task Force 14 was expected in Pearl Harbor on December 12.[214] The Buffalo squadron would reinforce the four remaining F4F-3s of Squadron 211 on Wake. Rear Admiral Frank Jack Fletcher, commanding Cruiser Division 6—*Astoria*, *Minneapolis*, and

---

211   Devereaux, 45-47.

212   Morison, 232-234.

213   Morison, Vol. 3 234.

214   Morison, Vol. 3, 235-236.

San Francisco—entered Pearl Harbor on December 10 and waited for TF-14 to arrive from San Diego to form a consolidated TF-14.[215] As the senior rear admiral, Fletcher would be in overall command.[216]

Task Force 11, under the command of Vice Admiral Wilson Brown, included carrier *Lexington*, three heavy cruisers—*Indianapolis, Chicago,* and *Portland*—Destroyer Squadron 1, and tanker *Neosho.* The force departed Pearl Harbor on December 14 after refueling and repairing refueling equipment on *Neosho.* Its mission was to bomb Jaluit in the Japanese-held Marshalls to distract attention from TF-14's mission to Wake.

Task Force 8, with *Enterprise* under the command of Vice Admiral Halsey, departed Pearl on December 20. Task Force 8 was to remain in a support position just west of Johnston Island and south of Midway— about halfway between Wake and Oahu—to provide support to either island. The location of the Japanese carrier Striking Force that had attacked Pearl Harbor was unknown at that time, and Admiral Stark in Washington was concerned about the security of the Hawaiian Islands. Whether a position more than 1,000 miles from both Wake and Pearl Harbor would have allowed timely support to either location was never tested.

The 492-foot seaplane tender *Tangier* in Pearl Harbor was also awaiting the arrival of TF-14, when it would join that force for the passage to Wake. *Tangier* was ready to disembark a detachment of the Fourth Marine Defense Battalion, together with their arms, ammunition, radar, fire control systems, and other equipment on Wake. TF-14, when fully constituted, would contain the air and ground force reinforcements for Wake, and also be prepared to make evacuations. If Pacific Fleet command decided to do a total evacuation, *Tangier,* in the opinion of Captain Charles H. McMorris of the Pacific Fleet staff, would be available

---

215 Morison, 237.

216 Morison, Vol. 3, 236-237.

to evacuate all persons—Armed Forces and civilians—on Wake Island, even with the Fourth Marine Defense Battalion still embarked. This appears in retrospect to be a heavy demand for a ship of that size.

The narrow and shallow channel between reefs at Wake meant that vessels larger than patrol boats had to stay offshore. Equipment offloading required the use of lighters, and evacuation required boats to bring personnel to the ships. Under battle conditions, including air and possible submarine attacks, execution of either reinforcement or evacuation would be hazardous. Amphibious ships anchor in position to carry out their operations, and without control of the air over the landing site the ships are sitting ducks to air attack. Any operation to disembark Marines or onload civilians could be accomplished only with enough air power to stop the bombers making daily attacks on Wake. If that could not be accomplished, any amphibious operation at Wake, whether for reinforcement or evacuation, was completely out of the question.

Tangier, with its tanker *Neches*, could make only thirteen knots with a following sea. Their speed dictated the speed of TF-14, and the resulting eight-day trip to Wake planned for a December 13 departure meant that TF-14, consisting of the three cruisers of Cruiser Division 6 with Rear Admiral Fletcher, *Saratoga* with Rear Admiral Fitch, and *Tangier*, was scheduled to arrive at Wake on December 21.

TF-14 departed San Diego on December 8 as scheduled but was delayed near Oahu by heavy weather and submarine scares. The force finally entered Pearl Harbor on December 15. On that day, *Tangier* and *Neches* were sent ahead for Wake. The rest of TF-14 departed Pearl on December 16 and caught up to *Tangier* a day later, after which the combined force proceeded across the Pacific to Wake. Because of the delay at Pearl Harbor, TF-14 would not arrive at Wake until December 23. To make an earlier arrival at Wake, *Tangier* and *Neches* could have been sent ahead several days before TF-14 arrived at Pearl, and the faster cruisers and *Saratoga* would have caught up with them farther along the route, but this was not done.

Vice Admiral Inoue, embarrassed by the failure of the first invasion attempt on December 11, was now taking no chances. Rear Admiral Kajioka was given an opportunity to save face from his earlier defeat. Early on December 20, Kajioka departed Kwajalein in the Marshalls with a new invasion force defended by four heavy cruisers and approximately 2,000 members of the highly trained Special Naval Landing Force. This force was scheduled to land on December 22. It would be supplemented by 800 garrison troops that would land in a second wave. Many of these forces had taken part in the Guam invasion and had moved approximately 1,400 miles to the Marshalls since that time. The heavy cruisers could pound the Marines from firing positions beyond the range of the artillery on Wake.

The daily flight of the medium bombers continued, now supplemented by seaplane tender *Chitose* and its complement of twenty-eight seaplanes, which bombed the Marine positions morning and afternoon.[217] The Japanese invasion was opposed by less than 500 US Marines.

Also on December 20, Pye ordered Vice Admiral Brown in TF-11 to abandon the feint on the Marshalls and steam north toward Wake. TF-11 could be near Wake by December 22. An earlier order to leave the Marshalls for Wake would have placed TF-11 in a position to intercept the approaching Japanese landing force, which had no carriers assigned to it for fighter protection. Pye informed Chief of Naval Operations Admiral Harold Stark in Washington of his order, who replied that both he and Admiral Ernest J. King, Chief of Naval Operations, after reading their messages and studying their charts, now considered Wake to be a liability. They authorized Pye to evacuate the personnel on Wake rather than reinforce them.[218] However, *Tangier*, the only ship capable

---

217   Morison, Vol. 3, 245.

218   Morison, 251.

of executing an evacuation, had been delayed waiting for *Saratoga* and could not be on the scene until December 23.

On December 21 at 0900, Japanese Val dive-bombers attacked Wake.[219] These planes were flown from carriers, so it was obvious the Striking Force, or a component of it, had moved to within operating range of Wake to support the amphibious landings. This was Carrier Division 2, comprising carriers *Hiryu* and *Soryu*, commanded by Rear Admiral Yamaguchi. All the Striking Force carriers had been trained to peak performance, and of the three carrier divisions, CarDiv2 was the best of the best. Had *Lexington* arrived by December 21 in time to oppose the Japanese landing force, it would have been confronted by CarDiv2—unless it could have intercepted the landing force well south of Wake, out of range of CarDiv2 planes.

On December 22 the Vals returned, this time escorted by Zero fighters. The Zeros shot down the last of the F4F-3 defenders, eliminating the last fighters on Wake. CarDiv2 planes were seen flying from the north, and they now supplemented the medium-range bombers and seaplanes flying from the Marshalls. CarDiv2 was supported by cruisers *Chikuma* and *Tone*, each with the same long-range search planes they had used at Pearl Harbor.

Late in the day on December 22, the lookouts on Wake saw a huge volume of light flashes on the horizon that showed the approach of a major Japanese fleet. Identifying heavy cruisers and knowing they would stay out of range of the five-inch guns on Wake, Major Devereaux sent the Marines manning five-inch guns to beach positions, manning machine guns. The three-inch anti-aircraft guns were altered to fire their guns horizontally.

As darkness fell small amphibious personnel ships were offloading the special landing force onto barges that would transfer them to the beaches. The three-inch gun crews set fire to ships discharging the

---

219   Devereaux, 84.

landing force. In the light of the fires, the machine gunners could see many barges with about fifty men in each and they took a fearsome toll on the invaders. Despite these casualties, hundreds were coming ashore against the dispersed forces of Marines. Patrols reported landings on the southern beaches of Wake and Wilkes, and the Marines met the invaders in ferocious fighting.[220]

A detachment of the landing force in rubber boats paddled into the channel between Wake and Wilkes and landed behind the Marine positions. Mortar and small guns on the landing ships dropped shells into Marine fortifications. Japanese landing forces were so numerous that they surrounded some positions, but Marines kept fighting even when there was no escape. One detachment of Marines held off hundreds of Japanese for several hours until all but one was killed or wounded.[221] Sometimes it came down to hand-to-hand combat, with Marines fighting Japanese troops with bayonets.

As dawn broke Marines saw Japanese in padded suits with tanks on their backs: flamethrowers. These were cut down by machine gun fire.[222] All along the beaches Devereaux could see Japanese flags showing their locations so that offshore bombardment would not be aimed at these positions. Commander Cunningham sent a message to Pye at Pearl Harbor: "The enemy is on the Island. The issue is in doubt."[223]

Just before Pye received the "issue in doubt" message from Cunningham, he received another message from Admiral Stark, who reminded Pye that concern was strong about the safety of the Hawaiian Islands and at the same time expressed the feeling that a successful relief of Wake would be of great "moral" value. He cautioned him to avoid unduly exposing ships by their protracted presence in one area." He added, "Wake was now considered a liability." It was signed by Stark,

220 Devereaux, 96.
221 Morison, Vol. 3, 248.
222 Devereaux, 107-108.
223 Morison, 248.

and a notation was added that Admiral King concurred.[224] In case the situation turned out badly, the two admirals in Washington were well covered by warning against all the possible outcomes.

Also on December 23, CarDiv2 was operating approximately 200 miles directly north of Wake, and *Hiryu* and *Soryu* were supplying aerial support for the landing forces. TF-14, with the carrier *Saratoga*, approached to approximately 325 miles northeast of Wake and refueled its destroyers. CarDiv2 was about 240 miles directly west of TF-14. The two carrier forces were within the operating range of the Japanese planes but beyond the 175-mile operating range of the US planes. Neither the CarDiv2 nor the TF-14 commands apparently was aware of the existence of the other force.

Monitoring the battle from Pearl Harbor, on December 23 Admiral Pye asked the two senior officers of his combined staff for written advice. Both agreed that neither fortifying Wake nor evacuating personnel was then possible against the air strength of the Japanese forces. Admiral Draemel, aware of the Japanese carriers of unknown strength within range of Wake, argued that risking the Pacific Fleet carriers in what was now a hopeless ground battle on Wake made no sense. Captain McMorris argued that it was possible for *Saratoga*, which had been delayed by destroyer refueling, to leave the destroyers behind and make a high-speed run toward Wake to launch an attack the following morning, December 24. TF-11, coming up from the south, would be close enough to Wake to participate. TF-8, still some distance away, would be brought into position to support the subsequent withdrawal. McMorris argued that refusing battle "would destroy service and public confidence."[225] If *Saratoga* left its destroyers behind and made a run toward Wake, however, it would be on a course with a closest point of approach (CPA) of 150 miles to CarDiv2, and discovery by CarDiv2 would have been

224   Graybar, Lloyd J. *The Journal of the National Archives*, Volume 12, 1980, 135-150.
225   Toll, 155.

inevitable. The reasons for leaving the refueled destroyers behind was not clear. In a battle north of Wake between *Saratoga* without escorts and the two carriers of CarDiv2, the odds would not have been good for *Saratoga*, and TF-11, still south of Wake, was too far away to participate.

Considering the options and the risks involved, Pye ordered the afloat forces to withdraw from Wake. As an interim commander for one week, he did not want to turn over a diminished fleet to Nimitz. The order to withdraw prompted great consternation aboard the ships. During this episode, despite two Pacific Fleet carrier task forces in the operating area of Wake Island, there had not been a shot fired or a plane flown against the enemy.

On Wake, Major Devereaux contacted Commander Cunningham, who thought of the 1,000 unarmed civilians on Wake. There were no relief forces forthcoming. Cunningham attempted to contact two submarines in the area to attack the Japanese fleet, but Pacific Fleet command informed him that the submarines had been ordered back to Pearl Harbor.[226] As the senior officer on the island, with no hope for relief and to prevent further casualties, Cunningham ordered the surrender of Wake Island.[227] Admiral Kajioka came ashore in dress whites with sword and medals to accept the surrender of all US forces on Wake. Surrender meant leaving all persons—Armed Forces and civilians—to their fate with the Japanese. After the US forces surrendered CarDiv2 departed for Japan.

Pye's presence as an interim commander in the Wake Island battle created confusion in the Pacific Fleet command and staff structure. Knox, while at Pearl Harbor, surely witnessed the Pacific Fleet command directing the battle over Wake. He could have retained Kimmel in command until the Wake battle was decided, or Nimitz arrived. Instead, he flew back to Washington, relieved Kimmel, and replaced him for

---

226 Morison, Vol. 3, 249.

227 Devereaux, 111.

a week with Pye—the week during which the Battle of Wake Island reached its climax.

In the fight for Wake Island, the Marines lost forty-nine men and the Navy three. Civilian deaths were 70, for a total on the US side of 122. The estimates of Japanese losses vary widely, from 381 to as many as 1,000.[228] The surrendered Marine garrison, small Navy and Army units, and more than 1,100 civilians were loaded onto a merchant ship for transportation to prisoner of war camps in Japan. Later most were moved to China. A contingent of 98 workers were kept behind on Wake as slave laborers to continue construction of facilities, now for the Japanese Army.

Those who survived the Japanese invasion of Wake would spend the remainder of the war in captivity, subjected to brutal conditions and atrocities by the Japanese Army. They were continually beaten with riding crops and bats and tormented by bloodsucking lice and bedbugs. They fought with rats for miserable scraps of food. Sanitation was nonexistent, and illnesses were rampant. This went on for nearly four years until liberation came in September 1945, soon after the Japanese surrender. Some men died in captivity, and many of those liberated had physical and mental health problems for the rest of their lives. Credit for those who survived is due primarily to Major Devereaux, Commander Cunningham, and the senior civilian managers, who maintained a form of discipline that instilled hope against the terrible cruelty inflicted on them. The ninety-eight workmen left behind on Wake were lined up and machine-gunned in 1943 when it looked like an invasion was coming. The Japanese officer on Wake who ordered the executions was hanged after a war crimes trial in 1947.

The US government, after several years of delay following the war, finally decided to compensate the survivors of Wake at the rate of $2.50 for each day they were in captivity, or slightly more than ten cents for each miserable hour they spent at the hands of their Japanese Army

---

228   Naval History and Heritage Command, 1941, "The Forsaken Defenders of Wake Island."

captors. No one has explained why the Morrison-Knudson workers were left on Wake to continue the construction project when war was imminent and similar civilian workers had been evacuated from Guam.

Admirals King and Stark, in direct control of the Wake operation during the Pacific Fleet command transition, knew Japanese air forces attacked Wake within hours of the Pearl Harbor attack, that possession of Wake was important to the Japanese, and that the Japanese had significant forces available for an assault. A reinforcement operation, dependent on *Saratoga* making the transit from San Diego, to be carried out in the face of strong opposition was a serious misjudgment. Waiting for *Saratoga*, with its eighteen F4Fs, hardly made sense when a major invasion attempt could be expected, including air support from the Marshalls and from the Striking Force after its attack on Pearl Harbor.

The Guam evacuation had been carried out months before Pearl Harbor when war was threatened. A similar move had not been made at Wake, despite its proximity to the Japanese forces on the Marshall Islands. The reinforcement force of Marines embarked on *Tangier* would not have added enough to repel the second Japanese invasion, as Major Deveroux had predicted prior to his assignment to Wake. After Pearl Harbor the best chance to avoid the surrender and subsequent brutal imprisonment of the Wake personnel was a complete evacuation of Wake by *Tangier* immediately after the Pearl Harbor attack. *Enterprise*, *Lexington* and *Tangier* were at Pearl Harbor on December 8 and available to get underway immediately. That combined force, commanded by Admiral Halsey on *Enterprise*, could have made the eight-day transit to Wake, arriving by December 16. Two squadrons of Wildcat fighters on the two carriers could have achieved air control over Wake, and the evacuation would have been completed in two days, prior to the arrival of CarDiv2. Instead, the time gained by the valiant Marines in repelling the first invasion attempt on December 11 was squandered.

The Wake debacle, coming just after the Pearl Harbor disaster, was the result of inept leadership from the Navy secretary down through the chain of command, including Admirals King and Stark. There was no organized inquiry over the battle for Wake, and none of them was ever held to account for the Wake debacle. It was going to be a long way back for the U.S. Navy.

Admiral Chester Nimitz
Photo Naval History and Heritage

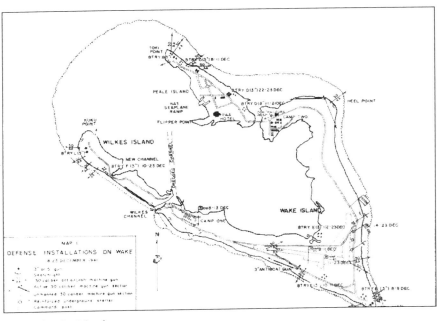

Chart of Wake Island
Photo Naval History and Heritage

CHAPTER 15

Pacific Fleet Carrier Raids

After the Striking Force carriers returned to Japan after the Pearl Harbor attack, Admiral Yamamoto decided to send them into the Indian Ocean to fight the British around Ceylon (Sri Lanka). His rationale for this move may have been to cut off the arms and equipment offloaded at Burma that supplied Chiang Kai-shek's army in China. He even may have thought that destroying the Royal Navy in the Indian Ocean would create an opportunity for Japan to take over the eastern portion of British-hating India. None of these considerations carries weight against the war then beginning with the ultimately powerful United States, however, and Yamamoto's decision to move the Striking Force into the Indian Ocean at that time raises serious questions about his strategic judgment.

After a short rest and celebration of their successful Pearl Harbor attack, the Striking Force was underway again. The carriers arrived at Truk on January 14 in preparation for the invasion of Rabaul, on New Britain Island at the northwest end of the Solomon Islands chain. On January 23 Japanese amphibious forces invaded, supported by the Striking Force carriers. The operation was completed by February 4. From there the Striking Force went west to Palau and then south through the Moluccas and the Banda Sea to attack Port Darwin on the northwestern coast of Australia on February 23. From there it was west into the Indian Ocean. There were only five carriers in the Striking Force at that point, as *Kaga* had run aground on a reef and was sent back to Japan for repairs.

By withdrawing from the central Pacific and allowing US carriers to operate virtually unopposed in the Pacific Ocean, Yamamoto allowed a rebuilding Pacific Fleet to fight back after Pearl Harbor and Wake Island. The question of Yamamoto's judgment is underscored because the attack on Pearl Harbor was terminated early, with only partial damage to Pacific Fleet ships and installations. The Pacific Fleet carriers, the primary targets of the attack, had survived and, with the withdrawal of the Striking Force, were now free to rampage almost anywhere in the Pacific—and even to attack Japan. By transferring his carrier forces to the Indian Ocean, Yamamoto withdrew at a highly critical time from the ocean where the outcome of the war would be decided.

Pacific Fleet command was at first concerned that a move south to Rabaul might be the first step toward an invasion of Fiji or, farther east, Samoa, blocking the route to Australia. Yamamoto, however, did not prioritize the central Pacific in his overall strategy. Despite earlier invasions of the Gilbert Islands and Wake, Yamamoto decided that his primary easternmost Pacific bastions would be Rabaul and Truk. He wanted Rabaul as a step toward control of the Coral Sea and as an approach to Australia from the north. Also, together with Truk, 700 miles to the north, Rabaul formed a defensive barrier for the planned invasions of the Dutch East Indies, 1,800 miles to the west. Yamamoto did not heavily fortify the Marshalls, Gilberts, and Wake, which could have been a defensive line for the Japanese in the mid-Pacific. The extensive reconnaissance units of ships and planes that had been organized into the Gradual Attrition Strategy, including the four-engine Kawanishi "Mavis" seaplane with a range of 2,500 miles, were not stationed east of Rabaul and Truk. As a result, the easternmost Japanese-held islands were exposed and open to surprise attack.

Admiral King made preserving the line from Midway south to Samoa and then west to Fiji, New Caledonia, and ultimately Australia his first priority.[229] To supplement carrier strength in the Pacific, he transferred *Yorktown* and its carrier task force from the Atlantic. *Yorktown* made the move from the Panama Canal to San Diego by January 6 in time to escort transports on a 4,300-mile transit to Samoa with the Second Marine Brigade embarked. On January 11, a Japanese submarine shelled the Pacific Fleet naval station at Pago Pago, Samoa, raising the prospect of a Japanese invasion of Samoa from the Gilberts. Nimitz directed Admiral Halsey on *Enterprise* to make the 2500-mile transit from Pearl Harbor to join *Yorktown* and protect Samoa as the Marines landed there on January 23, thus precluding a Japanese landing

Saratoga had been torpedoed west of Oahu on January 11 and would be out of action for six months, making *Yorktown's* arrival in the Pacific a timely addition. Together with *Lexington* and *Enterprise*, *Yorktown* made a Pacific Fleet carrier force of three. For some time after Pearl Harbor, *Enterprise* conducted patrols in the Oahu area, guarding against another surprise attack. Japanese submarines were also concentrated in the area, and *Enterprise* narrowly escaped being torpedoed on at least one occasion. In addition to hitting *Saratoga*, a Japanese submarine sank the oiler *Neches* on January 23. The loss of that ship prompted Vice Admiral Wilson Brown to cancel a *Lexington* raid against Wake for lack of a substitute oiler. The hyperaggressive King was pressing Nimitz to make attacks of opportunity on Japanese-held islands, and after the Marines had been offloaded at Samoa, the two carrier task forces went north on January 25 to attack the Marshalls on February 1.[230] Halsey, as the senior admiral, commanded the two forces.

Enterprise would lead the attack on the islands of Kwajalein, Wotje, and Maloelap, supported by a cruiser force under the command of Rear Admiral Raymond Spruance. A report from a Pacific Fleet submarine that had reconnoitered the area disclosed that Kwajalein had the

229   Morison, 257.

230   Morison, 262.

greatest concentration of ships and planes, and Halsey made that his prime target. The latter two were seaplane bases with less shipping. The *Yorktown* task force would attack the more southerly islands of Makin, Mili, and Jaluit.[231]

The Rabaul invasion was still ongoing when Halsey's forces attacked the Marshalls. The Striking Force was in the Rabaul area, about 1200 miles—or two days of twenty-five-knot steaming—from the Marshalls. Halsey could have been heading into a trap, but Japanese reconnaissance units that might have spotted Halsey's force well before it approached had been withdrawn from the Marshalls, and this allowed Halsey to move fast and surprise the Japanese forces there.

Approaching their targets from the east, the forces divided just before sunset on January 31: Halsey went farther north for *Enterprise* targets, and Fletcher headed west for those of *Yorktown*. Halsey executed a thirty-knot dash through the night and commenced launching dive-bombers and torpedo planes by moonlight on February 1.[232] As they flew through the night, the planes were guided to their target by radar plot officers on *Enterprise* giving continuous course corrections to the air group commander. The planes were over Kwajalein at daybreak. *Enterprise* planes sank a transport and a subchaser, and a second subchaser, a net tender, and a gunboat were badly damaged. A light cruiser, another transport, a minelayer, an ammunition ship, and a submarine tender also were damaged. Three Navy planes, including that of a squadron commander, were lost. Admiral Spruance's cruisers, *Northampton* and *Salt Lake City*, carried out shore bombardment primarily on Wotje in coordination with carrier air strikes. While this was happening, Fletcher, with *Yorktown* and cruisers *Louisville* and *St. Louis*, executed strikes on his three designated islands. Due to weather problems, *Yorktown* fliers damaged only two small ships and

---

231   Morison, 261.

232   Morison, 262.

a minelayer. Six planes failed to return. Around 1300, after nine hours in the Marshalls operating area and with their planes recovered, Halsey ordered a withdrawal.

Without long-range scouting, the Japanese had no warning of the attack before the carrier planes began dropping bombs. An alarm went out from the Japanese command in the Marshalls to the Striking Force. The Striking Force made a dash to attack Halsey's forces, but before any of their planes were within range Halsey's carriers were long gone. Although this was hardly a major victory, media throughout the United States carried it, trumpeting the first good news in the war since Pearl Harbor and Wake Island.

After *Saratoga* was torpedoed, its fighter squadron had been transferred to *Lexington*. Vice Admiral Brown, *Lexington's* task force commander, sensing the Japanese might not have had enough time since their invasion of Rabaul to build up their forces, now saw an opportunity to attack. Brown took the task force deep into Japanese waters toward Rabaul. On February 20 the task force approached Rabaul but was spotted early by a Mavis long-range search plane. The plane was shot down, but not before the pilot had radioed the approach of a Pacific Fleet carrier task force. Rear Admiral Goto Eiji on Rabaul sent a total of seventeen G4M "Betty" two-engine horizontal bombers in two flights against *Lexington*, foolishly attacking when Japanese fighters were still out of range to escort the bombers. The *Lexington* fliers, led by Lieutenant Commander Jimmie Thach, in wild aerial combat shot down all the bombers but one in the first flight—a disastrous result for the Japanese naval air force.

It was in this battle that Lieutenant Edward "Butch" O'Hare was pitted, virtually alone, against the second flight of eight bombers closing on *Lexington*. In a magnificent display of flying and aerial gunnery, he shot down five and possibly six planes and scattered the remaining ones when his ammunition was expended. His defense disrupted the attack and possibly saved his ship. For becoming the first air ace of the war in a single mission, O'Hare would be awarded the Medal of Honor for his bravery and superb flying that day. Sadly, he was lost later in the war. In a memorial to a native son, the city of Chicago named its international airport in his honor.

President Roosevelt took to the airwaves again on February 23 in another Fireside Chat to report to the American people on the progress of the war.

> *My fellow Americans:*
>
> *Washington's birthday is a most appropriate occasion for us to talk with each other about things as they are today and things as we know they shall be in the future. For eight years, General Washington and his Continental Army were faced continually with formidable odds and recurring defeats . . . In a sense, every winter was a Valley Forge . . . Washington's conduct in those hard times has provided the model for all Americans ever since—a model of moral stamina . . . The present great struggle has taught us increasingly that freedom . . . anywhere in the world depend[s] upon the security of the rights and obligations of liberty and justice throughout the world.*
>
> *I have asked you to take out and spread before you a map of the whole earth . . . The broad oceans which have been heralded in the past as our protection from attack have [themselves] become endless battlefields on which we are constantly being challenged by our enemies.*
>
> *Look at your map . . . Look at . . . China . . . Russia . . . the British Isles . . . Australia . . . the Dutch Indies . . . the Near East . . . The object of the Nazis and the Japanese is to separate the United States . . . and to isolate them from one another so that each will be surrounded and cut off from supplies and reinforcements. It is the old . . . policy of "divide and conquer."*

Roosevelt then examined each section of the world, summarized the progress to date, and described how these areas would be unable to carry on the fight, starved, or otherwise reduced if they were cut off.

> *I ask you to look at your maps again, particularly at that portion of the Pacific Ocean lying west of Hawaii. Before this war even started, the Philippine Islands were already surrounded on three sides by Japanese power. The islands that lie between Hawaii and the Philippines—these islands, hundreds of them, appear only as small dots on most maps . . . We knew that the war as a whole would have to be fought and won by a process of attrition against Japan itself. We knew that, to obtain our objective, many varieties of operations would be necessary in areas other than the Philippines.*
>
> *Our first job then is to build up production—uninterrupted production—so that the united nations can maintain control of the seas and attain control of the air—not merely a slight superiority, but an overwhelming superiority . . . We know now that if we lose this war it will be generations or even centuries before our conception of democracy can live again. And we can lose this war only if we slow up our effort or if we waste our ammunition sniping at each other.*
>
> *Ever since this nation became the arsenal of democracy— ever since the enactment of Lend Lease—there has been one persistent theme through Axis propaganda. This theme has been that Americans are admittedly rich, that Americans have considerable industrial power—but that Americans are soft and decadent, that they cannot and will not unite and work and fight.*
>
> *Let them repeat that now!*

Let them tell that to General MacArthur and his men.

Let them tell that to the sailors who today are hitting hard in the far waters of the Pacific.

Let them tell that to the boys in the Flying Fortresses.

Let them tell that to the Marines!

"These are the times that try men's souls." Tom Paine wrote these words on a drumhead . . . when Washington's little army of ragged, rugged men were retreating across New Jersey, having tasted nothing but defeat . . . And General Washington ordered that these great words written by Tom Paine be read to the men of every regiment in the Continental Army . . . Quoting Washington again, "The summer soldier and the sunshine patriot will, in this crisis, shrink from the service of their country; but he that stands it now deserves the love and thanks of man and woman . . . [T]he harder the sacrifice, the more glorious the triumph." So spoke Americans in the year 1776. So speak Americans today![233]

Even as the latest Fireside Chat was being broadcast into American homes from coast to coast, in the Pacific Halsey and the *Enterprise* force were approaching Wake Island, now held by the Japanese. On February 24, in a preliminary action, two heavy cruisers and several destroyers bombarded shore facilities and sank a patrol boat. The bombardment was carried out from a distance of 14,000 to 16,000 yards, outside the range of the Japanese artillery on the island. At the following dawn, *Enterprise* carried out an attack by thirty-six carrier bombers escorted by six fighters, inflicting further damage.[234]

From there Halsey sprinted northwest all the way to Marcus Island, about 600 miles east of the Japanese Bonin Islands and 950 miles from

---

233   Roosevelt, 105-112.

234   Morison, 268.

Japan. On March 4, in a moonlight launch, the planes flew 175 miles, the limit of their operating range, to attack shore facilities on Marcus. Guided by radar, the *Enterprise* planes attacked Japanese facilities at daybreak. There were no Zero defenders, but heavy antiaircraft fire brought down one plane.[235] Always looking out for his pilots, Halsey closed the range after the launch to shorten the distance of the return flights.

Marcus Island had little strategic value to the Pacific Fleet and was far from the southern route to Australia that King saw as crucial to his Pacific strategy. However, the attack caused considerable consternation to the Japanese. After the Marcus raid, Halsey and the *Enterprise* task force steamed back to Pearl Harbor, a voyage of 2,700 miles. They would not remain there long, as another mission was planned that would take them even closer to Japan. Although never disclosed, the Marcus raid might have been a test run for the more important mission to Japan that was planned for mid-April.

Considering another attack on Rabaul, Brown messaged Nimitz that the defenses there would require the strength of two carriers. Nimitz agreed, and ordered Fletcher on *Yorktown* to join Brown. They were supported by a surface force of cruisers and destroyers under the command of Royal Australian Navy Rear Admiral J. G. Crace, a tough and capable sea dog who shortly would demonstrate his capabilities in the Coral Sea. Meanwhile, the Japanese, moving to invade the island of New Guinea, landed troops at Lae and Salamaua on its northern coast. This landing put them within range of Port Moresby on the southern coast, which in turn would put them within range of Australia. All of this was consistent with Yamamoto's plan to control the Coral Sea and the northern and eastern coasts of Australia. Brown's battle plan shifted south from Rabaul on New Britain to the main island of New Guinea.

A move directly against the northern coast of New Guinea would expose Brown's force to attack from land-based planes from Rabaul to the north. A move to the Gulf of Papua, on the southern coast of New

---

235   Morison, 268.

Guinea, would be safe from Rabaul, but reaching Lae and Salamaua from the Gulf of Papua meant attacking over the high Owen Stanley Range that ran down the spine of New Guinea. The carrier planes, particularly the heavy Devastator torpedo planes, would have trouble crossing the mountain peaks, which varied from 10,000 to 12,500 feet. Close examination of the charts disclosed a pass that was only 7,500 feet above sea level, and Brown decided that all the planes, including the Devastators, could manage it.

On March 10 planes from *Lexington* and *Yorktown* cleared the mountains and made a combined attack on Lea and Salamaua. The Japanese had built an airstrip but no planes had yet arrived. Three transports were in the harbor at Lae and two more at Salamaua. There were minelayers, minesweepers, a seaplane tender, several destroyers, and the light cruiser *Yubari*, last seen at Wake and flagship of the convoy commander. Timing for the attack was ideal: there were no Zeros, and the attack caught the Japanese by surprise. The pilots reported three transports sunk, another damaged, and damage to the seaplane tender, the minelayer, and two destroyers. Later reports, however, showed that just one transport, one minesweeper, and a converted light cruiser were sunk. Exaggerated reports from fliers were to become typical of operations by both sides in the war, and seasoned commanders learned to discount such reports as they evaluated the results of battles.

Commanding the attacks of two carrier air groups operating together was the beginning of coordinated carrier operations for the Pacific Fleet, a skill the Japanese had already brought to a high level of expertise. *Lexington* returned to Pearl Harbor and joined the modern Navy by replacing its original cruiser eight-inch guns with antiaircraft weapons. Thach and O'Hare were rotated ashore for a well-deserved rest, and a new fighter squadron commander, Lieutenant Commander Paul Ramsay, came aboard. Twelve now-experienced fighter pilots stayed with *Lexington*.

Admiral William Halsey
Photo Naval History and Heritage

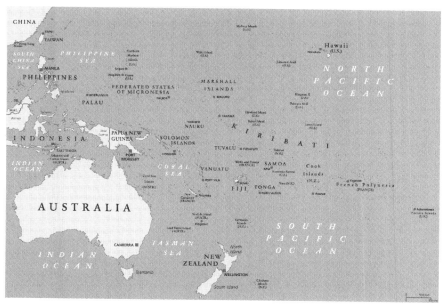

Chart of Central and Western Pacific Ocean.

CHAPTER 16

The Doolittle Raid on Tokyo

Ever since the Pearl Harbor attack, President Roosevelt had been looking for a way to take the fight to Japan. The raids on the Marshalls, Wake, Marcus, Rabaul, and New Guinea counted for something, but they were minor compared with the devastation and loss of life at Pearl Harbor and the pitiful defeat at Wake Island. In the general American public, the cry arose, "Remember Pearl Harbor!" Roosevelt challenged his service chiefs to come up with something that could reverse the sense of defeat and raise the mood of the US public.

It was not an easy assignment. For carriers to approach the Japanese mainland close enough for their planes to attack was suicidal. Before the carrier planes were even within range, swarms of land-based bombers and torpedo planes would overwhelm the carrier defenses and sink the ships. It would be like the *Prince of Wales* and *Repulse*, two Royal Navy ships that were sunk in the South China Sea in December, just after the Pearl Harbor attack. Launching land-based planes from a base in China, Russia, or the Aleutians was considered and discarded.[236]

In January 1942 Admiral King delegated the problem to two capable staff officers, Captains Francis S. Low and Donald B. Duncan. While observing a naval air training field with the outline of a carrier deck for novice carrier pilots to practice flight operations, it occurred to Captain Low that perhaps land-based planes could be launched from a carrier

---

236   Toll, 283.

beyond the range of detection by Japanese defenses. The clear flaw in the plan was that it was not possible for the planes to land on the carrier again.[237] The planes would have to continue beyond Japan and land on a friendly airfield. The obvious landing options were in China.

With this idea, King consulted with General Henry H. "Hap" Arnold, head of the Army Air Corps. Arnold brought Lieutenant Colonel James H. Doolittle, a highly experienced Army Air Corps flier, into the project. All discussions were top secret. Coordinating their efforts, Duncan and Doolittle concluded that a medium bomber, the B-25 Mitchell, had the range and flight characteristics to carry out the mission, could be accommodated on the flight deck of a carrier, and could take off with a minimum of forty knots of wind over the flight deck. Wind in the north Pacific at that time of year could be expected to be at least ten knots, so the carrier speed would need to be over thirty knots to produce a relative wind speed of forty knots as the carrier headed into the wind. The new carrier *Hornet*, commanded by Captain Marc Mitscher, with a top speed of thirty-two knots, was selected for the mission. The planes would be hoisted aboard *Hornet* with a crane and secured in place on the flight deck. Their wingspan was far too wide for the ship's elevators, and the planes would stay on the flight deck from the time they were hoisted aboard until they were launched for Japan.

Hornet, recently commissioned on the East Coast, was sent through the Panama Canal to arrive at Alameda Air Station, adjacent to San Francisco. Doolittle contacted an elite group of fliers, asking for volunteers for a dangerous mission that could make a significant contribution to the war effort. Details of the mission could not be divulged until later, but he had no trouble finding volunteers from among this highly patriotic group. The Army fliers trained with B-25s on an outline of a carrier deck, not knowing the reasons for the specific exercise. Following the training the pilots flew the B-25s to Alameda.

---

237   Morison, 390.

Captain Duncan flew to Pearl Harbor to brief Admiral Nimitz on the plan. Nimitz selected Admiral Halsey, his most experienced carrier commander, for the honor and responsibility of carrying out the mission. Security was tight, with the details restricted to a very few officers. Even Captain Mitscher was not aware of the mission until a few days before sixteen B-25s were hoisted aboard his ship on April 1. The Army assigned 70 officers and 130 enlisted men to the mission, and they came aboard. Escorted by the cruisers *Vincennes* and *Nashville*, four destroyers, and a tanker, the *Hornet* force departed Alameda on April 2.[238] The mission was announced to all hands the next day to enthusiastic cheers from ship's company and the Army Air Force guests. This was followed by detailed briefings to the fliers and their crews on the track of the flights, their targets, and the planned landing sites in China. The briefings included distributing Chinese money and other supplies that could be useful on the ground in China. Some of the spirited banter quieted down when the fliers were told that if captured by the Japanese they likely would be beheaded.

The total flight distance, from the projected launch 500 miles east of Japan to the airfields in Nationalist China south of Shanghai, was 2,400 miles. After dropping bombs on Tokyo, Yokohama, Nagoya, and Osaka, the planes would turn south, fly over the southern Japanese islands, cross the East China Sea, and then fly back over land to reach the Chinese airfields. Doolittle and twelve other pilots were to concentrate on Tokyo, and the other three bombers would target the other cities.

Moving west across the Pacific Ocean, on April 13 *Hornet* was at the international date line and latitude 38°N, 600 miles north of Midway, to rendezvous with Admiral Halsey on *Enterprise*. Cruisers *Northampton* and *Salt Lake City*, under the command of Rear Admiral Spruance, escorted *Enterprise*. Halsey was in command of the combined force, designated Task Force 16. The *Enterprise* air group under the command

---

238   Morison, 391.

of Lieutenant Commander Wade McClusky flew combat air control over the formation. *Hornet's* planes were below on the hangar deck and could not be raised until the B-25s departed.

Planning for Chinese landing fields with Chiang Kai-shek's government was difficult. Security within that government was lax, and the risk of the Japanese learning of the mission was very real. Chiang was told that US Army bombers would be flying toward them and needed landing fields, but he "did not get around to designating the fields until April 14"[239]—after the task force was already steaming for Japan, and four days before the mission was to be launched on April 18. Zhuzhou was the designated airfield, but Chiang still did not transmit current weather information in time to reach Doolittle aboard *Hornet* before the mission was launched. Because of a solid week of adverse weather, Zhuzhou was not serviceable. Unknown to the Army fliers, the Chinese canceled the plan to land and refuel the planes so they could proceed to airfields deeper into China. The air crews would likely end up bailing out over China, hopefully avoiding capture by the Japanese. As they prepared optimistically for their mission, they in fact were heading into a world of dark uncertainty.

TF-16 continued west, with the intention of launching the planes when they were 500 miles from the coast of Japan. About a thousand miles east of Japan, the weather changed to gale-force winds. Heavy spray reached the high flight decks of *Enterprise* and *Hornet*, and all flight operations were canceled. Refueling was hazardous; two sailors were swept over the side of their ships, and both were saved in heroic rescue operations. Further refueling was suspended, and the tankers were left behind as the task force increased speed and pounded through the huge swells.[240] The weather conditions were not unlike those encountered by

---

239   Morison, 393.

240   Toll, 287.

Japan's Striking Force on its eastern course for Pearl Harbor more than four months earlier.

At 0210 in the early morning of April 18, *Enterprise* radar picked up a contact to the southwest when the task force was about 700 miles from Japan. Halsey ordered a course change to the northwest. A radar operator reported another contact 42 miles ahead, and *Enterprise* launched a reconnaissance plane at 0715. The plane reported a Japanese picket boat, and it was clear that the Japanese had organized a defensive perimeter of picket boats 650 to 700 miles east of their coast. *Enterprise* planes quickly sank the boat, but not before radio operators picked up a transmission from it. Air forces in Japan surely had been informed of the approaching US force.

Halsey had hoped to get Doolittle within 500 miles of the coast of Japan, but now he could not risk his two carriers to an attack just to get them closer. Doolittle and his fliers would have to launch immediately, even though another 150 miles of flying added to the risks already inherent in the mission. Halsey sent the message to *Hornet*: "Launch planes. To Col. Doolittle and his gallant command, good luck and God bless you. Halsey."[241]

The task force was making high speed heading into a gale-force wind. The relative wind across *Hornet's* flight deck was seventy-five knots, well in excess of the minimum forty knots required to launch the B-25s, but the pounding into the heavy swells caused heavy pitching of the flight deck, made even more treacherous by the salt spray. The other ships of TF-16 were also pitching heavily and taking green water over their bows. *Hornet* deck crews, on the heaving deck, spotted the planes into final launch positions. Fuel tanks were topped up to their full capacity of more than 1100 gallons, and jury-rigged portable fuel container tanks also were filled to capacity. All unnecessary weight had been removed from the planes, even their radios. The ordnance crews brought the bomb

---

241   Toll, 288.

carts up on the forward elevator and rolled them into position under the planes. From there, four 500-pound bombs were lifted into position on each plane by sailors struggling to maintain their balance against the wind and the pitching flight deck.

Captain Mitscher came down from the bridge to see the planes off. Doolittle mobilized his flight crews, and they manned their planes. Mitscher and Doolittle shook hands, and Doolittle climbed aboard his plane. His would be the first plane off, and his distance on the flight deck would be the shortest. Engines were warmed up, and fuel was added to the tanks of each plane as they prepared for takeoff to compensate for the fuel consumed during the warm-ups. Sailors moved as carefully as they could between the flashing propellers, but one sailor lost his balance and lost his arm at the shoulder to a whirling propeller blade. He was taken to sick bay and survived.

The Navy flight control officer stood near the bow of *Hornet* with the assistance of a sailor who helped him brace against the wind. At 0725 the deck crew pulled the wheel chocks of Doolittle's plane and Doolittle stood on the brakes while his engines went to full throttle. The control officer circled his flag in the preparatory signal. He had to judge the rhythm of the ship's pitching, so that when Doolittle's plane got to the forward edge of the flight deck the bow would be lifting to its maximum height. Sensing the right moment, he dropped the flag and Doolittle released his brakes. The B-25 rolled down the deck, gathering speed through the spray, got to the edge as the bow was coming up, and was aloft. One by one the other pilots got their planes into the air. One plane was so low after leaving the flight deck that the wash from its propellers kicked up spray from the ocean, but the pilot was able to maintain control and gain altitude. By 0825 the last plane was aloft. There was no fuel to spare for a formation—the planes just trailed in a long line behind Doolittle. Immediately after the last plane was gone Halsey signaled the task force: Turn 090 (Straight east) Speed 25 (knots).

Thirteen B-25s were over Tokyo by 1215. Japanese defenses were caught by surprise because they assumed from the picket boat's report that the US carriers would take several more hours to get their planes within range. The message from the picket boat had failed to state there were two-engine planes on the enemy carriers, a detail that might have alerted Japanese air defenses that the planes had longer ranges.

The raid's targets in Tokyo were military or industrial, and the bombs caused some damage, but the main effects were surprise and shock. Inevitably there were misses, which regrettably caused civilian deaths. The three planes that headed for the three other cities dropped their incendiary bombs and flew on. None of the planes was lost over Japan. It was night by the time the planes were over China, where the lack of preparation by the Chinese was sorely felt. There were no airfields prepared or displaying a signal for the US pilots. Some of the planes actually flew over Zhuzhou, but there were no homing devices to guide them in, and the Chinese on the ground had no knowledge of the mission. They assumed the planes were hostile, so they extinguished the field lights and sounded the air raid alarm. Of the sixteen pilots who began the mission, eleven bailed out in the night after running out of fuel while searching frantically for landing sites. Of the other five planes, four made crash landings in China. The remaining plane developed a fuel leak while still over Japan and, knowing he would never make China, the pilot headed for Vladivostok in Russia. The Japanese Army inflicted very heavy reprisals on Chinese villages following the raid. The Japanese might have known the raid on Marcus was not just a random raid on another Japanese island. Japanese defenses had been found lacking. Yamamoto had stationed picket boats hundreds of miles off the coast of Japan, but that had failed against the Doolittle tactics.

The repercussions of the raid in the United States were spectacular. The American public was thrilled, and President Roosevelt, when asked where the planes had come from, jokingly said they flew from Shangri-La. Upon his eventual return to the United States, Colonel Doolittle was awarded the Medal of Honor for his leadership and skill in completing this spectacular mission. Of the eighty crew members that flew on April 18, seventy-one survived the mission and sixty-one survived the war. Reunions of the survivors were held annually on Doolittle's birthday beginning in 1946 as long as any of the original fliers lived.

On April 28 President Roosevelt again addressed the nation in another Fireside Chat:

> *My Fellow Americans:*
>
> *It is nearly five months since we were attacked at Pearl Harbor. For the two years prior to that attack this country had been gearing itself up to a high level of production and munitions. And yet our war efforts had done little to dislocate the normal lives of most of us. Since then we have dispatched strong forces of our Army and Navy, several hundred thousand of them, to bases and battlefronts thousands of miles from home. We have stepped up our war production on a scale that is testing our industrial power, our engineering genius, and our economic structure to the utmost. We have no illusions about the fact that this is a tough job—and a long one.*

He compared the will and patriotism of the people of the United States with those of the Axis powers:

> *In the German and Italian peoples themselves there is a growing conviction that the cause of Nazism and Fascism is hopeless—that their political and military leaders have led them along the bitter road which leads not to world conquest but to bitter defeat. They cannot fail to contrast the present frantic speeches of these leaders with their arrogant boastings of a year ago, and two years ago . . .*
>
> *We went into this war fighting. We know what we are fighting for.*

He summarized the progress of the war to date, noting the defeats that had been suffered. Good news had been sparse to date, but:

> *It is even reported from Japan that somebody has dropped bombs on Tokyo, and on other centers of Japanese war industries. If this be true, it is the first time Japan has suffered such indignities.*

He called on everyone to make sacrifices to win the war:

> *Not all of us can have the privilege of fighting our enemies in distant parts of the world. But there is one front and one battle where everyone in the United States—every man, woman, and child—is in action and will remain in action throughout the war. That is right here at home, in our daily lives, and in our daily tasks . . . Every loyal American is aware of his individual responsibility . . . Read the mail that floods into the White House . . . The one question that recurs is, "What more can I do to help my country in winning this war?"*

He recounted several examples of fighting men who displayed remarkable courage and patriotism:

> *These stories I have told you are not exceptional. They are typical examples of individual heroism and skill. As we here at home contemplate our own duties, our own responsibilities, let us think, and think hard of the example which is being set for us by our fighting men. Our soldiers and sailors . . . are the United States of America. That is why they fight. We too are the United States of America. That is why we must work and sacrifice. It is for them. It is for us. It is for victory.*

Doolittle raid on Tokyo
Photo Naval History and Heritage

CHAPTER 17

Coral Sea: Early Actions

An understanding of the Battle of the Coral Sea, and the Battle of Midway that followed immediately afterward, requires the perspective of events that occurred several months prior to the engagements themselves. The Pearl Harbor attack occurred simultaneously with the first major moves of Japanese forces south from Japan into islands of the southern and western Pacific Ocean. By early 1942 these forces had conquered the entire Dutch East Indian network of islands, including Borneo, Celebes, Sumatra, Java and Bali, the Philippines, Burma, Malaya, Timor, New Britain, New Ireland, and the northern coast of New Guinea. Islands farther east—Guam, Wake, and the Gilberts—also had been added to their empire. Sinking *Prince of Wales* and *Repulse* in the South China Sea in December 1941 fortified their position against the British, and within a matter of weeks the great British base of Singapore, their "Gibraltar of the Far East," had fallen. All this new empire was added to the former German island colonies, Marianas, Carolines, and Marshalls, dating from the Versailles Treaty. Japan's conquest of Rabaul gave them an excellent harbor, and this became the most important southern base for the Combined Fleet.

The exuberance of the Japanese was boundless. Their expansion to the South Seas had been dramatic—done in less time than originally thought possible, and with minimal losses. The oil fields of Borneo, Sumatra, and Java had been taken from the Dutch, despite their attempts to deny the oil to the Japanese through their "scorched-earth" policy. The apparent success of the Dutch colony supplying their much-needed oil was a further incentive to embrace what was later described as victory disease: the belief that Japanese military and naval might was invincible.

The original Japanese ambition was to invade and occupy Australia. An assembly point was needed to do this, and this was identified as Port Moresby, on the southeast coast of New Guinea. Plans were drawn up for the invasion of Port Moresby, but the Japanese army was adamantly opposed to an Australian invasion that would require ten to twelve army divisions and a massive fleet of transports.[242] Realizing after further consideration that control of Australia could be accomplished equally well by cutting off the supply chain from the United States, the Japanese plan evolved into an easterly movement along the Solomon Islands chain. Invading Tulagi would give them control of the central Solomon Islands, with airfield and port capabilities. They planned to continue along the Solomon chain leading to invasions of Santa Cruz, New Hebrides, and Fiji. The meager US facility at Noumea on New Caledonia would be overwhelmed easily. When that was accomplished, the Imperial Japanese Navy would sever the US-Australia link, prevent a US buildup, and force Australia out of the war.

Yamamoto anticipated that the Pacific Fleet would make an all-out effort to preserve the Australia link, and the showdown between the Combined Fleet and the Pacific Fleet he was looking for could take place east of the Coral Sea, perhaps around Fiji. Port Moresby, south of the Solomons, added little to the revised Australian cutoff strategy after plans for an invasion of Australia had been cancelled. The recently acquired bases at Lae and Salamaua on the northern Papuan coast could provide protection for Rabaul from Army Air Force bombers based in northern Australia. Port Moresby itself could be neutralized by bombing its airfields until Australia was forced out of the war. But, with the plan for the Port Moresby invasion in place, it was almost easier for

---

242   Costello, 218.

the Japanese command to go ahead with it than to make changes. In those heady days of victory disease, anything seemed possible. In fact, to proceed with the Port Moresby invasion was outright carelessness.

In mid-April the Striking Force came back from its ill-advised venture in the Indian Ocean. The Pacific Fleet carriers had not been destroyed in the Pearl Harbor raid and were roaming free, raiding Japanese islands. On April 18 came the Doolittle Raid on Tokyo, and Yamamoto realized he had limited time to defeat the Pacific Fleet. He knew that once the Americans had time to build their naval forces, the Combined Fleet would be overwhelmed. Had the Striking Force executed the Fiji-Samoa strategy right after Pearl Harbor, instead of venturing into the Indian Ocean, they could have moved against the US link to Australia immediately. The Pacific Fleet carriers would have come into the area to prevent it, and Yamamoto would have gotten the showdown he wanted. All that was forfeited by the Striking Force move into the Indian Ocean, and now the Doolittle Raid demanded action.

Yamamoto was concerned that pursuing the Australian cutoff strategy would require too much time because additional island invasions would be necessary at New Caledonia and Fiji. Perhaps realizing his mistake sending the Striking Force into the Indian Ocean, and now feeling the pressure of staging a confrontation sooner rather than later, he was moving toward a confrontation at Midway. There were some senior officers in the Japanese navy who had grave doubts about the feasibility and risk of the Midway operation. In a one-on-one confrontation with Yamamoto, Vice Admiral Kondo Nobutake, commander of the Second Fleet, expressed strong and well-reasoned objections to the Midway plan and argued forcefully for the New Caledonia-Fiji strategy. Once the Combined Fleet had engaged in a battle with the Americans around Fiji, the Striking Force would have the support of land-based aircraft from bases they would build in the Solomons and the other islands they would invade. The Pacific Fleet would have only their own ships. At Midway the reverse was the case. The Striking Force would be on its own—the nearest

Japanese base was at Wake, which was out of range—while the Pacific Fleet would have the support of their aircraft based on Midway itself, in addition to their own carrier fleet.

The Doolittle Raid had created a crisis of confidence in Navy leadership, however, and Yamamoto tolerated no further discussion. The Striking Force, supported by large elements of the Combined Fleet, would move against Midway immediately. The attack would take place the first week of June, and there would be no delays. After a dazzling string of victories, Yamamoto was confident the Navy could accomplish anything he desired. The Port Moresby invasion through the Coral Sea would also proceed as planned, despite the need to divide the Striking Force to do so. The Mahan principle of never dividing one's fleet would be ignored. It should have been a choice between the Coral Sea and Midway, and Yamamoto clearly would have opted for Midway; the Coral Sea plan would have been scrapped.

CarDiv5, coming back from the Indian Ocean, was assigned to the Port Moresby operation. In addition to the large fleet carriers *Shokaku* and *Zuikaku*, CarDiv5 was assigned two heavy cruisers and six destroyers of Cruiser Division Five. This assignment meant that the senior commander of CarDiv5 would be the recently promoted black shoe Vice Admiral Takagi Takeo, commander of Cruiser Division Five. The CarDiv5 carrier commander remained Rear Admiral Hara Tadaichi in *Zuikaku*. Upon its detachment from the rest of the Striking Force, CarDiv5 was ordered to Truk. Although consideration was given for the carrier *Kaga* to be part of the Port Moresby operation, that idea was dropped so that *Kaga* could prepare for Midway.

Two invasion forces were assembled at Rabaul to execute the invasion plan. The smaller invasion force, consisting of two transports with naval marines onboard, was escorted by two destroyers and other support ships. It would invade Tulagi in the central Solomons on May 3 to establish a seaplane base there. The larger force, consisting of eleven transports conveying army and naval marine units, would depart Rabaul on May 4, transit the Jomard Pass at the northwestern edge of the Coral Sea, and invade Port Moresby on May 10. That force was supported by six destroyers and other escort ships.

In addition to CarDiv5, two other naval afloat commands assembled at the island of Truk. The Covering Force was charged with protecting the Port Moresby landing force and consisted of the light carrier *Shoho*, four heavy cruisers, and destroyers. The Support Group would construct a seaplane base at Tulagi following the amphibious landings there. It consisted of a seaplane carrier, two light cruisers, and several gunboats. The land-based 25th Air Flotilla at Rabaul, operating under separate command, was within range for possible assistance.[243] The overall commander of the entire Port Moresby operation was Vice Admiral Inoue Shigeyoshi, commander of the Fourth Fleet, embarked on a light cruiser in port at Rabaul. No fewer than ten admirals were in command of the various elements of Japanese naval and air forces as they began to execute the invasion plan.

The Japanese command assigned several operations to CarDiv5 that had to be executed in sequential order. On the way to the Port Moresby engagement, CarDiv5 carriers would deliver nine additional Zero fighters to Rabaul. After delivering the Zeros, they were to be north of the Solomon Islands of Santa Isabel and Malaita on May 3 to provide air support for the amphibious landings on Tulagi. Following this operation, CarDiv5 would round the eastern tip of the Solomons at San Cristobal Island, enter the Coral Sea from the east, and, in a pincer movement with the Covering Force coming from the west, crush any Pacific Fleet ships caught between them. Finally, the CarDiv5 aircraft, together with land-based planes from Lae and Rabaul, would fly air support over the Port Moresby invasion itself.

All these tasks together were a tall order for CarDiv5. During operations the Zero fighters would have to be split between escorting attack

---

243 Morison, Vol. 4, 10-12.

planes to their targets and flying combat air patrol over their own ships. Before the Port Moresby landings could proceed, the Japanese command would have to consider whether sufficient aircraft, including carrier planes and land-based aircraft from Lae and Rabaul, but after losses from earlier carrier operations, would be available to provide adequate air cover over Port Moresby during the landings.

The carefully crafted plan called for the Tulagi invasion force to be supported by the Covering Force and CarDiv5 while the Support Force assembled the seaplane base. The Covering Force and Support Force would steam south of the Solomon chain and approach Tulagi on a generally southeast course. The Covering Force would provide gunfire support if needed as well as limited air cover from *Shoho*. CarDiv5 would provide the primary air cover with the powerful force of Zeros embarked on *Shokaku* and *Zuikaku*.

After the landings had been completed on Tulagi, Covering Force would withdraw to the west and await the arrival of the Port Moresby invasion force coming through the Jomard Pass. Support Force also would move west to establish another seaplane base in the western Coral Sea at the Deboyne Islands in the Louisiade Archipelago. The Covering Force, including the small carrier *Shoho*, could be called into action if a Pacific Fleet force appeared in the Coral Sea south of the Solomons.

The second phase of the plan called for the Port Moresby amphibious assault to occur on May 10. By that time seaplane scouting bases would have been operating on Tulagi and Deboyne. From those positions Support Force seaplanes could provide scouting throughout the Solomons and the Coral Sea. Any American task force should be discovered by the seaplane scouts or by land-based planes from Rabaul, and destroyed by CarDiv5 and the Covering Force. The invasion fleet itself was to transit Jomard Pass in the Louisiade Archipelago, supported by air cover from land bases and carriers.

Opposing the Port Moresby invasion was TF-17, composed of carriers *Lexington* and *Yorktown*, plus destroyer escorts and support vessels.

Lexington had recently spent three weeks in Pearl Harbor for a full replenishment, departing on April 16 for the Coral Sea. *Yorktown* had been in the south Pacific since February and saw its share of action during that time. MacArthur's air groups in Australia were available for possible long-range support. MacArthur had Army Air Force B-17s and Royal Australian Air Force planes at Port Moresby and four Australian airfields. On March 18, the Eighth Bombardment Squadron, composed of A-24 dive-bombers, had been sent to Port Moresby. In mid-April, P-39 and P-40 Air Cobra fighters were added to the Port Moresby air complement. On April 30 these air forces made attacks against Lae and Salamaua. These air groups were prepared to oppose the advance of the two carriers of CarDiv5, the Covering Force, and the Port Moresby invasion force.

The two Japanese carriers were relatively new, and both were capable of speeds of 34 knots and tight turning diameters. On the US side, *Yorktown* was commissioned in 1937 and compared favorably in performance with the Japanese ships. *Lexington*, originally commissioned as a battle cruiser in 1927, was later converted to an aircraft carrier. She was larger, slower, and not as maneuverable. CarDiv5 had more experienced pilots, more advanced airplanes, and significantly better torpedoes. TF-17 had radar and better anti-aircraft armaments.

Flight operations on TF-17's two carriers were not as well-developed as those of the far more experienced crews and pilots of CarDiv5, but the Pacific Fleet's most potent weapon was the SBD Dauntless dive-bomber. The Dauntless carried bombs up to 1,000 pounds. It was designed and constructed with perforated trailing edge split wing dive flaps that restricted the terminal velocity in a dive to 300 knots. It could dive at 70 degrees and maintain lift in its wings, which made it slightly maneuverable during its dive. This was important because a dive from 20,000 feet at 300 knots took 40 seconds, and leveling off at 1,500 feet meant a net dive time of about 35 seconds. A target ship moving at 30 knots traveled more than 500 yards during the same time—and would maneuver to avoid being hit.

A formation of Dauntless dive-bombers could maintain a "V of Vs" compressed defensive formation against enemy fighters right up until the time came to push over into their dives. Once in a dive, the plane's rear gunner could defend against enemy Zeros. The Zero, with speed above 300 knots flying level, could not control its speed in a dive and would shoot past a Dauntless with its extended diving flaps. If the plane was spotted by lookouts, the shipboard antiaircraft gunners had just seconds to orient their guns, and the Dauntless presented a small, head-on target shape that was difficult to hit. In addition, some of the older Japanese anti-aircraft guns could not elevate to the high angle needed against dive-bombers. By comparison, the Japanese Val did not dive steeper than 60 degrees and carried either one 500-pound bomb or two 123-pound bombs. The Val was a very good attack plane with a long range, but it did not dive as steeply or carry bombs as heavy as the Dauntless.

The US Devastator torpedo plane, despite its name, was slow and obsolete. It carried a WWI vintage torpedo that had been designed for submarines and destroyers, and it had not been satisfactorily modified to compensate for a drop from aircraft. The torpedoes, once dropped, did not maintain course or depth, and the explosive mechanism frequently did not work when the torpedo made contact. By comparison, the very capable Japanese torpedo plane, known as Kate to Pacific Fleet fliers, had excellent torpedoes and had proved its deadly effectiveness in earlier combat.

When Admiral Nimitz took command of the Pacific Fleet in late December 1941, he organized and mobilized the shocked and demoralized naval personnel at Pearl Harbor in the aftermath of the Japanese attack and the surrender of Wake Island. However, he had the problem of the micromanaging Admiral Ernest J. King, Chief of Naval Operations, creating separate issues from his office in Washington. King, ever since the war began, had taken the position that Australia was vital to the war effort and sea routes to that country must be maintained at all costs. He perceived the rapid movements of Japanese forces into the southern and western Pacific as a threat to Australia, and to counter that he ordered two carriers kept in the southwest Pacific as a standing policy, with other forces added as necessary.

Admiral Halsey arrived at Pearl Harbor with TF-16 from the Doolittle Raid on April 25, seven days after the Doolittle fliers were launched. *Enterprise* and *Hornet* were replenished by May 1. Relying on his intelligence staff that may have been confused by decrypted messages showing Japanese movements before and after the Port Moresby invasion, Admiral King demanded that Halsey depart for the Coral Sea immediately.[244] Upon meeting up with Admiral Fletcher aboard *Yorktown*, Halsey as senior officer would assume overall command. An additional two carriers would create a dominant force against CarDiv5 and the other Japanese forces. However, in company with the necessary but slower support train, TF-16 could not arrive at the eastern edge of the Coral Sea before May 10. Because the Japanese invasion plan was to begin on May 3, TF-16 could not arrive in time to take part in the battle unless there were delays or the action continued for more than seven days. Neither was very likely to occur, but King's order directed Halsey's movements.

The impending confrontation between the carrier task forces would be the first battle in history between two opposing naval air attack groups. The surface ships of each force would never sight each other. On May 1, the same day that CarDiv5 departed Truk, Lexington with Rear Admiral Aubrey Fitch, an experienced aviator, met up with *Yorktown* in the Coral Sea, approximately 300 miles west of the New Hebrides islands.[245] The overall commander would be cruiser commander Fletcher, the more senior rear admiral. Nimitz ordered Task Force 44, commanded by Rear Admiral J. G. Crace of the Royal Australian Navy, which had been part of the southwest Pacific naval forces in Australia, to rendezvous with

244   Cincpac Op Plan 23-42, 29 April, 1942, as in Morison, Vol. 4, 16 fn.
245   Morison, Vol. 4, 21.

TF-17 on May 4. TF-44 consisted of HMAS *Australia* and two additional cruisers, plus two American ships, cruiser *Chicago* and destroyer *Perkins*.

Maintaining full fuel tanks was always a priority with Fletcher. The Yorktown group fueled from the oiler *Neosho* beginning May 1, and the group under Fitch did likewise from the oiler *Tippecanoe*. Fitch at first estimated that his group would not complete the fueling until May 4 because of adverse weather conditions, but when the weather improved his ships completed refueling by midday on May 3, one day ahead of schedule. Observing radio silence, he did not contact Fletcher or make an aerial message drop to advise him of the change in schedule.

Fletcher got word of the Tulagi landings in the afternoon of May 3 from units of Army Air Force planes operating from northern Australia. He decided to steam north immediately at high speed through the night to attack at first light on May 4.[246] For reasons unknown, Fitch did not get the same message. Fitch had steamed west following the completion of his fueling on May 3 for his scheduled May 4 rendezvous with TF-44, and so was not far away when Fletcher received word of the Tulagi landings. Another opportunity for a message drop was missed, this time from Fletcher to Fitch, which could have ordered the junior admiral to join him on the dash north. As a result, Fletcher took the *Yorktown* group alone to attack Tulagi.

Meanwhile, Covering Group and Support Group, having remained in the area long enough to see the landings completed on May 3, withdrew to the west to prepare for their next operations. By first light on May 4, they were well away from the area. CarDiv5, which had been charged with providing air support over the Tulagi invasion force, was delayed by bad weather while attempting to deliver the nine Zeros to Rabaul. The delivery was part of a planned buildup of air power on Rabaul, and there was no need for it to be completed immediately. Admiral Takagi could have decided to keep the planes on board so he could support the Tulagi

---

246   Morison, Vol. 4, 24.

landings on May 3 and deliver the Zeros later. Instead, he decided to stay and wait for good weather to deliver the Zeros, even though it meant CarDiv5 would not be within range to fly air support over Tulagi.

Flying air support over an amphibious invasion was far more important than delivering Zeros to add to a standby reserve, but this was lost on black shoe Admiral Takagi. This poor judgment, and violation of direct orders, exposed the Tulagi landing force to unexpected attack. CarDiv5 had barely begun to carry out the tasks assigned to it in the Port Moresby invasion plan, and it had already failed a major assignment. As a result, CarDiv5 was more than 700 miles from Tulagi when the landings took place and was still out of range when the TF-17 planes were preparing to attack on May 4.

Yorktown arrived south of Guadalcanal at 0630 on May 4 and launched twelve torpedo planes, thirteen scout planes, and fifteen bombers[247] for Tulagi, range about 100 miles. The weather was perfect for the carrier pilots: a heavy overcast enveloped their carrier, and this condition prevailed up to 20 miles from Tulagi, which was in the clear. Even though the Yorktown group was under an overcast that provided good protection from scouts and possible attacks, black shoe commander Fletcher, assuming there was no opposition to his attack planes, held back all the Wildcat fighters as combat air patrol (CAP) over Yorktown and its escorts. A CAP of six planes, working in three shifts, was maintained throughout the day.[248] As a result the SBD dive-bombers and TBD torpedo planes were sent against Tulagi without fighter protection. Takagi's decision to wait for good weather near Rabaul was a fortunate one for Yorktown's torpedo and bomber pilots, who otherwise would have been met over Tulagi by a hornets' nest of Zeros from Zuikaku and Shokaku with no defending Wildcat fighters.

---

247   Naval History and Heritage Command, Battle of the Coral Sea – Combat Narrative, 5.

248   Morison, Vol. 4, 26.

The dive-bombers had targets of minelayers, minesweepers, barges, transports, destroyers, and other minor craft. Thousand-pound bombs were dropped with only minor results for the huge amount of munitions expended. Japanese defenders threw up heavy antiaircraft fire. The planes returned to *Yorktown* for refueling and rearming, and two more attacks were carried out with similar results. Despite inflated reports of ships sunk, the torpedo planes had no hits except for a minesweeper. In the afternoon, Fletcher released some Wildcats that destroyed three seaplanes in a strafing attack. One torpedo plane was lost, and two other planes were forced down but the pilots were rescued. The last planes were recovered just after 1600, and *Yorktown* headed south to rendezvous with Fitch.

Had CarDiv5 been on station to provide cover for the Tulagi landings, the *Yorktown* planes would have fared much worse. In addition, the separation of the two carrier forces would have been just 120 to 140 miles, and a Japanese plane could have followed one of the (possibly few) surviving *Yorktown* planes back to its carrier and then notified the Japanese command. A carrier battle might have been fought south of Tulagi on May 4 between the two carriers of CarDiv5 and a depleted *Yorktown*, but this did not occur. As a result of the *Yorktown* raid, the Japanese command now knew there was an American carrier force in the Coral Sea. But Fletcher and Fitch, even with intelligence indicating that a large force of Japanese ships was operating in the area, including carriers, did not know specifically of CarDiv5 or its location.

After his dash south from Tulagi and the rendezvous with Fitch, Fletcher took the opportunity to fuel from oiler *Neosho* during the afternoon hours on May 5. Although his intention was to proceed northwest toward the expected encounter with the Japanese around the Louisiades, fueling required steaming into the southeast wind. The same southeast course was required to launch and recover search planes. Overnight on May 5-6, Fletcher headed northwest to close with Japanese forces expected north of the Louisiades. Fueling continued during most of May 6, followed by resuming the northwest course. After fueling was completed, *Neosho* and the escorting destroyer *Sims* were ordered south. Fletcher logically expected to engage CarDiv5 looking north and west as escorts for their amphibious force. Search planes were active in all directions but were inhibited by a large overcast to the north of the US force.

Meanwhile, CarDiv5 rounded the eastern tip of San Cristobal Island late in the day of May 5 and entered the Coral Sea from the east under the overcast. Overnight on May 5-6, CarDiv5 was on a northwest course, passing between Guadalcanal and Rennell Island. At 0930 on May 6, Takagi ordered a course change to the south, which put CarDiv5 on an intercept with the TF-17 carriers.

During May 6 neither force was aware of the close proximity of the other; at 1800 they were only about seventy miles apart. TF-17 searches did not spot the Japanese under the overcast. Takagi, under the overcast, surprisingly conducted no searches. Had Takagi ordered searches on May 6, he quite likely would have found TF-17 to the south, with *Neosho* refueling *Yorktown* in broad daylight. Black shoe cruiser commander Takagi perhaps thought the overcast made flying too difficult, such as when he waited for good weather to deliver the nine Zeros to Rabaul. Perhaps he thought the overcast made him safe, or that the land-based and seaplane reconnaissance would supply the intelligence he needed. Perhaps he did not consult the junior but more experienced carrier force commander, Rear Admiral Hara. A seaplane spotted TF-17 about midday, but its report got lost—along with a major opportunity for a Japanese victory at the Coral Sea.

Late in the day Takagi reversed course to the north to make his own refueling rendezvous and then proceeded to the northwest. As a result, May 6 passed without any significant incident and became a squandered opportunity for the Japanese. Takagi was only in the early phase of the plans for the Port Moresby invasion and had already made two significant misjudgments. Although senior to Hara he did not have the experience or mentality of a flier, and that void characterized his command decisions during the Coral Sea battle.

TF-17 continued generally northwest until, at 0625 on May 7, it was just over 100 miles south of Tagula Island, the eastern tip of the Louisiades. At that point Fletcher turned north to search for Japanese forces transiting the Solomon Sea heading south to the Jomard Pass. He ordered TF-44, Crace's surface force, to continue on the current course to a point south of Jomard Pass. Regardless of the outcome of the expected encounter with a major Japanese carrier force, Fletcher wanted Crace's group in position to block any Japanese ships transiting Jomard Pass. Without any intelligence to the contrary, Fletcher logically operated with the expectation that on his northerly course he would meet the Japanese carrier and invasion forces in the Solomon Sea as they approached the Louisiades and Jomard Pass. He was still unaware that CarDiv5 had rounded San Cristobal and was coming up behind his force from the east.

Crace's TF-44 continued on a westerly course on May 7, taking it south of the Louisiades and heading for a position south of the Jomard Pass. However, the ubiquitous Japanese seaplane scouts were in the area looking for Pacific Fleet carriers and spotted TF-44. Just before 1400 a squadron of single-engine land-based bombers attacked. Crace had his ships in a tight diamond formation and, operating at high speed, executed severe tactical maneuvers to avoid the Japanese bombs while throwing up a huge volume of antiaircraft fire. No hits were scored on Crace's ships. Immediately afterward, a squadron of land-based two-engine planes appeared, armed with torpedoes. More skillful maneuvering by Crace, and the torpedo attack failed. Five planes were shot down. Finally, a high-flying squadron of the two-engine planes dropped bombs from 15,000 feet, and these were dodged. In a magnificent performance of seamanship by Admiral Crace and his battle force, his ships suffered no damage, and he continued on course for the area south of Jomard Pass.[249]

Meanwhile, Fletcher's TF-17, now under overcast and squalls, still expected CarDiv5 to be north of them in the Solomon Sea. In fact, CarDiv5 was approximately 100 miles to the east, moving northwest. *Lexington* and *Yorktown* launched search planes at first light to the north and west. Within two hours a *Yorktown* plane reported sighting two carriers and four heavy cruisers. Fletcher accepted this report as CarDiv5, and ordered a full attack from both carriers, 93 planes total. The search plane returned to *Yorktown* two hours later, where Fletcher, to his great consternation, discovered that an error in the coding had resulted in cruisers being identified as carriers. All was not lost, however, as an Army Air Force plane operating from a base in Australia correctly identified a carrier about thirty miles from the cruisers' location. The TF-17 attack was vectored to the new sighting north of the task force, which turned out to be the Covering Force and its lone small carrier *Shoho*.

Lexington's group leader, Commander William B. Ault, led the *Lexington* air group of dive-bombers and torpedo planes against *Shoho*. At about 1300 the pilots dropped 1,000-pound bombs on and around *Shoho*. Several hit their target, and others were damaging near-misses. *Yorktown* planes arrived after the *Lexington* squadrons had heavily damaged *Shoho* and only added to the demolition. *Shoho* went down, and a radio message flashed across the ocean and subsequently around the world, "Scratch one flat top!"[250] It was the most significant tactical victory for US forces in the Atlantic or Pacific since the war began, five months earlier.

While all this was happening, Japanese search planes from Rabaul found TF-17 and reported its position to Admiral Inoue. This report, however, was not received by Takagi. Had the report been received in

249 Morison, Vol. 4, 38.

250 Morison, Vol. 4, 42.

a timely manner, Takagi could have launched an attack on TF-17 while the planes from *Lexington* and *Yorktown* were attacking *Shoho*. Instead, a CarDiv5 scout that had been searching since first light reported a carrier and cruiser had been sighted south of CarDiv5's location. Takagi launched an all-out attack, led by the senior air group commander, Lieutenant Commander Takahashi Kakuichi.

However, soon after the attack had been sent south, Takagi received a report from a Covering Force cruiser floatplane that correctly showed the position of TF-17 to be about 100 miles to the west of CarDiv5. What to do? Takagi concluded that the carrier task force must have divided, and calculated that the force sent south could make its attack, and there would still be time to recover, refuel, and rearm his planes to make a second attack on the forces to his west.

The "carrier" to the south turned out to be the oiler *Neosho*. Since it was riding high in the water after being drained of fuel, young and enthusiastic eyes at high altitude mistook it for a carrier, and the destroyer *Sims* was misidentified as a cruiser. Flying over these ships, Takahashi realized he had a problem. Was this a case of misidentification or error in the scout report, or were the carriers somewhere else nearby? He ordered a 100-square-mile search, which consumed an hour and turned up nothing. By this time it was approximately 1200. He could have aborted the mission but decided instead to send the slower torpedo planes back to their carriers and have the Val dive-bombers attack *Neosho* and *Sims*.

Sims took station behind *Neosho* and its gunners repelled the first wave of attackers. But Takahashi's Vals were too powerful for the single destroyer, and it was hit with several bombs. *Sims* broke in half and sank, taking almost all her crew with her into the depths of the ocean. *Neosho* took several hits and was set on fire, leading the Japanese pilots to assume she was sinking. Four Vals were lost to antiaircraft fire. *Neosho* drifted aimlessly for several days until she was found, having lost most of her crew, some of whom had separated from *Neosho* on rafts.

In a matter of hours, the enormous repercussions from untrained, unseasoned, unprofessional, and in some cases insufficient scouting became apparent. Both American and Japanese forces had the opportunity to win a substantial victory on May 7 while their enemy was chasing after a target that was ordered from erroneous scouting information. TF-17, by luck as much as any other factor, earned a partial victory with the diversion of its force to *Shoho*. CarDiv5 could have made a massive attack on TF-17, but instead expended its power on an oiler and a destroyer. It was not good enough to put young, untrained eyes on an important scouting mission to reserve a few more seasoned aviators for attack. A scouting mistake could waste an entire day and expose a major force to destructive attack from the enemy. The same could be said for exaggerations of battle damage. False, self-serving information fed back to commanders as sunk ships, when they were only damaged, led to mistakes and lost opportunities. All these factors played out over several days in the Coral Sea, and subsequent battles would see replays of these events in similar situations.

Hara was readying his planes for an attack on TF-17 but was delayed by the late recovery of the dive-bombers that had destroyed *Neosho* and *Sims*. In the overcast they could not find the carriers for more than an hour after they returned to their carriers' expected position. Again, what to do? Launching an attack at that point meant a night recovery. Many of his pilots were not ready for night operations.

Fletcher had recovered his planes from the attack on *Shoho* by about 1500 and considered another attack on the remaining cruisers of the Covering Force. There were two options: a late day attack with his planes or a night attack with his destroyers. The first option meant a night landing, with inevitable losses that could be significant and weaken his force for the battle he fully expected on the following day. The second was unpredictable, and Fletcher calculated that it was better to prepare his destroyers for antiaircraft defense the next day. All that risk was not worth it for an attack on just cruisers. There was another consideration.

His scouts still had not discovered the location of CarDiv5, despite the scattered, frantic messages from *Neosho* as it was attacked. On the other hand, judging from the volume of Japanese traffic, it appeared that the Japanese scouts had discovered his own position. A Japanese attack could come at any time, and in that case he would need all his air and naval antiaircraft power to defend his own force.

Admiral King, after reading a report of the battle, criticized Fletcher as being timid. The excellent quality of Fletcher's judgment late in the day on May 7 can be discerned from the opposite decision made by Takagi. When the planes from the attack on *Neosho* and *Sims* were finally recovered, he ordered *Shokaku* and *Zuikaku* to launch some of their best pilots, who were trained in night operations, into the darkening gloom to attack TF-17. After rearming and refueling, a total of twenty-seven Vals and Kates were launched without fighter protection less than two hours before sunset. The weather was uncertain, and his pilots failed to find any American ships. They were returning to their carriers when TF-17 radar picked them up. Wildcats were launched against them, and nine were shot down at the cost of only two Wildcats.

In a weird incident that shows how risky and dangerous night flying was, several Japanese planes flying in scattered fog mistook the Pacific Fleet carriers for their own carrier and attempted to land. As a result, one was shot down. Without good direction back to their carriers, the remaining planes were in trouble. A desperate Admiral Hara turned on his ship's searchlights to guide them in, but even with that assist, eleven planes were lost attempting an extremely difficult night landing in fog. Out of twenty-seven planes that were launched earlier in the evening, only six were recovered.

The superbly trained torpedo crews on the Japanese destroyers and cruisers, who had scored devastating hits with their Long Lance torpedo attacks in earlier engagements in the Indian Ocean, were left sitting by their torpedo launchers. The black shoe Admiral Takagi should have had a keen appreciation for the potential power of a torpedo attack.

Had Takagi ordered an attack of destroyers and cruisers late in the day, they could have reached the American force by about midnight and, employing their expertise in night surface tactics, possibly could have inflicted serious casualties on TF-17, perhaps even hitting one of the carriers. Instead, with limited experience or understanding of flight operations and the risks he was about to impose on the pilots, he ordered the night air attack. It was another major Takagi misjudgment and a disaster of the first order. In adverse weather and at night, Takagi squandered some of the best, irreplaceable pilots in a hopeless attack. The mission failed to inflict any damage on the TF-17 carrier forces, and more than 75 percent of the Japanese planes and pilots were lost. It resulted in very significant gaps in the attack forces available for the showdown battle the following day.

Prior to the night attack, Fletcher was still uncertain of the position of CarDiv5. However, radar was able to track the surviving CarDiv5 planes as they returned to their carriers and establish its position. The Japanese knew TF-17's position and knew where to send their attack force the next day. Because of Takagi's disastrous night attack, Fletcher now knew where to send his.

On May 8, both sides were ready for action. The scouting mistakes, lost communications, miscalculations, and other problems of the previous days were in the past. Each side knew where the enemy force was, and May 8 promised to be the showdown. The scouting missions, contacts with the enemy, and attacks on the opposing force would occur at approximately the same time. It was going to be a truly mano-a-mano battle, carriers versus carriers.

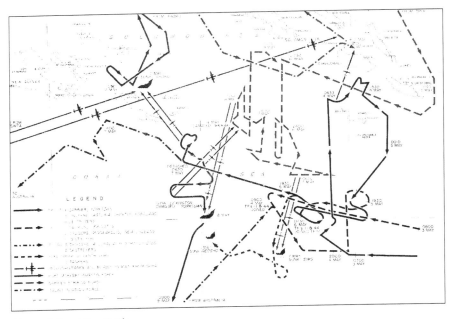

Chart of Coral Sea Battle
Photo Public Domain, wikpedia.org

Admiral Frank Jack Fletcher
Photo Naval History and Heritage

CHAPTER 18

Coral Sea: The Carrier Battle of May 8

Through the night of May 7-8, CarDiv5 moved north to stay within a 150-mile band of overcast that extended northwest to southeast for several hundred miles. As dawn was breaking over the Coral Sea, CarDiv5 turned south and remained under the overcast. TF-17 was in the clear to the southwest. Admiral Fletcher realized he needed the most experienced air officer to run the air battle, and early on May 8 he designated Admiral Fitch to be officer in tactical command as the showdown battle was developing. Although junior to Fletcher, Fletcher needed "to allow him [Fitch] complete freedom of action for his carriers and air groups."[251]

CarDiv5 launched seven scouts at 0615 in a search pattern oriented toward the south, based on a position from a scouting report made the day before. At 0700 Takagi ordered CarDiv5 south at high speed to close the range with TF-17 but still stay in the overcast. Takagi could have opened the range with the American force to give his longer-range planes an advantage, but he elected to be more aggressive and closed the range to allow his planes more time on station over TF-17. Meanwhile, TF-17 launched eighteen scouts at 0625 from *Lexington*. Most were sent northeast toward the position discovered the night before. A few were sent on other courses to be sure there was not another enemy force that had not yet been discovered.

---

251 Morison, 49.

A CarDiv5 scout made contact with TF-17 and transmitted the position, course, and speed back to Takagi at 0822. Hara began launching the attack from *Shokaku* and *Zuikaku* immediately. Eighteen Zero fighters, thirty-three Val dive-bombers, and eighteen Kate torpedo planes were formed up and heading southwest by 0915. A scout from *Lexington* made contact with CarDiv5 also at 0822 and radioed position, course, and speed back to TF-17. Fitch ordered an immediate launch from *Lexington* and *Yorktown*, and at 0840 both carriers began launching planes. *Yorktown* completed its launch by 0915, and eight Wildcat fighters, twenty-four dive-bombers, and nine torpedo planes headed northeast. The US and Japanese planes simultaneously flew on reciprocal courses to attack each other's task forces, but in the vast expanse of the skies they failed to catch sight of each other as they flew. *Lexington* did not complete its launch until 0925, which meant its group of nine Wildcats, twenty-two dive-bombers, and twelve torpedo planes was 10 minutes, flying time, or about 22 miles, behind the *Yorktown* group. Visual contact could be maintained while the two groups were in the clear, but once in the overcast that no longer would be possible.

At 0930 another scout plane piloted by a more senior and experienced pilot also found the Japanese force and determined that a navigation error had been made in the earlier reported position. The real position was forty-five miles farther north. The correction was radioed to the two carrier groups, already in the air. For whatever reason, the *Yorktown* group picked up the message and the *Lexington* group did not. Because the Japanese carrier fleet was under heavy overcast, this corrected position was a crucial piece of information.

Arriving over CarDiv5 at 1035, the Yorktown dive-bombers circled, awaiting the torpedo planes to make a coordinated attack. Hearing the engines above them, the Japanese took advantage of this delay to launch more CAP Zeros. The two carriers were about seven miles apart. *Zuikaku* got under heavy low clouds, and *Shokaku* headed into the wind to launch its planes. The *Yorktown* attack began, with the torpedo planes making their runs toward the enemy carriers. The twelve *Yorktown* torpedo planes headed toward *Shokaku*, divided into two sections for an anvil attack. The anvil tactic, sometimes called the scissors tactic, was a simultaneous attack of torpedo planes against opposite sides of the target ship, each from 45 degrees off the bow. The purpose was to make it difficult for the target ship to evade the torpedoes. If the ship turned one way to thread the track of oncoming torpedoes, the torpedoes launched at the other side would hit it broadside. If the ship didn't turn, torpedoes on both sides had a chance to hit. Ten torpedo planes attacked the starboard side of Shokaku and two to port. The CAP Zeros of CarDiv5 attacked, but the Wildcat escorts held them off. *Shokaku* took evasive action, and at thirty-four knots had the advantage against the slow American torpedoes. There were no hits, or if there were hits the torpedoes failed to explode.[252]

While the torpedo planes were making their runs, the seven-plane *Yorktown* scouting squadron loaded with 500-pound bombs made their dives. The windshields fogged as they descended quickly into warmer, moist air. Leveling off at 1,500 feet, they dropped their bombs more by guesswork than by sighting, and all seven exploded harmlessly in the ocean. The seventeen planes of the bomber squadron followed the scouting planes. Dropping down in sequence, like a waterfall, there were several misses and then one hit. Immediately after the first hit, Lieutenant John J. Powers, who had proclaimed earlier he was determined to make a hit, dove down to 300 feet and dropped a bomb on the flight deck of *Shokaku*. This was inevitably a suicide move, for there was no chance for survival at that altitude. The blast tore his plane apart, and Powers and his rear gunner fell into the ocean. Lieutenant Powers would be awarded a posthumous Medal of Honor for his "gallantry and

---

252   Morison, Vol. 4, 50.

intrepidity" for this and earlier actions. Fires raged, and *Shokaku* lost the ability to operate planes.[253]

About 1113, thirteen minutes after the TF-17 planes began their attacks on CarDiv5, planes from *Shokaku* and *Zuikaku* attacked TF-17. This was the first major carrier battle for the Pacific Fleet, and there were some serious misjudgments in the defense tactics. TF-17 started the battle with eighteen Wildcats available to fly CAP. Nine were patrolling; the other nine were spotted, warmed up, manned, and ready to launch at a moment's notice.

The TF-17 command had picked up messages from the Japanese scouts, obviously reporting their position back to CarDiv5. Given the time of the report, the distance between the two task forces, and the time required for the Japanese to launch, form up, and fly to TF-17, Fitch knew to expect an attack about 1100. The nine Wildcats flying CAP had been in the air since early morning. When the time of the Japanese attack was calculated, the air controller should have determined when those nine CAP planes needed to be rotated in to refuel so they were ready as 1100 approached. This was not done, however, and the Wildcats were held in the air. Radar picked up the Japanese planes at 1055, when they were 70 miles away. At that point it was too late for the Wildcats in the air to land, refuel, and launch again. They started the battle needing to conserve fuel and were restricted to low altitude and the area immediately around the carriers.

The remaining nine Wildcats were launched as soon as the incoming attack was spotted on radar. Six CAP planes were sent out long range at low altitude to intercept torpedo planes. Low altitude was where the American torpedo planes, the Devastators, would have been found. However, the Kate torpedo planes had much greater maneuverability and could approach and drop torpedoes from a higher altitude. The Kate pilots could first see the American fleet from 35 miles away. The

---

253   Morison, Vol 4, 50.

Kates came in over a cloud layer while the six long-range CAP planes were looking under it, and they were past the long-range CAP before the CAP pilots knew they were there.

The remaining CAP of three Wildcats, meant to defend against dive-bombers, were at 10,000 feet, but the Val dive-bombers attacked from 14,000 feet. The CAP should have been at the highest possible altitude because it is more advantageous to be above, ready to dive, than to be below, trying to climb. This was particularly true for the Wildcats, since their climbing ability was sluggish compared with the agile Zeros that could be defending the Vals.

In addition to these miscalculations, there were too few American fighters on their carriers to defend against attack. Lexington's commanding officer, Captain Frederick Sherman, had held back eighteen dive-bombers from the attack against CarDiv5 to defend against torpedo planes attacking TF-17. The dive-bombers were too slow to engage in dogfights with Zeros, but, stationed close to the carrier, the hope was they could be effective defenders against the slower Kate torpedo planes as they made their attack runs.

As the Japanese attack group approached, the air group commander, flying high above the scene, assessed the situation. This was the same Lieutenant Commander Takahashi who had led the attack on *Neosho* and *Sims* the day before. As they approached, Takahashi saw two carriers, one larger than the other. He divided his eighteen Kate torpedo planes into two sections, fourteen for the larger carrier (*Lexington*) and four for the smaller (*Yorktown*). The flight of fourteen was divided into two waves of seven each. He also divided the Val dive-bombers into two sections. The Kates would go in first, with Zeros flying above and slightly behind. The dive-bombers would follow immediately in a coordinated attack.

As the Kates approached the American carriers about six miles (or 12,000 yards) out, one of the Wildcat pilots at 10,000 feet looking for Val dive-bombers spotted the two waves of Kates below him. Diving at high speed on the second wave, he shot down one Kate before the Zeros could stop him. The second wave was now reduced to six planes.

At 8,000 yards, the Kates approached the first screen of dive-bombers acting as defensive CAP. Again assuming the Kates would be at about the same altitude as the US Devastators, they were too low and too slow, and the Kates flew by unscathed. However, the escorting Zeros were right there, and, in a totally lopsided dogfight, the Zeros sent four CAP dive-bombers into the ocean. In less than two minutes, four young Navy pilots, all decorated from previous engagements, were gone. It looked like using dive-bombers for CAP defense was a bad idea.

At 4,000 yards, the second screen of dive-bombers met the Kate torpedo planes. These dive-bombers had better altitude than the first group, and the Zeros were farther behind because it had cost them time to shoot down the first line of defense. Two Kates were shot down, and the first wave was reduced from seven to five.

The first wave of Kates came in against *Lexington* using the anvil tactic, which the Japanese torpedo planes had practiced to a fine art. They were now missing two planes, but they came in with two on the port side of *Lexington* and three to starboard. The execution of the anvil attack was good but not perfect. As soon as Captain Sherman saw torpedo splashes on the starboard side, he turned *Lexington* straight into the torpedoes to thread their tracks. All three passed harmlessly on either side of the ship. Two torpedoes dropped to port were on their way, but Sherman had time to avoid them, too. *Lexington* evaded all the torpedoes in the first wave.

The second wave of Kates was right behind the first, pressing in with another anvil attack. Four attacked the port side and two to starboard. Anti-aircraft fire destroyed the Kates on the starboard side, but four planes dropped their torpedoes to port. They had to dodge the close-in Wildcats and were well inside 1,000 yards when they dropped their torpedoes, closer than the ideal range. Two passed under *Lexington* because the torpedoes had not had enough time to adjust to a constant depth. The other two, however, exploded against the port side, blowing 30-foot holes in the hull below the waterline and instantly killing sailors in the engineering spaces. The ocean poured in, and *Lexington* took a seven-degree list to port. Good damage control limited the list to just that.

Yorktown was next. The four remaining Kate torpedo planes attacked on the port side of *Yorktown*. They did not employ the anvil tactic, and good maneuvering by Captain Elliott Buckmaster of *Yorktown* avoided all the torpedoes.

Now it was the dive-bombers' turn. Takahashi led nineteen Vals against *Lexington*, dropping in a stream from 14,000 feet in their usual 60-degree dives. Each Val carried one 500-pound bomb or two 132-pound bombs. The scanty CAP over *Lexington* climbing for altitude had little effect on the Vals, and sparse antiaircraft fire was the last line of defense. With all these advantages for the Japanese pilots, the results were disappointing. The dive-bombers scored no hits on *Lexington* with the 500-pounders, and only two minor hits with the 132-pounders. Near misses did little damage. The two 132-pounder hits caused loss of life in a Marine anti-aircraft battery as well as a young ship gunnery officer and several crew members. It had no further effect on ship operations. The losses in the Val squadrons from the long campaign in the Indian Ocean, as well as from the night attack just hours earlier, were evident in these pitiful results.

Meanwhile, *Yorktown* was under attack from fourteen Vals. Moving at thirty knots and being more maneuverable than *Lexington*, *Yorktown* made it difficult for the Val pilots to line up their dives. Nevertheless, one 500-pounder hit the flight deck amidships and penetrated four decks before exploding. Firefighters quickly brought the damage under control. A near miss damaged external hull plates, and the concussion penetrated inward far enough to cause a leak in a fuel tank. *Yorktown* started trailing oil. Once again, however, the dive-bomber attack was largely unsuccessful. *Yorktown* ended the battle with one bomb hit that was brought under control, some damaged hull plates, and modest oil leakage. A hasty repair to the hole in the flight deck, and *Yorktown* was able to continue flight operations. This was a different Japanese carrier force than the one that attacked Pearl Harbor.

Back at CarDiv5, the *Lexington* attack group had not picked up the corrected position of the Japanese fleet and, under the overcast, had difficulty finding them. All eighteen dive-bombers of one squadron could not find the Japanese at all and, running low on fuel, turned back with three Wildcat escorts. The entire *Lexington* air group was reduced to eleven torpedo planes, four dive-bombers, and six Wildcats, all under the leadership of Commander Bill Ault. At 1140, after executing a box search, they found CarDiv5 and commenced an attack.

The Zero CAP was drawn away by the Wildcats, and instead of facing the CAP at higher altitude, Ault saw an opportunity to go in low. He led his group of four Dauntlesses in a glide bombing attack against *Shokaku*. Each plane carried a 1,000-pound bomb. Three missed, but one hit. It was the third hit on *Shokaku* with a 1,000-pound bomb, and *Shokaku* was now out of action.

Even though three Wildcats were shot down in a dogfight with the Zeros, it opened up a clear shot at *Shokaku* for the torpedo planes. The eleven planes started their attack by separating into two groups of nine and two and executing an anvil attack. The two went in at the port side of *Shokaku*, and the captain turned his ship away. In so doing, he set up a broadside attack by the other nine planes, which all dropped torpedoes—but not a single one scored a hit.

The battle now evolved into a dogfight, with Zeros, Wildcats, and Dauntlesses streaking in and out of clouds, taking shots of opportunity as they showed themselves. It was one thing for the Dauntlesses to form a screen against Kates at low level as the Kates made their torpedo runs, but engaging Zeros in a high-level dogfight was another thing entirely. Bill Ault was not one to back out of a fight. He flew his Dauntless to the limit of its ability, but his plane was just too ponderous and slow against the Zeros. Hit by machine gun fire, he was wounded, and his plane was damaged and losing fuel. He tried to get a directional signal back to *Lexington*, but it didn't work. He knew he was never going to make it back. He made one last transmission: "So long people. Remember, we got a 1000-pound hit on the flattop." Ault and his crew disappeared over the ocean and were never heard from again. The heavily damaged *Shokaku* headed back to Japan.

Meanwhile, back at TF-17, the Japanese attack was tapering off and the surviving planes were heading back to their carriers. Commander Takahashi remained over the scene in his Val and again considered the situation. He was bitterly disappointed with the performance of his planes, particularly the dive-bombers. Yes, his torpedo planes had scored twice against the large carrier, but it appeared to have survived. It was listing but making good headway, with no sign it was sinking. The torpedo attack on the small carrier was a total failure.

Flying conditions over the American fleet had been excellent, and Takahashi had seen the poor deployment of the American CAP. Nevertheless, out of thirty-three Vals making attacks, there had been only one big hit on the small carrier. The large carrier was clearly old and not very maneuverable, but it was hit only twice with small bombs that probably hadn't done much damage. Some of his best pilots had been lost the night before in the disastrous late attack on TF-17, and those who survived were furious with Admiral Takagi for sending them on such a risky and hopeless mission. The price for that decision had now been paid.

Takahashi knew the brash young pilots in his group would report to Admiral Hara that they had sunk two carriers and who knew what else. He concluded that another attack was necessary to finish the job *against* the Americans. He had to radio all this to Admiral Hara immediately, get back to *Zuikaku* as fast as possible, and get another attack launched. Just then, a Wildcat pilot returning to his carrier saw a single Val below and ahead of his plane. Seeing it as just one more opportunity in this battle, he dove on the Val, guns blazing. Takahashi never saw him coming. His Val caught fire, turned over, and headed straight down. The message to Admiral Hara never got sent. Both air group commanders, Ault and Takahashi, ended their lives that day in the ocean.

Onboard *Lexington* the portside list was corrected by pumping fuel oil to starboard tanks. Planes were returning from the attack on CarDiv5 and landing on both *Lexington* and *Yorktown*. Young pilots were reporting two Japanese carriers sunk. Planes also were returning to CarDiv5, but *Shokaku* was out of action and dispatched. All returning planes were taken aboard *Zuikaku*. Young pilots were reporting two American carriers sunk. Taking these reports at face value, and considering that they had lost the service of *Shokaku*, Takagi recommended withdrawal, to which Inoue, getting his reports aboard his cruiser at Rabaul, concurred. CarDiv5 turned north.

Meanwhile, the torpedo hits on *Lexington* had caused leaks in the gasoline tanks deep in the bowels of the ship. Gasoline spread along the lower decks, and even more insidious were the heavy combustible fumes that built up throughout the lower spaces. At 1242 the fumes erupted in a huge explosion, the first in a series of explosions that spread fire throughout the ship. Despite the valiant efforts of firefighters, repair parties, and every available man, the battle to save the ship became hopeless. Just after 1700 Admiral Fitch called down from the flag bridge to Sherman, "Let's get the boys off, Ted." Sherman reluctantly agreed. The procedure to abandon ship was orderly, and Captain Sherman was the last man off. *Lexington* became a burning hulk, and finally just before 1900 an escorting destroyer was ordered to torpedo what remained. The torpedo exploded, and the ship sank.

Admiral Yamamoto, aboard his flagship in the Inland Sea of Japan, received the battle reports of the returning pilots claiming two carriers had been sunk and Inoue's order to break off the action. He knew the pilots' reports were probably exaggerated and immediately ordered *Zuikaku* to reverse course to the south "and annihilate the enemy." *Zuikaku* reversed course, but TF-17, minus *Lexington*, was long gone. It was Admiral Takagi's final blunder in the Battle of the Coral Sea. At the same time as *Zuikaku* was making its final dash south, Admiral Halsey and TF-16 were still several hundred miles east of the battle scene on the King-ordered dash to join TF-16 in the Battle of the Coral Sea.

Both Japanese carriers survived Coral Sea and would appear in later engagements in the Pacific War. *Zuikaku* had lost many planes and pilots in the crippling night action of May 7 and the main carrier battle of May 8. These losses followed earlier losses suffered in the Indian Ocean. Unlike American squadrons that could move from carrier to carrier, Japanese air groups were integral to the carrier to which they were assigned. The losses to the *Zuikaku* air group at the Coral Sea were just too many, and the ship would be in training mode for several months while a new air group was integrated into its operations. *Shokaku* would be undergoing major repairs for several months. Particularly bitter for the Japanese navy mid-level commanders and surviving pilots was the hard realization that the entire purpose of the Port Moresby operation was to prepare for the invasion of Australia, an operation that already had been cancelled.

The Battle of the Coral Sea is considered by many observers as something close to a draw. In fact, it was a major defeat for the Japanese and a major win for the Pacific Fleet. The Japanese would go into the Battle of Midway with four carriers instead of six. For purposes of Midway, *Zuikaku* and *Shokaku* might as well have been sunk. A third of the Striking Force carriers would be out of action for the largest and most consequential battle of the Pacific War. In addition, they suffered irreplaceable pilot losses. The Pacific Fleet would go into the battle with three carriers instead of four, but they would have many planes based on Midway itself. As Yamamoto knew, the great industrial base of the United States was mobilizing a huge naval force that would eventually overwhelm the Combined Fleet. Midway was the last chance for the Japanese to avoid defeat in the Pacific War, and the foolish decision to engage in the Coral Sea lengthened the odds against them.

CHAPTER 19

Midway: The Japanese Advance

Yamamoto liked to think about sea battles in terms of powerful forces and annihilating victories, such as Admiral Togo had achieved against the Russian battleship fleet in 1905, when Yamamoto was a young ensign. He knew the Striking Force had to destroy the Pacific Fleet carriers that had escaped the Pearl Harbor raid, or he faced defeat. The plan Yamamoto devised was to invade a place he thought the Americans would be compelled to fight, set a trap, and destroy the Pacific Fleet carriers in one titanic battle. The place was Midway.

Japanese instincts for deception and intricate, coordinated movements dictated his battle plan. The Striking Force of six carriers had been reduced to four from the damage and plane losses suffered by *Shokaku* and *Zuikaku* at the Coral Sea battle a month earlier. No matter. The four remaining carriers—*Akagi*, *Kaga*, *Hiryu*, and *Soryu*, still under the command of Vice Admiral Nagumo—would launch an air attack on the US facilities on Midway at first light on June 4. The carriers would be supported by two battleships and sixteen other cruisers and destroyers.

An amphibious invasion force of 5,000 troops were embarked on sixteen transports. The invasion force would be supported by two battleships, four new cruisers, and escorting destroyers. Troops would go ashore after the planes of the Striking Force had destroyed the defenses on the island, which were expected to be meager. The battleships and cruisers of the amphibious force could provide shore bombardment before and during the landings if necessary. When the American carriers rushed to the scene from Pearl Harbor, they would be met by aircraft of the Striking Force. Then the main body of the fleet, consisting of the 76,000-ton *Yamato*, with Yamamoto embarked, plus six other battleships and a huge fleet of cruisers and destroyers, would deliver death and destruction to the carriers of the Pacific Fleet. The various units of the fleet would be dispersed beyond the range of Midway-based reconnaissance planes to disguise the size of the entire force. However, that also meant the units would be too far away from each other to afford mutual support.

It is curious that the man who had developed the First Carrier Striking Force into the deadliest naval force on the planet still believed that the final devastation of the American fleet at Midway would be delivered by battleships. Despite his development of the carrier force, its unprecedented attack on Pearl Harbor, and its victories in the south Pacific and Indian Ocean prior to Midway, Yamamoto compulsively remained a battleship admiral.

Rear Admiral Yamaguchi had questioned the disposition of the Japanese fleet. He proposed that the surface forces of the Combined Fleet be reorganized into three to four task groups, each with a carrier nucleus, and each screened by battleships, cruisers, and destroyers. The Main Body combined with the carrier Striking Force could have accomplished this. However, his ideas fell on the deaf ears of the "gun club" battleship admirals, who had been trained to organize their ships in a battle line opposing an enemy line, a tactic navies had used for centuries. Yamamoto did not consider Yamaguchi's advice when planning the Midway attack.[254] The prescient Yamaguchi was ahead of his time, as later in the war and for decades afterward this would become the doctrinal configuration of the carrier battle group.

So that the Japanese knew what to expect, a flotilla of submarines was to be stationed outside Pearl Harbor to inform Yamamoto when the

---

254   Fuchida, 127.

Pacific Fleet sortied from the harbor. In addition, a Mavis four-engine seaplane with an operating range of more than 2,500 miles would overfly Pearl Harbor to confirm that the Pacific Fleet carriers were still there. It would be refueled by a submarine at French Frigate Shoals, between Midway and Oahu, and from there proceed to Pearl Harbor. A separate amphibious attack on Attu and Kiska, two western islands in the Aleutian chain of Alaska, was scheduled for June 3. Capture of these islands would extend the operating range of Japanese forces and possibly be a springboard for raids on the northwest US mainland. Altogether, nearly 200 ships were involved in this dispersed but massive fleet movement.

The two battles, Coral Sea and Midway, are a continuum. As a result of Coral Sea, Yamamoto was without the two carriers that had just fought there. He sent the four remaining Striking Force carriers, just back from the Indian Ocean, into battle at Midway with depleted pilot strength and ships needing repair and upkeep. The crews, particularly the pilots who fought perilous missions in the Indian Ocean on nearly a daily schedule, were exhausted. Oil dripped from aircraft engines on the hangar deck. As a fighting fleet, the Striking Force going into the Midway battle had been underway almost continually since departing for Pearl Harbor in late November 1941. It was hardly more than half the strength of the superbly trained and ready air groups on the six carriers that attacked Pearl Harbor. All this while the Japanese battleships, like pampered poodles, rode at anchor in the Inland Sea of Japan, inter-rupted only occasionally by training exercises. Nevertheless, Yamamoto declared that the battleships would win the showdown with the Pacific Fleet at Midway.

The Striking Force carriers were to be sent out front, to tempt and smoke out the Pacific Fleet carriers while the battleships lay back, ready to pounce. Pounce on what? Yamamoto seemed to think his carrier planes would merely wound the Pacific Fleet carriers, destroying their flight decks so that his battleships could then deliver devastation with their huge guns. It apparently did not occur to him that if Mahan had been writing in 1940 instead of fifty years earlier in 1890, he would have understood the power of carriers and developed his strategy differently. Aircraft on the Japanese carriers were as follows:[255]

CarDiv1
Akagi

Zero Fighters	21
Dive-bombers	21
Torpedo/Attack Aircraft	21
Total Aircraft	**63**

Kaga

Zero Fighters	30
Dive-bombers	23
Torpedo/Attack Aircraft	30
Total Aircraft	**83**

CarDiv2
Hiryu

Zero Fighters	21
Dive-bombers	21
Torpedo/Attack Aircraft	21
Total Aircraft	**63**

Soryu

Zero Fighters	21
Dive Bombers	21
Torpedo/Attack Aircraft	21
Total Aircraft	**63**
Total Aircraft, All Carriers	**272**

---

255   Morison Vol. 4, 88.

CHAPTER 20

Midway: The Pacific Fleet Response

Both Admirals King and Nimitz knew, from decoded Japanese messages, that the Japanese were planning to continue their advances. The question was: where. Formulating strategy involved the Naval Intelligence Service in Washington—in particular Rear Admiral Richmond Kelly Turner, who argued that the Japanese buildup would be aimed at northeast Australia, New Caledonia, and Fiji, and would begin between June 15 and 20. King accepted Turner's intelligence evaluation, and that meant his estimate of the time the target would be attacked would be late.

Nimitz had available to him the Hypo Group, the cryptography unit housed in a smoke-filled basement in Pearl Harbor. Unbeknownst to the Japanese, Hypo had been hard at work deciphering the J-25 naval code. The cryptographers, led by Japanese linguist Lieutenant Commander Joseph J. Rochefort, succeeded in decoding increasing numbers of messages and compiling more and more data. Rochefort kept Admiral Nimitz informed of Japanese movements over the first few months of 1942, including specific information about the Japanese plans for Midway several weeks before the June 4 target date. Coordination between the Naval Intelligence Service in Washington and the Hypo Group at Pearl Harbor was poor, and because the officers in Washington were senior to Rochefort their evaluations dominated the reports given to King. "Shortly before battle was joined in the Coral Sea, the Hypo Group informed Admiral Nimitz of a forthcoming enemy offensive in the central Pacific that threatened to be far more powerful and dangerous than the one about to be stopped" at the Coral Sea.[256] Nevertheless, acting on intelligence generated by Naval Intelligence in Washington, King demanded that two carriers be kept continually in the south Pacific. Because of the poor communications between the two intelligence units, there was no comparison of information or attempts to reconcile different evaluations. King failed to resolve these issues and just relied on the information from his immediate intelligence staff.

Admiral Halsey, embarked on *Enterprise* in command of TF-16, had been underway almost continuously since Pearl Harbor, covering thousands of ocean miles to carry out support of amphibious landings on Samoa and raids on the Marshall Islands, Wake, and Marcus. *Enterprise* and *Hornet* launched the Doolittle Raid on April 18, and TF-16 returned to Pearl Harbor on April 25. On King's orders they were underway again on May 1 for a 7,000-mile round trip to the Coral Sea, arriving in the area after the battle had been fought.

The identity of the target of the forthcoming Japanese attack was confirmed by a cleverly executed message sent in the clear about water being in short supply on Midway. As hoped, the Japanese picked up the message, and Hypo soon decrypted a Japanese report of a water shortage on "MI." This confirmed that the target of the Japanese attack was Midway. With this news, in addition to the aircraft and personnel already stationed on Midway, Nimitz ordered more Marine Corps F4F Wildcat and F2A Buffalo fighters, Army Air Corps B-26 and B-17 bombers, and a detachment of Marine Corps infantry to Midway.[257] Rochefort confirmed that the attack on Midway would be in early June.

TF-16 returned to Pearl Harbor on May 26 in good order, with one huge exception: Halsey, the 60-year-old commander, arrived back completely exhausted and ill. After six months of intense underway operations, culminating in the fruitless mission across the Pacific to the

---

256   Morison, Vol. 4, 261.

257   Morison, Vol. 4, 85–86.

Coral Sea, Halsey had lost twenty pounds and had contracted a serious case of dermatitis. Nimitz took one look at him and sent him straight to the Pearl Harbor hospital. The Navy's most experienced and highly regarded carrier force commander would sit out the Battle of Midway.

The challenge for Nimitz was to choose Halsey's replacement for commander of Task Force 16. Rear Admiral Aubrey Fitch, the seasoned carrier commander who had been officer in tactical command for the final day's carrier battle at the Coral Sea, was unavailable. He had moved back to the West Coast to take command of a task force built around the now-repaired carrier *Saratoga*. Halsey recommended his cruiser and screen commander, Rear Admiral Raymond Spruance. Spruance was not an aviator and had never had an aviation or carrier command, but he would be backed by Halsey's experienced staff. Halsey had known Spruance for many years and had confidence in his capabilities and judgment.

Nimitz had to consider whether a non-flier without a carrier task force command or even the ship command of an aircraft carrier was the best choice to take over Task Force 16. But Nimitz had also come to value Spruance's abilities, and he accepted Halsey's recommendation. Fletcher, also not a flier but a task force commander who had just fought the Coral Sea battle, would remain in command of Task Force 17. As the senior rear admiral, Fletcher would be in overall command. Halsey, the ultimate sea warrior, would watch from his hospital window as the two task forces departed Pearl Harbor for Midway.

There was another aspect to the last-minute shift in the command structure. Over the previous year, Halsey had examined the operations of American carrier aircraft in a series of exercises. In July 1941, in a secret exercise at a remote lake, he had sixteen torpedo planes drop torpedoes against a stationary target at the center of the lake. Not even one torpedo came close to hitting the target. During the raid against the Japanese-held Marshall Islands in February 1942, torpedo bombers were sent against unarmed ships trapped in a lagoon after a dive-bomber sank a tanker in the channel. Ten planes launched their torpedoes against these trapped, stationary targets, causing no damage. The torpedoes either went off course or failed to explode on contact.

At the Battle of the Coral Sea, the torpedo planes had scored no hits, but the dive-bombers had scored three hits against the carrier *Shokaku* using high-explosive, point-detonating bombs. (Armor-piercing bombs, such as the Japanese had used at Pearl Harbor, were not available to the Pacific Fleet at that point in the war.) It was clear to Halsey that torpedo attacks were unreliable at best, and the primary aerial attack force in the U.S. Navy had to be the Dauntless dive-bomber. It is unknowable whether Halsey would have employed the torpedo planes at Midway, but the forthcoming battle would be fought without the benefit of Halsey's expertise and judgment.

This first encounter between Japanese and US carrier planes led to evaluations of flying tactics. Lieutenant Commander Jimmy Flatley, a fighter squadron leader flying from *Yorktown*, analyzed the encounters at Coral Sea and made important observations, which he reduced to writing for other Navy pilots. Flatley observed that the Zero pilots depend on their maneuverability and speed to make fast attacks because they know their light planes are highly vulnerable to gunfire. Because of the Zero's speed, particularly when climbing, it was extremely important to never try to outclimb a Zero. Attacking them from above is the best tactic, and they will dive away to avoid getting hit. It was important to stay above a Zero in a dogfight because a Wildcat can lose altitude fast but not gain it when up against a Zero.[258] These observations would prove valuable when the next encounter occurred.

At Coral Sea the scouting was grossly deficient, and that deficiency had squandered an opportunity to strike a deadlier blow against the Japanese carrier force. Fortunately for the Pacific Fleet, Japanese scouting had not been any better. Whatever lay ahead was unknown but almost

---

258   Young, 57-58.

surely would involve heavy fighting. The risk was huge. Even with crucial intelligence in his possession, Nimitz had to consider that the ranges of the Striking Force aircraft were greater than the Pacific Fleet equivalents. The difference in operational ranges between Pacific Fleet planes and Striking Force planes, 175 miles versus 240 miles, or 65 miles, was over two and a half hours of carrier steaming time at 25 knots. If Japanese scouts discovered the Pacific Fleet carriers early in an engagement, the Striking Force planes could attack when their carriers were still out of range of Pacific Fleet planes.

In the Great War, it was said of British Admiral John Jellicoe before the Battle of Jutland that he was the only officer in the British armed forces who could lose the war in a single day. While a defeat at Midway would not necessarily lose the war for the United States, losing the carriers in a single day would mean that Japan would occupy Midway and once again threaten Pearl Harbor. The West Coast of the United States would be a potential target for Japanese raids, and the military would have to shift forces from the European theater to defend it. The amphibious landings on Morocco, planned for later in 1942, would have to be postponed.

Alternatively, destruction of the Pacific Fleet carriers would remove any threat to Japanese island bases in the Pacific and allow the Striking force to move west into the Indian Ocean again and establish a new base, such as at the Maldives. The Japanese fleet then could move all the way to the Red Sea and the Persian Gulf. Churchill's great fear was for the Axis forces in North Africa to link up with the Japanese navy, cutting off the buildup of the British Eighth Army in Egypt and the massive supply of tanks moving through the Persian Gulf to Russia. If that were to occur, there would be no battles at El Alamein and Stalingrad in late 1942 and January 1943. The Pacific War, and by association the Allied war effort, would be set back significantly. The outcome of the entire war could become uncertain.

On May 27 Commander Edwin T. Layton, the CINCPAC intelligence officer, had a meeting with Nimitz. Nimitz demanded that Layton make his best determination of "the dates and dispositions the enemy intends to take." Layton determined that the Japanese fleet would approach from the northwest and launch an attack on Midway Island at first light on June 4.[259] Nimitz's first question was whether he had confidence in the accuracy of the decoded messages and the comprehensive picture of the Japanese advance that the intelligence staff had developed. A negative answer would mean there was too much uncertainty in the situation, and the risk of exposing the carriers was too great. After exhaustive review, Nimitz decided that the intelligence was reliable, and he could risk the carriers to thwart the Japanese advance. Nimitz had decided to put his own staff intelligence above the conflicting evidence being made in Washington. The next step was to devise a plan that would give his forces the best chance to win. Nimitz had a week to formulate the plan.

The greater range of the Japanese planes was a critical factor. In order to launch an attack, Pacific Fleet carriers had to get to their maximum operating range of 175 miles without being discovered. If they closed the range before dawn, Pacific Fleet would have the advantage of being able to advance closer to their own operating range from the projected position of the Japanese carriers before first light. CINCPAC fleet aviation officer Captain Arthur Davis, who was charged by Nimitz to anticipate the most likely Japanese tactics and devise the best counter-measures, recognized the vulnerabilities of the carriers and advised that attacking the enemy before being attacked oneself should be the guiding strategy.

Based on the intelligence gathered by Rochefort and his staff at the Hypo Group, Layton determined that the Japanese command would approach Midway on a course of 135 degrees and launch their planes for Midway on the same course. The Japanese would want to close

---

259   Layton, 430.

the range quickly and launch planes into the slow southeast wind, but they were limited by the slowest ship, *Kaga*, and so would be moving at twenty-six knots. With this information, Layton calculated the movement of the Japanese fleet by simple dead reckoning along course 135. Nimitz issued Operation Order 29-42 for the disposition of ships and planes. He also positioned submarines along the expected track of the Striking Force.

Nimitz decided to use the land-based PBY Catalinas on Midway to carry out the scouting for the American forces. It was crucial for the PBYs to locate the Japanese fleet as early as possible on June 4, and for the carriers to be in position to launch a surprise attack before the Japanese knew they were there. That meant they had to have early and excellent scouting. The PBYs would report their contacts to Fletcher and Spruance on the carriers and to Captain Cyril T. Simard, the commander on Midway. The Japanese on their ships could sight a PBY and still not know that an American carrier force was in the area. This was particularly important because the Japanese were not aware that Pacific Fleet forces had detailed knowledge of their battle plan.

A semicircular search pattern covering 180 degrees was developed, with vectors like spokes of a wheel radiating out from Midway. The search pattern was oriented to the northwest, from 200 degrees around to 020 degrees. A total force of twenty-two PBYs was to be employed, and each plane would fly straight along its vector to search for the Japanese formations. PBYs had a maximum operating range of 700 miles. At the end of their vectors they would turn left 90 degrees and fly for several miles before turning again to fly straight back to Midway. The left turn taken at the farthest point of each vector meant that the return leg would survey a different area of the ocean and provide the best possible search result.

The Nimitz plan called for the PBYs to take off at 0430, and Layton calculated that one of the PBYs would encounter the Striking Force at about 0600, when it had flown 175 miles from Midway. The position, course, and speed of the contact would be reported to all Pacific fleet units. Layton calculated how much time would elapse from the PBY report until the Midway planes would launch, form up, and fly on course 315, the reciprocal of 135 degrees, up the track of the expected movement of the Japanese ships. By combining the speed of the Japanese carrier force and the speed of the planes and allowing ten minutes to form up, Layton predicted that the planes should intercept the Japanese carriers about 0720, or an hour and 20 minutes after the PBY report. During that time, the Japanese carriers, moving at 26 knots, would have advanced approximately 35 miles, placing them 140 miles from Midway. Layton's calculations showed 140 miles from Midway to be the interception point for the planes from Midway.

Nimitz was determined to devise a plan that would give his forces the best chance of success. A basic military and naval battle tactic, concentration of force, is to assemble and focus one's forces on the most important and vulnerable point of the enemy forces. Concentration of force is a tactic as old as Hannibal, who 2,200 years earlier concentrated his elephants to break the Roman lines. Nelson at Trafalgar and Togo at Tsushima concentrated their forces against an enemy fleet by "Crossing the T"—having their ships in a battle line achieve a position perpendicular to the opposing line and focusing their fire on the first or second ships in the enemy's line. Now, in the age of air power, Nimitz knew the maximum number of attacking planes from both Midway and the carriers concentrated simultaneously over the Japanese fleet would have the best chance to overwhelm the Zero defenders and deliver the most potent attack. The best tactic to achieve that was a flank attack from the carriers, arriving over the target at the same time as the planes from Midway.

The next step in the plan was to establish the position for the carriers at 0600 so the carrier planes could arrive simultaneously with the planes from Midway. Layton would have drawn a perpendicular line from the 140-mile interception point, bearing 045 degrees from that point. (A perpendicular from the Japanese course of 135 degrees is 045 degrees.) He would have marked a point on the perpendicular line 140 miles from the interception point to establish the position of the carriers. On receipt of the PBY contact message the carrier planes would fly on a course of 225 degrees, the reciprocal of the 045 degree course, to the interception point. Speeds of different airplane types would be adjusted so that they all arrived over the interception point at the same time. The location for the Pacific Fleet carriers at 0600 also measured 200 miles straight north of Midway Island. The 200-mile point north of Midway would be used as the navigation point by the carrier command.

When a PBY reported contact with the Striking Force carriers, expected around 0600, planes from Midway would take off and fly on course 315 degrees. The carriers would launch their planes on course 225 degrees. Adjustments would be made by the carriers to compensate for wind speed, direction, and other factors to achieve a simultaneous attack with the Midway planes. The attack plan, properly executed, would result in all the attack planes from both Midway and the three carriers arriving over the Japanese fleet at the same time in a combined, concentrated attack at about 0720. If all went well, Pacific Fleet would achieve a victory over the Striking Force by 0800 to 0815.

Because the Japanese force attacking Midway still would be in the area of Midway at 0720, the Pacific Fleet attack would be against just the reserve force. If the Pacific Fleet attack on the Striking Force resulted in serious damage to the flight decks of the carriers, even without sinking the ships the returning Midway planes, expected around 0830, would be unable to land.

TF-17 with the carrier *Yorktown*, damaged from Japanese bombs at the Battle of the Coral Sea, arrived back in Pearl Harbor early on May 27, trailing fuel oil from leaking tanks. It moved into dry dock, and 1,400 workmen immediately descended on the ship to begin repairs. Admiral Nimitz, in wader boots, went into the dry dock to see the damage for himself. In three days the workmen made temporary but sufficient repairs to *Yorktown* so that she was ready for action again.

Spruance moved from the cruiser *Northampton*, where he had flown his flag, to *Enterprise*. In the late afternoon and evening of May 27, Admirals Nimitz, Fletcher, and Spruance; Pacific Fleet staff officers under war plans officer Captain Charles McMorris; and commanding officers of the ships held a conference at Pacific Fleet headquarters. The navigation point, 200 miles north of Midway, for the carriers to launch their planes is confirmed in the June 14, 1942, report of ComCruPac (Commander of Cruisers in the Pacific), i.e., Admiral Fletcher):

> *ENTERPRISE and HORNET maintained their air groups in readiness as a striking force. During the night of June 3-4 both forces [TF-17 and TF-16] proceeded for a point two hundred miles North of Midway. Reports of enemy forces to the Westward of Midway were received from Midway and Commander-in-Chief, Pacific Fleet. These reports indicated the location of the enemy Occupation Force but not the Striking Force.*[260]

The ComCruPac report refers to PBY scouts on June 3, when the Occupation Force was contacted and the Striking Force was still under heavy clouds. Further confirmation of the Nimitz plan and the ordered position of the carriers to be 200 miles north of Midway at 0600 on June 4 is contained in accounts of at least three published contemporary historians who had the opportunity to interview participants: Richard Bates, Samuel Eliot Morison, and E. B. Potter.[261]

---

260   262 Report of Commander Cruisers, Pacific Fleet (Adm. Fletcher), To: Commander-in-Chief, United States Pacific Fleet, Subject: Battle of Midway, 14 June 1942, Pearl Harbor, T.H., Para. 3, included as Enclosure (H) in United States Pacific Fleet, Advance Report – Battle of Midway, 15 June 1942.

261   Bates, Richard, The Battle of Midway, U.S. Naval War College, 1948, 108. Morison, Samuel Eliot, *Coral Sea, Midway, and Submarine Actions* (Naval Institute Press, 1949), 102. Potter, E.B., *Nimitz (Naval Institute Press, 1976),* 87.

The advantages of the concentration of force are obvious, but the plan did involve risks. The Japanese used the E13A1 catapult-launched float-planes, nicknamed "Jakes" by Pacific Fleet fliers. Jakes were launched from the cruisers *Tone* and *Chikuma* for their primary searches and had a range of more than 1,100 miles with a cruising speed of 138 knots. At slower speeds they could stay aloft for 14 hours. The Jake floatplanes, launched at 0430 and traveling at 138 knots, would cover more than 200 miles of their search track by 0600. A Jake launched at 0430 could discover the Pacific Fleet carriers approaching the position 200 miles north of Midway at approximately the same time as a PBY flying from Midway would discover the Striking Force. In that event there was the likely confrontation of the Pacific Fleet planes with the reserve force Zeros. An attack by the reserve force on the Pacific Fleet carriers also was possible. Whether such a confrontation would occur would depend on the readiness of the reserve force and the effectiveness of the search executed by the Japanese scouts.

On May 28, TF-16, *Enterprise*, and *Hornet*, together with their escorting cruisers and destroyers, sortied from Pearl Harbor. They were bound for a location designated as Point Luck, 1,100 miles away and 320 miles northeast of Midway. Once clear of the harbor, it was time to tell all hands the mission of the task force. Spruance issued a statement, beginning with the Japanese battle plan:

> *An attack for the purpose of capturing Midway is expected.*
> *The attacking force may be composed of all combatant types,*
> *including four or five carriers plus transports and train vessels.*

He continued with an outline of the strategy to counter the Japanese attack and the subsequent events that would govern his judgment as the engagement continued:

> *If our presence remains unknown to the enemy, we should*
> *be able to make surprise flank attacks on the enemy carriers*
> *from a position northeast of Midway. Further operations will*

be based on the outcome of these attacks, damage inflicted by
Midway forces, and information of enemy movements.

Spruance's mention of "surprise flank attacks" refers to the part the carrier planes would play in the concentration of force in the Nimitz battle plan.

In 1805, as the British fleet headed into battle at Cape Trafalgar, Vice Admiral Horatio Nelson drew on the patriotism of his sailors and raised a flag hoist that still reverberates in the lore of the Royal Navy:

England expects that every man will do his duty

Heading for the fateful rendezvous with the Japanese at Midway, the restrained, understated Spruance was not given to the same stirring rhetoric as Nelson. However, like Nelson 137 years earlier, he drew on the patriotism of his sailors as he alerted every man to the high stakes of their mission:

The successful conclusion of the operation now commencing
will be of great value to our country.[262]

Yorktown, with Fletcher embarked and repairs completed, was underway from Pearl Harbor with TF-17 on May 30 to rendezvous with TF-16 at Point Luck. Two black shoe, surface warfare admirals took command of the carrier forces heading into the largest and most important carrier battle of the war.

Because of the major losses at the Coral Sea, the air groups on *Yorktown* had to be heavily reconstituted. *Saratoga* was completing repairs on the West Coast from the torpedo damage suffered in January, and air units from that ship were available to rebuild the fighter, torpedo, and dive-bomber squadrons on *Yorktown*. Units from *Lexington*, sunk at the Coral Sea, also were ordered in, and *Yorktown* went to sea with a strong air arm. Bombing Three, Torpedo Three, and Fighting Three

---

262   Toll, 402.

with twenty-seven new F4F-4 fighters, all from *Saratoga*, would replace most of *Yorktown*'s air arm. Only Bombing Five remained of its original complement.

With his ships underway, Nimitz sent the following to his task force commanders:

> *Letter of Instructions.*
>
> *In carrying out the tasks assigned in Operation Plan 29-42 you will be governed by the principle of calculated risk, which you shall interpret to mean the avoidance of exposure to attack by superior enemy forces without good prospect of inflicting, as a result of such exposure, greater damage to the enemy. This applies to a landing phase as well as during preliminary air attacks.*[263]
>
> C. W. Nimitz

The two American task forces made contact on June 2, and overnight Fletcher moved the forces to a position northeast of Midway.

The American carrier forces were as follows:[264]

Total Midway Aircraft

Task Force 17

Wildcat Fighters	25
Dive-bombers	37
Torpedo Planes	13
Total Aircraft	**75**

---

263   Cincpac File No. A16-3/A4-3/ FF12(12)/(16) Serial 0115, May 28, 1942.
264   Morison, 90-91.

Task Force 16

Enterprise

Wildcat Fighters	27
Dive-bombers	38
Torpedo Planes	14
Total Aircraft	**79**

Hornet

Wildcat Fighters	27
Dive-bombers	38
Torpedo Planes	15
Total Aircraft	**80**
Total Carrier Aircraft	**223**

The Japanese command estimated about fifty aircraft would be stationed on Midway. However, because of the success of American intelligence, aircraft based on Midway, including those recently moved to the island in anticipation of the attack, were more than double the Japanese expectation. Antiaircraft batteries also were increased. Total aircraft on Midway were as follows:[265]

PBY Catalina Scouts	32
TBF Avenger Torpedo Aircraft	6
F4F Wildcat Fighters	7
F2A Buffalo Fighters	20
SB2U Vindicators	11
SBD Dive-bombers	16
B-26 Bombers	4
B-17 Bombers	19
Total Midway Aircraft	**115**
Total US Aircraft, Ashore and Afloat	**338**

---

265   Morison, 92-93.

At the Coral Sea, Rear Admiral Fitch was put in tactical command of the Pacific Fleet air operations prior to the culminating air battle on May 8. Although he was junior to Fletcher, Fletcher delegated this command to Fitch because of his training and experience in carrier operations. As the Midway battle loomed, Fletcher did not have Fitch to take over air operations.

Lt. Commander Joseph Rochefort
Photo Naval History and Heritage

Lt. Commander Edwin Layton
Photo Naval History and Heritage

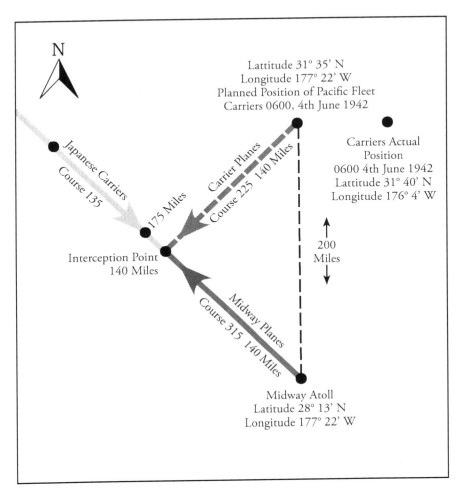

N

Lattitude 31° 35' N
Longitude 177° 22' W
Planned Position of Pacific Fleet
Carriers 0600, 4th June 1942

Carriers Actual
Position
0600 4th June 1942
Lattitude 31° 40' N
Longitude 176° 4' W

Japanese Carriers
Course 135

175 Miles

Carrier Planes
Course 225 140 Miles

200
Miles

Interception Point
140 Miles

Midway Planes
Course 315 140 Miles

Midway Atoll
Latitude 28° 13' N
Longitude 177° 22' W

Nimitz Attack Plan

CHAPTER 21

Midway: Opening Actions

The Japanese Striking Force of carriers approached Midway from the northwest under cloud cover. The southernmost force, the amphibious task force, was in the clear on June 3. Starting at first light on June 3, the twenty-two PBYs radiated out from Midway on their assigned search vectors. Fletcher supplemented the PBY search with scouts from *Yorktown* that searched to the north.

The PBYs discovered the first minesweeper units of the amphibious force 700 miles west of Midway. They found the main amphibious force itself at 0930. The only planes with enough range to reach this force were the B-17 bombers, and these were launched upon receiving the report. No hits were scored despite heavy bomb loads dropped from high altitude on the slow-moving transports. Later that night, a force of PBYs fitted to carry torpedoes managed to do minor damage to a tanker with a torpedo. Yamamoto's orders were to maintain radio silence, but the amphibious force commander, in view of this startling development, reported the attack to Yamamoto. Nagumo also received this information.

The B-17 and subsequent PBY attacks made it abundantly clear to Yamamoto and Nagumo that the approaching Japanese force was no longer a secret from the Americans. The great advantage the US forces had going into the Midway battle was the Japanese being unaware that the US cryptologists had broken their code and that the Pacific Fleet was prepared to attack the Japanese fleet. It was important to maintain that secrecy and wait until the Japanese carrier forces appeared along the track as planned so that the combined Pacific Fleet forces from Midway and the carriers could execute the concentration of force.

It was obvious to naval commanders on both sides that an amphibious force of eighteen transports and two battleships would not be operating alone without carrier support. By attacking the first Japanese formation to appear, the far less important amphibious force, 700 miles distant, the Japanese were aware they had been discovered. Pacific Fleet would be looking for an additional support group, and were prepared to take action against the Japanese force. The Japanese, in turn, could be expected to increase their own scouting for US forces, plan counterattacks to US actions, and take evasive maneuvers.

The Japanese attack plan was based on secrecy and surprise. But now there was no surprise, and someone in the Japanese command should have considered revisions to their plan. Yet Yamamoto and Nagumo continued to operate under the existing plan as if their mission were still a secret and the Pacific Fleet carriers were still in Pearl Harbor. It was a major mistake by the Japanese, and a fortunate break for the Pacific Fleet.

Two axioms of warfare are worth citing at this point. A brilliant nineteenth-century military strategist, Prussian Field Marshal Helmuth von Moltke, in his theories on war, stated that no battle plan survives first contact with the enemy.[266] First contact had been made, early on June 3, but Yamamoto proceeded as if it made no difference. He saw no need to reevaluate his battle plan because he assumed the Pacific Fleet carriers were still in Pearl Harbor. Second, an ancient strategy: a commander will try to get the enemy to attack the component of his force that he least minds losing. The Japanese were leading with their

---

266   Hughes, Daniel J. (ed.) *Moltke on the Art of War: selected writings* (Presidio Press: New York, New York, 1993), ISBN 0-89141-575-0. 45-47.

carriers, the most valuable and most vulnerable component of their entire navy.

Two important Japanese reconnaissance missions set up to track Pacific Fleet movements had both failed. The submarine refueling rendezvous of the Mavis scouting flight at French Frigate Shoals was discovered by the code breakers, and ships were dispatched to prevent the refueling. In addition, the submarines outside Pearl Harbor had reported nothing, but that was expected because Yamamoto assumed the American carriers would not sortie until the Midway attack began. Unfortunately for the Japanese command, the submarines were behind schedule and had not arrived on station until May 30, after both task forces had departed. No report from the submarines was interpreted by the Japanese to mean that the carriers were still inside Pearl Harbor. In fact, they were approaching the battle zone.

As a result of all these events, Yamamoto and Nagumo had no information about the presence of Pacific Fleet carriers, in Pearl Harbor or anywhere else. However, several days earlier, another Japanese submarine near Midway had reported an unusually high level of aircraft, ship, and boat movements around the island in the weeks prior to June 4. In addition, despite the extensive use of the undersea cable between Pearl Harbor and Midway, Japanese communications units had picked up a high volume of urgent radio transmissions among Pearl Harbor, afloat units, and Midway. All this information had been ignored.

The next day, June 4, at 0430, as the Striking Force approached Midway on course 135 degrees, the Japanese executed their scouting plan: a seven-spoke, semicircular pattern oriented to the east. Four scout aircraft from two cruisers would fly 300 miles out on a line of bearing from the carrier force, turn left for 60 miles, then fly back to their ships. The four easternmost sectors would be flown by reconnaissance floatplanes from the cruisers *Tone* and *Chikuma*, two planes from each ship. The two southernmost sectors were flown by Kate Type 97 attack/torpedo planes from *Kaga* and *Akagi*. The northernmost sector was flown by a floatplane from the battleship *Haruna* and was just a 150-mile scan.

The search plan was scanty and left gaps, even assuming ideal weather conditions and alert crew performance. However, weather conditions on June 4 were anything but ideal. The Striking Force had emerged from fog and heavy overcast that had prevailed for several days. In the morning hours, there was a 50 percent cloud overcast at 1,000 to 3,000 feet over the ocean, combined with occasional squalls. The *Tone* #4 scout, flying on a relative bearing of 100 degrees from the carrier force, was delayed until 0500. This would be a factor as the day's events progressed. Likewise, *Chikuma* #1 apparently flew over part of the Pacific Fleet force at 0630 and failed to catch sight of it.

In previous missions, including many of their island invasions and at Coral Sea, the Striking Force had been supplemented by land-based aircraft, particularly for scouting. But now the Striking Force was beyond the range of the nearest island base at Wake. The lack of land-based air support had been one of the major criticisms of the Midway plan from the beginning, but Nagumo had not assigned extra planes from his carrier force to compensate for the lack of land-based scouting. The implications of inadequate or erroneous scouting at Coral Sea should have been obvious and built into Japanese battle doctrine, but this was not done. Commander Fuchida had recommended a two-stage search, with a second wave following shortly after the first, but Nagumo did not implement it. Had Nagumo thought carefully and realistically, he would have realized he had no confirmation that the American carriers were still in Pearl Harbor—either from the failed overfly, submarines, spies, or any other source.

On June 4, the Japanese pilots began manning their planes at 0415, and at 0430 they launched their attack. Formed up quickly by 0445 into one large armada of 108 planes, it headed southeast, straight for Midway. It would be over Midway by 0630. The planes on the Midway attack came from all four carriers: thirty-six Type 99 Val dive-bombers, thirty-six Type 97 Kate torpedo/attack planes, and thirty-six Zero fighters. CarDiv1, *Akagi* and *Kaga*, contributed its complement of dive-bombers. CarDiv2, *Hiryu* and *Soryu*, supplied its attack aircraft, fitted with point-detonating bombs. Each of the four carriers contributed nine Zeros. Lieutenant Tomonaga Joichi of *Hiryu* led the attack, substituting for Commander Fuchida, who had developed appendicitis shortly before the mission.

While the attack force was winging its way toward Midway, the remaining reserve force had two missions: maintain a CAP over the Striking Force and be prepared to launch an attack if the scouts discovered an opposing naval force. Of the aircraft held in reserve, the forty-five attack bombers of CarDiv1 were armed with torpedoes, and the thirty-six dive-bombers of CarDiv2 were ready to be armed with armor-piercing bombs. A total of eighty-one attack planes remained on the four carriers, plus thirty-six Zeros designated to fly CAP over the Striking Force, for a total reserve force of 117 planes.

The "A" team of the Japanese carrier pilots was kept in the reserve force because, if an opposing fleet were encountered, it was better to have their best pilots flying against maneuvering, defended ships. The "A" team included Lieutenant Commander Egusa Takashige of *Soryu*, the star dive-bombing pilot and squadron leader. His dive-bombers had destroyed the British cruisers *Dorsetshire* and *Cornwall* when the Striking Force attacked Royal Navy forces in the Indian Ocean three months earlier. Leading the torpedo squadrons was the flamboyant Lieutenant Commander Murata Shigeharu of *Akagi*, who had perfected the torpedo attack tactics for the shallow waters of Pearl Harbor. He had personally led the planes that sank battleships *Oklahoma*, *California*, and *West Virginia*.[267] The "B" team could fly the Midway mission against static land targets.

---

267 Parshall and Tully, *Shattered Sword* (Potomac Books, 2007), 131-132.

This organization of the reserve force makes it clear that encountering an opposing fleet was considered, at least at one time, a real possibility. Why Nagumo did not follow this with adequate scouting is one of the imponderables of this battle. In addition, it was far from clear how the thirty-six Zeros, operating from all four carriers, were organized to provide CAP defense and at the same time be prepared to escort an attack force. The attack force itself would need to be raised from the hangar deck, spotted, launched, and escorted at the same time as all four carriers were committed to CAP operations with the Zeros.

The Midway attack force was structured to make it easier to organize the attack, since all of one type of aircraft came from the same carrier division. Nagumo apparently gave little thought to the organization of the reserve force on the carriers, because each division was left with just one type of aircraft. A division of two carriers could not independently mount a coordinated attack of dive-bombers and torpedo/attack planes. As a result, the entire remaining reserve force needed to operate as a single unit to mount a coordinated attack should they be deployed against an opposing naval force. All flight decks would be committed to spotting and launching aircraft, and the Zeros in the sky would not be able to replenish themselves for at least thirty minutes during the spotting, warm-up, and launch. Moreover, at the planning sessions aboard *Yamato* in early May, Yamamoto had specifically ordered Nagumo to maintain a ready reserve capability after the Midway strike force was launched. Having all four carriers committed to CAP operations was in direct violation of Yamamoto's order.

Japanese air commander Fuchida later stated that it would have been far better for Nagumo to have split his force by carrier division to carry out the two missions he had been assigned. One division should have been assigned to the attack on Midway, leaving the other division in reserve with armed aircraft already spotted on the flight decks, ready to attack immediately if required. Fuchida, however, does not describe how this would be organized.

In a split assignment, the designated carrier division for the Midway attack would have to make two launches to get all its planes aloft, with a subsequent time loss. This was a small price to pay for having the reserve force in position to make an immediate attack if the scouts discovered an enemy force after the departure of the Midway planes. To accomplish this, the Zeros from the reserve carriers would be launched to conduct CAP operations together with the first wave of the Midway force. After the second wave of Midway planes had departed the reserve Zeros would have clear decks on the Midway carriers to continue CAP operations. While this was happening the planes of the reserve force would be raised and spotted on the decks of their carriers. This modest departure from doctrine about Zeros being assigned to specific ships made such a plan viable.

The first launch of the Midway force could have orbited until the second launch was made, or moved out toward the target immediately. In the latter case the Midway force would have made a two-wave attack. Even in a two-wave attack, the Zeros in the second wave, with their 300-plus-knot speed, could have caught up to the first wave to add protection prior to the first wave arriving over the target. The extensive range and endurance of the Zeros would have allowed them to stay over the target during the second attack wave.

Nagumo was confident that the powerful, unbeaten Striking Force was invincible, and he proceeded with his game plan unchanged. This assurance persisted even after the report a day earlier of the US attack on the amphibious group. Yamamoto, in his sumptuous quarters aboard *Yamato*, still observing radio silence, was in self-imposed exile and unable to deal with rapidly changing events. The late and scanty search put up by the Japanese resulted in their failure to discover the American presence until much later than almost surely would have occurred with a comprehensive search effort. As a result, the "A" team of Japanese pilots were sitting in their ready rooms awaiting developments.

The crucial importance of comprehensive, accurate scouting was still lost on both the Striking Force and the Pacific Fleet task forces. The Pacific Fleet command thought the 0430 PBY search would provide all the information needed. It assumed the concentration of force attack would be triggered by a PBY report, the attack would be carried out promptly, and no further scouting would be necessary. It made no provision for on-station monitoring to track subsequent developments after the first PBY report. If the concentration of force was not executed adequately for any reason, the Pacific Fleet force would be left without follow-up scouting information.

The B-17s would have been better employed to supplement the search of the PBYs and give updated positions of the Japanese fleet, and they had the added ability to defend themselves from Zero attack. This was stated in later Pacific Fleet evaluations. Further experience would show that attempting to bomb fast-moving, maneuvering ships from 18,000 feet was a hopeless exercise.

The Japanese, relying on the perceived secrecy of their mission and the submarine and Mavis reconnaissance, thought that scanty search from the Striking Force was enough. Neither side had learned much since grossly inaccurate reports resulted in serious mistakes and lost opportunities in the action at the Coral Sea. Both sides at Midway were deluded by the perceived confidence in the secrecy of their mission and the circumstances they believed were under their control. With more comprehensive, very early search and better battle plan organization, the Striking Force might have discovered Pacific Fleet carriers and launched an attack when the Pacific Fleet planes were still beyond their operating range. The Pacific Fleet operated with the confidence that their intelligence breakthrough was unknown to the Japanese, and with the advantage of surprise they could win, even with shorter-range, less-capable aircraft and less-seasoned pilots.

CHAPTER 22

Midway: Nagumo's Decisions

A t first light on June 4, in a repeat of the previous day's search, twenty-two PBYs took off from Midway to search outward for up to 700 miles to find the Japanese carriers. At 0534 a PBY pilot saw wakes in the distance and sent a preliminary ship-sighting message. At 0603 the pilot sent a more complete message to Midway, and to TF-16 and TF-17: "Two carriers and battleships bearing 320, distant 180 [miles from Midway], course 135 [degrees], speed 25."[268] Observers on the Striking Force saw the PBY. The Japanese radio operators determined that the PBY had transmitted a message, presumably reporting the contact. CAP Zeros attempted to find the PBY and shoot it down, but it was able to elude its attackers.

On receipt of the PBY report, every flyable plane on Midway took to the skies as soon as they could get aloft. Avengers, B-26s, and Marine Dauntlesses flew to attack the Japanese carriers. B-17s that had taken off earlier bound for another attempt at the amphibious force were diverted toward the carriers. Buffalo fighters and the few F4F Wildcat fighters climbed for altitude to defend Midway. Radar on Midway and a report from a different PBY showed the Japanese carrier planes closing on Midway.

Simard kept the four F4Fs and the twenty obsolete Buffalo fighters to defend Midway. The Avengers, B-26s, and Marine dive-bombers went

---

268   Morison, 103.

against the Striking Force without fighter protection from Midway. Simard may have decided that the distance to the Japanese fleet was too great for the Buffaloes to be effective once they arrived over the battle area, and the best use of them was to defend Midway. Also, the carrier planes from Task Forces 16 and 17 that should be arriving at the same time over the Japanese fleet would have Wildcat fighter squadrons as part of the force, and the Wildcats were more advanced and more capable than the Buffaloes in a dogfight with Zeros.

Midway came under attack at 0620. Running into stiffer anti-aircraft fire than expected, the attack aircraft and dive-bombers nevertheless inflicted significant damage to fuel storage and pumping equipment as well as structures and other facilities. The Buffaloes did their best to defend Midway, but they were hopelessly outclassed in a high-altitude, free-wheeling dogfight with Zeros. Out of the twenty that went into the air that day, only seven returned. There were no Zero losses against the Buffaloes. The runways were left untouched so they could be put into service immediately after the amphibious invasion secured the island. However, resistance on the island was not subdued by the Japanese attack, and at 0705 mission commander Tomonaga sent Nagumo a message: "Another attack is required."

Meanwhile, minutes after Tomonaga's message to Nagumo, the first American planes from Midway reached the Striking Force. Coming in low, the six Avengers, carrying torpedoes, focused on *Hiryu*. The four B-26s, also carrying torpedoes, targeted *Akagi*. The Japanese carriers had Zeros in the air and quickly launched more—about thirty in total— that attacked the two flights of US aircraft. The Avengers were hopeless against the Zeros, and several were shot down immediately. Two Avengers dropped their torpedoes at *Hiryu*, but they were too far away when they dropped. The American torpedoes travelled at only thirty knots, but *Hiryu*, which at flank speed could make thirty-four knots, simply turned away. There were no torpedo hits, or even good chances for hits, and in the end the Zeros sent five of the six Avengers flaming into the ocean. The attack force from the Pacific Fleet carriers, which in the attack plan were to arrive simultaneously with the planes from Midway, did not appear. As a result there were no protecting Wildcats for the attack planes from Midway.

Meanwhile, the B-26s that made a run at *Akagi* dropped two torpedoes that missed widely. *Akagi* had to maneuver, but the attack was not a serious concern. The Zeros closed in and began shooting down the B-26s. One went into the ocean, and two escaped after their ineffective torpedo drops. It is impossible to know if any of the torpedoes would have exploded even if they had struck a Japanese ship. The fourth B-26 was badly shot up and about to crash into the ocean. Its pilot apparently realized he was not going to make it back, and if he was going to die he was determined to take out the bridge of the Japanese flagship. The aircraft, trailing smoke, bored in straight at the *Akagi* bridge—and straight at Nagumo. Nagumo and his staff were immobilized, facing death, but at the last moment the B-26 veered slightly, missed the bridge by a few feet, and fell into the ocean.[269] The B-26 pilot went to his death thinking his last effort on this Earth had failed. In fact, he may have done as much as anyone that day to bring about the victory he gave his life to achieve.

Nagumo's reaction was pure panic. At 0715, immediately after the encounter with the B-26, he decided to launch another attack on Midway Island. He ordered a change in the ordnance of the aircraft on all four of the carriers, from torpedoes and armor-piercing bombs to high-explosive bombs, to make another attack on Midway.[270]

But why? The immediate purpose of the air attack against Midway was to soften up the island's defenses for the amphibious landings. But the amphibious force was at least a day's steaming away, and it was still just 0715 in the morning. There was plenty of time for another attack later in the day. Moreover, the Midway attack was just the bait. The Pacific

---

269   Parshall and Tully, 152.
270   Morison, 107.

Fleet carriers were the priority and the most dangerous adversary. The ultimate purpose of the air attack on Midway was to draw the Pacific Fleet carriers into combat. By ordering a change in ordnance, Nagumo created a situation where an immediate, full deck launch against Pacific Fleet carriers, should they appear, was not possible. In addition, it created disorder in a highly structured, highly disciplined force. His keen strategist and adviser, Commander Genda Minoru, was suffering from a severe fever and was incoherent. Fuchida, Nagumo's other key adviser, who was recovering from an appendectomy, had staggered to the bridge in a very weakened condition and was sprawled on the deck.

The racks that held the bombs on Val dive-bombers were the same for high-explosive bombs as for armor-piercing bombs. Changing bomb types could be accomplished relatively quickly. But on the Kate torpedo/attack aircraft, it was a far more complicated and time-consuming operation. It meant not just changing from torpedoes to bombs but also unbolting the racks that held the twenty-one-foot, 1,000-pound torpedoes and bolting on different racks that held bombs. This, then, was a four-step process: unload the torpedoes, unbolt torpedo racks, install bomb racks, and finally load bombs. The hangar deck crews struggled to carry out these orders.

Timing was also a factor. Changing ordnance on all the torpedo/attack planes beginning at 0715 would require an hour and a half, plus another 30 minutes to spot and launch the planes. All in, beginning the process at 0715 meant the Japanese carriers were committed to ordnance changeover and launch until at least 0915. With the Midway attack aircraft returning about 0830, there would not be time to launch a second attack before the Midway aircraft, running low on fuel, had to land. In addition, instead of lowering the torpedoes down the hoists to the magazines and then sending up the bombs, in the scramble to save time the torpedoes were stowed on bulkhead racks on the hangar deck to load bombs quickly. Nagumo, the black shoe battleship admiral who converted to carrier force commander late in his career, did not understand the details of these logistical and timing complications. Yamamoto's orders were to maintain the aircraft in reserve armed with anti-ship ordnance and ready to attack American carriers should they appear, unexpected as that was. That meant ready to launch, not be in the middle of an ordnance changeover.

Three months earlier in the Indian Ocean, the Japanese assault on the British base at Ceylon had been interrupted by the sudden opportunity to attack Royal Navy cruisers *Dorsetshire* and *Cornwall*. Nagumo had ordered planes prepared for a second attack on the base but reversed himself with news of the two cruisers. Yamaguchi's dive-bombers had converted quickly to armor-piercing bombs, but the torpedo rearming had not gone smoothly. Nonetheless, the dive-bombers sank the two cruisers by themselves. Now Nagumo was faced with a similar situation. Had he learned nothing from that experience? And would the complicated rearming of torpedoes repeat itself, causing delays? In the Indian Ocean battle, Nagumo had been bailed out by the stellar performance of his dive-bombers. Could he count on the same result this time?

On the *Hiryu* bridge, an increasingly worried Rear Admiral Yamaguchi Tamon considered the situation. A PBY patrol scout had made a radio transmission just after 0600. The PBY had to have come from Midway. The attack on the Striking Force at 0710 also had clearly come from Midway, 140 miles away. To be over the Japanese fleet at 0710 meant that they had taken off immediately at 0600, in response to the PBY report, which in turn meant that the Americans had prepared for the attack the previous day, or even earlier. Furthermore, B-26s normally would not be stationed on Midway; they would have been flown in from Pearl Harbor, indicating an even earlier preparation. The secrecy of the Japanese mission clearly had been compromised at least several days before, and the Americans had had time to prepare their defenses and counterattack.

There had been no positive confirmation that the American carriers were still in Pearl Harbor. If the Americans had several days to prepare, they could have deployed their carriers to be able to attack the Striking

Force before the Japanese submarines were in position off Pearl Harbor. With the mission's secrecy blown and the location of the American carriers unknown, would the Americans not throw everything they had against the Japanese, including carriers? The American carriers had been constantly on the move, making raids against the Marshalls, Marcus, Rabaul, New Guinea, and even Tokyo. Why did Yamamoto think they would now be tied up at their piers in Pearl Harbor and their sailors lolling on Waikiki Beach?

At 0715 Nagumo knew the 108 aircraft he had launched against the air and naval facilities on Midway had made their attack. A message from a *Kaga* pilot, relayed through *Kaga* to Nagumo, reported heavy damage to the Midway facilities. It was entirely possible that the damage inflicted on Midway could prevent the US forces from getting off any future attack. The Americans had sent a paltry force of ten planes against the carriers, without fighter protection and armed with slow torpedoes. They had scored no hits and their pilots were hopelessly inexperienced. The Zeros had swept them aside with little difficulty.

Then came the message from the *Tone* scout aircraft at 0728: ten enemy ships sighted, 100 miles away. Ship types, undisclosed. Nagumo messaged frantically to the scout aircraft: identify ship types. No reply from the scout.

On the *Hiryu* bridge, Yamaguchi was now desperate. The Japanese didn't know where the American carriers were, but they knew their mission was compromised. Why would there not be carriers in an American force of ten ships? His CarDiv2 carriers were ready with dive-bombers, and he could spot, warm up, and launch a full deck load in thirty minutes. CarDiv1 could complete their launch with whatever ordnance was currently loaded on its planes in another 15 minutes. Some of the Zeros had been refueled and rearmed, and others with their great speed could catch up to the slower dive-bombers. If they launched immediately, they had little to lose even if the American force had no carriers, and it would clear the decks for the returning planes from Midway, beginning about 0830.

Still nothing from Nagumo. Yamaguchi understood that the Zeros had beaten off one attack, but there could be another one. Why had Nagumo not ordered a course change? They could send a destroyer back down the returning flight course to intercept the aircraft returning from Midway and guide them back to the carriers' new position.

Nagumo had made his career as a battleship and cruiser admiral. When he was assigned command of the Striking Force, his seniority meant that he was never required to get into the details of flight operations, nor did he make the effort to do so. He depended on his experts, Commanders Fuchida and Genda, for that, but now both of them were debilitated. Nagumo was suddenly on his own. At this crucial time, the cost of his failure to learn the complicated factors that played into carrier operations suddenly exploded. Now, when every minute counted, it was too late to learn the complexities involved in loading different munitions on different types of planes on the hangar deck, too late to learn how the planes were organized and spotted on the flight decks, too late to learn the flight capabilities of his different types of planes, and far too late to know how to integrate all those factors into a fast-moving and efficient operation with the planes and ordnance available at that moment. Commander Genda, his brilliant operations officer, couldn't make the decisions for him now. It was all up to Nagumo. At 0730 on June 4, 1942, years of shipbuilding, training, and strategic planning had all come to this moment. Teams of highly trained pilots, flight deck personnel, mechanics, and hundreds of other sailors were ready and awaiting his command. The entire course of the battle, of the Combined Fleet, and even perhaps of Japan were going to bear the results of his decisions, then and there.

He thought for fifteen minutes—a lifetime in a carrier battle. Then came the order from Nagumo at 0745: "Prepare to carry out attacks on enemy fleet units. Leave torpedoes on those attack planes which have not yet changed to bombs."[271] But there was no order to launch an attack or to change course. Yamaguchi was incredulous. Had Nagumo lost his mind? Did he not understand that in a carrier battle, blasting holes in an enemy carrier flight deck with high-explosive ordnance, thereby shutting down flight operations, was the number-one priority? A destroyed flight deck makes a carrier a helpless target. Sinking the ship is secondary at that point, and the existing ordnance could take a carrier out of action, quickly and effectively. The exhausted deck crews struggled to comply with this latest order.

At 0745, even in this confused state, Nagumo had forty-five minutes to order an attack with whatever ordnance the aircraft were carrying at that time and then land the returning Midway force at 0830. After that, he had a choice between launching an attack and losing the Midway force or landing the Midway force to refuel and rearm, hoping the Americans would not attack for two hours, or if they did the Zeros flying CAP would be able to fight them off.

Nagumo's decision was to choose that last option. Landing the Midway force would take at least thirty minutes. It would take another ninety minutes to refuel and rearm the entire Striking Force after the Midway planes had landed, plus the time to spot and launch, for an attack by the entire Japanese air fleet. Adding up all that meant a full-force attack no earlier than 1100.

The alternative choice Nagumo might have made was an immediate attack by the available aircraft. Naval historians Jonathan Parshall and Anthony Tully have analyzed the potential attack force that was available to Nagumo at 0745 on June 4. *Akagi* had eighteen torpedo planes in reserve, but in the half hour since the ordnance change order had been given, about one-third would have been changing over to bombs and were unavailable. The net result was that *Akagi* had twelve torpedo planes immediately available for spotting and launching. *Kaga*

---

271   Morison, 107.

had twenty-seven torpedo planes, and about the same proportion, eighteen, would have been available for immediate launch. Nagumo had a total of thirty torpedo planes between the two carriers. *Hiryu* and *Soryu*'s dive-bombers did not need to change brackets and could just load armor-piercing bombs. *Hiryu* had eighteen dive-bombers and *Soryu* had sixteen, for a total dive-bomber attack of thirty-four planes. Nagumo, even after his panic attack at 0715 that had cost him a half hour and fifteen torpedo planes, still had immediately available a combined attack force of sixty-four planes.

One of Nagumo's possible concerns was the attack planes flying without fighter protection. He did not know the state of readiness of his Zeros, which had been flying CAP on a rotating basis since 0430 and had been engaged in an intense defense against US planes attacking from Midway. However, there were thirty-six Zeros not on the Midway strike force, and at least eighteen of them should have rotated back recently for rearming and refueling and thus be available to escort the attack.

One of the results of not splitting the two missions of the Striking Force between the two carrier divisions was that Nagumo was not up to speed on the readiness status of the Zeros. Had either carrier division been responsible for the single mission of having an attack force ready, that division commander could have focused on the state of readiness of his force. He would have been able to decide about launching an attack based on the aircraft available to him, particularly the Zeros. The "A" team of Japanese pilots was ready, but Nagumo was frantically groping for information on the American ships before making his decision about launching an attack. Everything was now resting on the crew of one lonely scout plane.

Compounding the situation further, fifteen minutes after Nagumo ordered the halt in the ordnance change, at about 0800 a force of sixteen Dauntless dive-bombers piloted by Marines from Midway led by Major Lofton R. Henderson made a glide bombing attack. Many fliers in this force had never flown in combat and were flying their planes loaded with bombs for the first time. They were completely incapable of making the dives from 15,000 to 20,000 feet that characterize a dive-bomber attack by experienced pilots. Instead, Major Henderson led his force in from 9,000 feet in a gradual glide attack toward the Japanese fleet.

The Zeros swarmed over these slow-moving ducks, and Major Henderson was the first to crash into the ocean. One by one the planes that followed flew into the Zero deathtrap. A few bombs were dropped without effect. Half of the planes escaped because the Zeros were running low on ammunition and did not press their attacks after a plane dropped its bomb. No hits were made on the Japanese carriers. The Zeros rotated back to their carriers for a quick refueling and rearming stop, then set off again.

After the last of the Marine Dauntlesses were dispatched, B-17 bombers, which had been headed toward the amphibious fleet and were diverted to attack the Striking Force, appeared over the carriers at 0810, flying at 20,000 feet. No Zeros were encountered at that altitude. Despite some misses near *Soryu*, the bombs did no damage, and the B-17s retired.[272] They were followed almost immediately by a squadron of Marine Corps Vindicator bombers, slow and with minimal defenses. The Zeros swarmed over them. Realizing that continuing their approach to the carriers would be suicidal, they changed their target to the battleship *Haruna*. Many bombs were dropped but no hits were scored on *Haruna*. Nine out of the original eleven returned. This was the final attack from Midway Island and the last involvement of any Midway force in the battle.[273]

Many brave fliers from Midway, unsung heroes all, went to their deaths in the ocean that morning with hardly more than a scratch on a single Japanese ship. But their constant hammering on the Striking Force meant that the Zeros had to stay in the air defending the carriers and continually land for refueling and rearmament. Even any Zeros originally assigned to defend the high-altitude space against dive-bombers were drawn down to defend the sea-level attacks. The attacks from Midway created delay and confusion within the Japanese command. Nagumo's order to change ordnance, and as a result be unprepared for an attack on Pacific Fleet carriers, was a direct result of their sacrifice.

Then at 0820 the dreaded news came from the scout: "There appears to be a carrier in the American force of ten ships." In the iron-clad discipline of the Imperial Japanese Navy, the mere suggestion from a junior commander to a senior under battle conditions was unthinkable, even mutinous. Nevertheless, Yamaguchi sent a message to Nagumo, "Recommend an immediate attack." It was received by Nagumo at 0830.

At 0830 the Japanese commander faced an agonizing choice: a window of time between 0830 and 0900 that he could use to either land the Midway force or launch an attack. Yamaguchi knew the composition of his reserve force that was ready to launch, and his calculation from the bridge of *Hiryu* on June 4, 1942, would not have been significantly different from an analysis decades later. CarDiv2 had a potent force of thirty-four dive-bombers ready to spot, warm up, and launch in thirty minutes, together with as many Zeros as were ready to fly. CarDiv1 could launch thirty torpedo planes, plus available Zeros, 15 minutes later—a powerful force.

But all this was at the cost of unknown numbers of returning Midway planes that would ditch in the ocean if they could not land on their carriers. Yamaguchi could not know the number of planes that would ditch if the order came to launch an attack. It could be a quarter, half, or three-quarters of the Midway force. Destroyers would pick up most of the crews. To Yamaguchi the choice was clear: the Striking Force had to launch an attack. If some, or even many, of the returning Midway force were lost, that was too bad. The survival of the Japanese carriers, and the attack on the American carrier, was more important than saving the Midway planes and crews.

Yamaguchi knew that American PBY scouts had discovered them two and a half hours earlier, and the Striking Force had been under attack for an hour and a half, apparently from Midway. Now they had confirmation of an American carrier within its attack range, and that meant planes even now could be winging toward them. Moreover, why had they not yet seen any high altitude dive-bombers, the most potent force in the American naval arsenal? There was no reply from Nagumo to Yamaguchi's message and no order to attack.

It is impossible to know exactly what went on in Nagumo's mind at 0830, but several important considerations are apparent. Japanese naval doctrine was to attack with a massive, coordinated force. To do otherwise was a violation of an established fundamental. Disciplined operations also were vital, and the unfortunate rearming of the planes earlier had created a confused situation that he believed should be rectified before taking further action. In addition, the Zeros had repelled all the Pacific Fleet attacks so far, and the US aircraft, torpedoes, flying skills, and tactics had been unimpressive.

One might speculate on Nagumo's emotional state of mind at this point. His force had been subjected to nearly continuous attacks over the previous hour and a half, one of which was a personal near-death experience. None of these attacks, including the sudden appearance of an American carrier force within striking distance, had been expected. In the final analysis, faced with surprising developments and a confused situation, he took the conservative approach and fell back on doctrine. He ordered the returning Midway attack force to land.

At 0855, as the Midway planes were landing, Nagumo sent Yamamoto a message regarding the scouting report and his intentions:

"Enemy composed of one carrier, five cruisers, and five destroyers sighted at 0800 in position bearing 10 degrees, 240 miles from Midway. We are heading for it."[274] Nagumo would land the returning Midway

---

274   Parshall and Tully, 198.

planes, and when the planes were all landed at 0917 he would execute a turn and head for the US force. Admiral Nagumo had just made a fateful decision. He had just forfeited his chance to launch an attack and, as it turned out, his best chance to win the Battle of Midway.

Admiral Chuichi Nagumo
Photo Naval History and Heritage

CHAPTER 23

Midway: Pacific Fleet Carriers Attack

Admiral Nimitz had decided not to make any changes in his force structure prior to the Midway battle. That meant TF-16 would be composed of the battle-seasoned *Enterprise* with the new *Hornet* and its inexperienced air crews. TF-17 had the experienced *Yorktown* with Fletcher embarked in overall command of both task forces.

Enterprise and *Yorktown* were the veterans of several engagements, including, in the case of *Yorktown*, the Battle of the Coral Sea. *Yorktown* suffered air crew losses at the Coral Sea, but experienced air crews from *Saratoga* and *Lexington* had largely replaced the depleted *Yorktown* fliers. The *Yorktown* deck crews and hangar-deck mechanics had combat experience.

Hornet was a new carrier, having been commissioned at Norfolk just a few months earlier. After commissioning, *Hornet* was rushed to the Pacific through the Panama Canal. At Alameda the Doolittle B-25s had been hoisted aboard the flight deck, while *Hornet's* own squadrons were held below on the hangar deck. Many *Hornet* pilots were recent flight training graduates and did not have many hours in the planes they were flying. The new torpedo planes, the Avengers, were beginning to replace the obsolete Devastators, but it was the Devastators that were still aboard the Pacific Fleet carriers, including *Hornet*. Making barely 100 knots when carrying a torpedo, Devastators badly needed fighter protection in any confrontation with Zeros.

Lieutenant Commander Jimmy Thach, commander of the Fighting Three squadron from *Saratoga*, had seen extensive action on *Lexington* and was now the Wildcat fighter squadron commander aboard *Yorktown*.[275] This was a strong addition. Thach built on the points about combat with Zeros that Jimmy Flatley made after the Coral Sea battle and devised a tactic that became known as the Thach Weave. In the Thach Weave, a Wildcat pilot would have a wingman fly a parallel course. A Wildcat being attacked by a Zero would turn toward his wingman, drawing the Zero into pursuit. The Wildcat's wingman would then turn toward the first Wildcat and hit the Zero as it pursued the first Wildcat in a rapidly closing, head-on confrontation. Properly employed, Thach was convinced this tactic would allow the Wildcat to match the Zero in combat. The *Yorktown* pilots were organized in pairs to employ it. Another version of the Thach Weave was two pairs of Wildcats flying together as a team, one plane behind the other on each side. This variation allowed more opportunities to hit the Zeros.

Lieutenant John C. Waldron commanded the *Hornet* torpedo squadron, Torpedo Eight. Torpedo Eight was made up of a few lieutenants but mostly of young, inexperienced ensigns recently out of flight school. None of the ensigns had flown with a torpedo before. There was time for some flight training on the way to Midway, but not much. Waldron put his young fliers through intense mental and physical training in the meager time allowed. Daily classroom sessions focused on target lead angles, fighter evasion tactics, and antiaircraft defense. The forty-two-year-old Waldron tried to instill in his young rookies in a matter of weeks what he had learned in years of flying. With daily drills he built confidence in his squadron, and Torpedo Eight went into battle with the best attitude that young, inexperienced fliers could have.[276] Yet they had heard enough stories about the Zeros at Coral Sea to know that combat was going to

---

275   Keith, *Stay the Rising Sun* (Zenith Press, Minneapolis, 2015), 69.
276   Toll, 400-401.

be rough. On June 3, the night before the battle, Waldron assembled the Torpedo Eight squadron in the ready room for their final session:

The approaching battle will be the biggest of the war, and may be the turning point. It is to be known as the Battle of Midway. It will be a historical and, I hope, a glorious event. We have had a very short time to train, and we have worked under the most severe difficulties. But we have done the best humanly possible. I actually believe that under these conditions we are the best in the world. My greatest hope is that we encounter a favorable tactical situation. But if we don't and worse comes to worst, I want each of us to do his utmost to destroy our enemies. If there is only one aircraft left to make a final run-in, I want that man to go in and get a hit. Good luck, happy landings, and give 'e m hell. May God be with us all.[277]

The young fliers wrote letters home and arranged their affairs as best they could, because they knew, almost surely, that not everyone was going to come back.

At first light on June 4, the twenty-two PBY search aircraft from Midway launched on their assigned vectors, covering the 180-degree arc from 200 degrees to 020. At 0430 the seven Japanese search planes launched from their ships. Both sides scanned the ocean for contacts. The B-17s took off from Midway, heading for the Japanese amphibious force they had attacked the day before.

"After sundown Fletcher swung southwest intending to be 200 miles north of Midway at dawn on 4 June, and again ready to fight according to plan."[278] At first light Fletcher ordered *Yorktown* planes to scout north and northeast. Scouting duty for *Yorktown* meant delaying any attack by his most experienced carrier and air crews. Fletcher might

---

277 Morison, 117.

278 Lundstrom, John B., *Black Shoe Carrier Admiral* (Naval Institute Press, 2006), 239.

have considered more carefully whether it was worth taking his carrier out of action just to supplement the search already covered by the PBYs.

Given the comprehensive information in the decoded Japanese messages, and the contact from the previous day that confirmed the Japanese movements, a lot of offensive power that would surely be needed was deferred for the sake of additional scouting. If Fletcher considered that additional scouting was needed, he could have ordered the floatplanes on the cruisers to carry it out and kept *Yorktown* ready for action. By taking *Yorktown* out of position to be the first to engage, he removed his most experienced carrier at a time when enemy action was imminent. It left *Hornet's* inexperienced fliers and crew, and Spruance, who was not a flier and had never before had a carrier command, most likely to see first combat.

A PBY on a northwest course sent a message announcing contact with the Japanese carrier force:

At 0[5]34—from Flight 58 to Radio Midway "enemy carriers."

At 0[5]53—from Flight 58 to Radio Midway "many planes heading Midway."

At 0[6]03—from Flight 92 to Radio Midway "2 carriers and battleships bearing 320° distance 180 course 135 speed 25."[279, 280]

Fletcher and Spruance on Task Forces 17 and 16 received the messages, as did the air command on Midway and Nimitz at Pearl Harbor. Upon receiving the message and seeing the staff plotters mark the position on the chart, Nimitz walked over to the chart table to compare the position with the one made a week earlier by Commander Layton.

---

279   Action Report of ENTERPRISE, From: The Commanding Officer, To: The Commander-in-Chief, U. S. Pacific Fleet, Via: Commander Task Force 16 (Rear Admiral R. A. Spruance, U. S. Navy) At Sea, June 8, 1942.

280   Actual times transmitted were in Time Zone -10, Pearl Harbor. Above times are converted to Time Zone -12, Midway.

After looking at the chart, Nimitz turned to Layton. "'Well, you were only five minutes, five degrees, and five miles out,' Nimitz remarked to me with a smile," Layton wrote in his memoirs.[281] It was a great compliment to Layton, Rochefort, and the entire Hypo intelligence team at Pearl Harbor.

Planes from Midway were launched immediately after receiving the 0603 report. At 0607, Fletcher ordered Spruance in TF-16 to "proceed southwesterly and attack enemy carriers when definitely located. I will follow as soon as planes recovered."[282] However, at 0607, TF-16 and TF-17 were more than 60 miles to the east and north of the planned attack position, 200 miles north of Midway. They also were about 200 miles from the interception point. TF-16 was beyond its maximum operating range of 175 miles and had to close the range by at least 25 miles before it could launch planes. A carrier steaming at 25 knots required an hour to cover that distance. If Fletcher planned to conduct a search, his reason for not doing so from the position 200 miles north of Midway is unknown. The new launch time for TF-16 was set for 0700.

Because the carriers were out of position, the plan for achieving a concentration of force with the planes from Midway had failed. The first Midway planes were over the Japanese carriers between 0710 and 0720. At 0700, assuming no delays, the TF-16 launch would be just beginning, and they were starting from farther away. The Midway planes would arrive alone over the Striking Force, and the Zeros would attack them as they arrived. Wildcat fighters from TF-16 could not intercept the Striking Force for more than another hour, in the best case. Without fighter support the Zeros would take a heavy toll. Suddenly it became apparent that King's foolish order directing Halsey to make the hopeless dash to the Coral Sea a month earlier was having heavy repercussions.

---

281   Layton, Edwin T., *And I Was There* (Konecky & Konecky, 1985), 438.

282   Morison, 103, 113.

After Fletcher detached Spruance, TF-16 proceeded southwest. Spruance had to calculate a new interception plan. The original course of 255 degrees for the TF-16 planes was now obsolete because the Striking Force would continue on its southeast course as TF-16 was closing the range. To launch an attack at the earliest possible time, he had to calculate a course that would allow a launch at maximum range directly to a new interception point. Without updated scouting reports, the only projection available was the original dead reckoning track. Spruance calculated a new interception point and ordered a course of 240 degrees for the ships of TF-16. TF-16 would close the range to 175 miles in one hour, and the carriers would turn into the wind and launch their planes. That position was at the outer limit of the planes' operating range, particularly the torpedo planes, but it was a decision Spruance made to get an attack off as early as possible.

These events showed the result of the failure to have a backup scouting plan. If the concentration of force plan failed for any reason, the Pacific Fleet forces would be left only with the information from 0603, which was getting older by the minute. A backup scouting plan would have updated the information sent in the first report. Without fresh data, the admirals were facing uncertainty. It was possible there were four carriers in the formation that had been spotted, and because of the cloud cover and the dispersed formation only two carriers were seen. It could also mean there were more carriers at a different location. Backup scouting would have clarified the number of carriers in that formation.

The PBYs had been flying since 0430, were now out nearly 400 miles, and had found no other contacts. Fletcher had *Yorktown* planes conduct shorter searches to the north. Spruance, with two air groups under his command, understood the importance of dealing with the reality he knew. He was not going to send one air group on a search mission without any contact information and send the single remaining air group against at least two other carriers. He would launch the air groups of both *Enterprise* and *Hornet* at the two identified Japanese carriers. He did not unify the commands under the senior air group commander, Commander Stanhope Ring, because the increasing uncertainty of the movement of the Striking Force needed independent decisions by each air group commander. He also decided to launch total air groups into the attack for maximum power and operating options, holding back only CAP fighters.

A rapid and flawless execution required 20 minutes for the *Enterprise* and *Hornet* air groups to launch and form up from the pre-spotted positions on their flight decks. Launching from 175 miles instead of 140 miles added approximately 15 minutes to the original projected one-hour, 20-minute flying time. Steaming into the wind to launch planes at an angle away from the intended track added another 15 minutes. Beginning flight operations at 0700 meant that the TF-16 air groups could not expect to intercept the Japanese carriers before about 0910, and that time assumed excellent execution and no delays.

The Japanese scout found the Americans at 0728, when the delayed *Tone* floatplane made its first meager, inconclusive report. That report arrived while the Striking Force was under attack from the Midway planes, and because of Nagumo's order to change ordnance at 0715, the Striking Force hangar decks were a mass of confusion. Meanwhile, Fletcher, having headed *Yorktown* into the southeast wind to launch and recover scouts, took *Yorktown* farther out of range.

The PBY pilot who reported contact with the Striking Force continued flying on his assigned vector. If he could have stayed on station longer he almost surely would have seen all four Japanese carriers and been able to provide that information. Better scouting also would have provided updated data on the position, course and speed of the Striking Force. Without updated scouting, if the Japanese carriers slowed their advance or changed course, Spruance's dead reckoning projections would be wrong and the carrier planes would be searching open ocean.

The delayed attack Spruance ordered began at 0700, and the *Enterprise* dive-bombers launched and were forming up over the ship. There was a problem on the *Enterprise* flight deck, however, and the launch of the torpedo planes and fighters was delayed. During the *Enterprise* launch, radio operators picked up the Japanese scout aircraft over TF-16 and intercepted the scout's 0728 "ten ship" message, obviously giving its position. If the Japanese were ready they could launch an immediate attack on the Pacific Fleet carriers.

This was a devastating piece of news. The great advantage the Americans had had up to 0728 was the secrecy of their operations from the Japanese. The carriers were supposed to be back in Pearl Harbor. Even the B-17 attack on the amphibious force a day earlier had not changed those circumstances. Now that advantage was gone. But it was worse than that—now the tables were turned. The Japanese scout was staying on station, sending continuous contact reports back to Nagumo.

The earliest interception time of 0910 meant that the Japanese carriers had more than three hours to move from their position in the 0603 report, and at twenty-five knots they could be seventy-five miles in any direction by the time the American planes could hope to intercept them. Would the TF-16 air groups fly over empty ocean while their own carriers were attacked? Spruance thought of the order from Nimitz about calculated risk, and not exposing his force without the probability that he could inflict greater damage on the enemy force than his force would suffer. He also had an order from Fletcher to launch a strike when the position of the Japanese carriers had been identified.

Spruance knew the Japanese aircraft had attacked Midway an hour earlier, but he had no way of knowing if all the carrier air groups had been used for the attack. If they had used their entire force and launched in two waves, as they had done at Pearl Harbor, they would have to be rearmed and refueled before being ready to launch again. But it was more probable that only part of the total attack force had been employed. Nagumo would not need that many planes for the attack on the modest shore facilities he would have expected at Midway. Further, it was very unlikely, now that the United States and Japan were at war, that he would leave his carriers without both offensive and defensive capabilities. The Striking Force had at least four carriers with more than 200 planes. It all pointed to a reserve force on Nagumo's carriers, ready to launch.

The Pacific Fleet fliers were not as experienced as the Japanese, but Spruance had confidence in their bravery, skill, and judgment. He was not a carrier admiral or even a flier, but he knew that the fundamental axiom of carrier warfare was to make the first attack. As he stated in his foreword to Fuchida's landmark history of the Midway battle, *Midway: The Battle That Doomed Japan,* he had "a strong desire to hit the enemy carriers with our full strength as early as we could reach them."[283]

Spruance had been impressed with Lieutenant Commander Wade McClusky, the air group commander, whose planes were now circling overhead. Weighing it all together, he made up his mind. His order went out by blinker light to McClusky: "Proceed on mission assigned." The thirty-two *Enterprise* dive-bombers and scouts headed away. The die was cast.

If his judgment was correct, his fliers would find the Japanese carriers at a vulnerable time, as their Midway attack wave was returning. If he was wrong, the Japanese even now could be sending a deadly force against his carriers. That would be followed by a second wave of rearmed and refueled attack planes—unless the planes now being launched from *Enterprise* and *Hornet* could find the Japanese carriers first.

The delay in the launch of the *Enterprise* torpedo planes and Wildcat fighters, combined with the earlier departure of the dive-bombers, meant that if they encountered the Japanese fleet it was going to be difficult for the *Enterprise* group to have a coordinated attack of dive bombers and torpedo planes. Nevertheless, the torpedo planes and fighters got launched, and trailed the dive-bombers by 50 to 75 miles.

---

283   Spruance, ADM Raymond A. Foreword for Fuchida, *Midway: The Battle That Doomed Japan* as quoted in Hone, Thomas C., Ed., *The Battle of Midway,* 284.

The fighters climbed to 20,000 feet to see a broad expanse of ocean and be ready to dive to attack. The torpedo planes, carrying their heavy torpedoes, flew close to the water under the scattered cloud cover, more than three vertical miles below the fighters and dive-bombers. The *Hornet* air group was delayed while Commander Ring formed them up into one large formation.

Preparing to launch the *Yorktown* attack at 0830, Fletcher still had no confirmation about the positions or movements of any Japanese carriers beyond the original PBY report. He knew that the PBY pilot had reported just two carriers. As a result, Fletcher held back the seventeen SBD dive-bombers of VS-5 to attack another formation of carriers if one were discovered. If another Japanese carrier force of two or even three carriers did turn up, how effective could one squadron be against the expected formidable CAP defenses? In addition, by 0830 the twenty-two PBYs from Midway had been flying their search patterns for almost four hours. At 124 knots the PBYs would have covered approximately 500 miles of their search pattern and would be starting their return leg. Since none of them had reported any contacts with Japanese carriers beyond the one reported at 0603, it was a strong indication that there was not another carrier group in a different location.

Fletcher sent seventeen dive-bombers and twelve torpedo planes in the 0830 launch against the known contact protected by only six F4F Wildcat fighters, out of twenty-five flyable F4Fs onboard. Thach's objection to such a small fighter commitment was to no avail; Fletcher's first priority was to defend his ship. The fighters under Thach were assigned to protect the torpedo planes, but it was going to be tough if they faced serious opposition from a large Zero force.

Nagumo took evasive maneuvers while beating off the attacks from Midway that slowed his progress on the southeast course. Otherwise, he maintained his course of 135 degrees until 0917, when all his carriers had recovered the planes returning from Midway. He then changed course to 030 in response to the scout's report, a northeast heading that would close with the Pacific Fleet carrier force. Because the Striking Force had maneuvered to avoid attacks from the Pacific Fleet planes from Midway, they were behind the plots on the dead reckoning track. With the course change to 030, the projected intercept point for the *Enterprise* and *Hornet* planes was now completely wrong. On course 240 degrees, they would find nothing.

Meanwhile, the Japanese floatplane flitted from cloud to cloud over the American task forces, making periodic reports. Had even one PBY been kept over the Striking Force to provide updated position reports, the entire air wings of *Enterprise* and *Hornet* could have changed course and attacked while Nagumo was recovering or reorganizing his air group. Better scouting organization and execution could have compensated for a tardy and protracted launch of the TF-16 attack. The reality was that oversights in the planning and execution of the Pacific Fleet scouting effort put their entire naval force in serious jeopardy.

Admiral Raymond Spruance
Photo Shutterstock editorial

CHAPTER 24

Midway: Teetering on a Knife-Edge

The *Hornet* air group proceeded on course 240 degrees from the carrier. Ensign George Gay, appointed navigator of Torpedo Eight by Lieutenant Commander Waldron, kept careful track of the squadron's course.[284]

Waldron had had time to think after the squadron launched. He reasoned that the Japanese force would not continue to close on Midway indefinitely, but at some point would change course to maintain an operating distance from Midway. That meant they would turn either northeast or southeast. Waldron probably was not aware that a Japanese scout had discovered the US carriers, but by this time he may have thought it probable that his carrier had been found. Waldron knew a scout would report the US forces northeast of their own formation, and in response the Striking Force would close the range. Taking all these factors into consideration, Waldron calculated that the real intercept point for his squadron would be north of the dead reckoning track projected earlier.

At that point, a furious disagreement broke out between Waldron and air group commander Ring. Over the air group radio frequency, Waldron told Ring he was flying on the wrong course. Ring informed Waldron that he was in command of this mission, the debate was in

---

284 Gay, Ens. George, *Sole Survivor*, 115.

violation of the ordered radio silence, and that Waldron was to obey orders and stay on the course Ring had ordered.

After failing to convince Ring that his analysis was correct, Waldron, in an action that constituted a mutiny, executed a right turn to the northwest for himself and the entire Torpedo Eight squadron of fifteen planes. Torpedo Eight was mostly under cloud cover, and the Wildcat fighters were high above it. The fighters continued on course, and Waldron and his squadron were on their own.

Ring and the rest of the *Hornet* group on course 240 passed the point where they could have expected to intercept the Striking Force. It was unclear to Ring whether the Japanese had passed ahead or were behind on the dead reckoning track. If they were ahead, it meant the Japanese were between the *Hornet* group and Midway. In a move he believed was protective, Ring took his group to the southeast toward Midway.

At about 0925, within a few minutes of Nagumo's course change, Torpedo Eight intercepted the Striking Force. Flying low, without any fighter protection, they bored in on the Japanese carriers. The carriers maneuvered away, and the Zeros leaped onto the slow-moving Devastators, shooting them down one by one. Flying at more than twice their speed, the Zeros made repeated passes over the attackers, doing wingovers and loops to double back over their targets. The Devastators launched a few slow torpedoes to no effect.

In a matter of minutes, this young, proud squadron was a mass of burning, sinking flotsam on the ocean. Some planes were torn apart or exploded. A blue wing with a white star stuck out of the water here, a burning aircraft floated there, a sinking aircraft with a blood-spattered canopy somewhere else. Some fliers were struggling, some were wounded, some shouted for help, some were drowning, some were trapped in their sinking aircraft, some just floated on the water face down. This band of brothers, this flower of American youth, was now strewn on the ocean. Waldron was last seen trying to get out of his burning plane. One member of Torpedo Eight survived.[285] There was not so much as a scratch on a Japanese ship. It was all over by about 0940.

Torpedo Six, the *Enterprise* torpedo squadron, flew steadily on course 241 over three vertical miles below its protecting fighters. Close to the ocean surface, they were mostly under the cumulus cloud cover. One of the crewmen saw a faint wisp of smoke on the horizon. He told his pilot, who in turn radioed the squadron commander, who turned the squadron in that direction. The fighters, high above the clouds, failed to see this course change, and failed to pick up a message. The fighters continued on course, and Torpedo Six investigated the wisp of smoke on their own. This led them directly to the Japanese carriers just as the last planes of the *Hornet*'s torpedo squadron ended up in the ocean.

Torpedo Six attacked the Japanese carriers, and it was like the attack of Torpedo Eight all over again. The carriers turned away, and the Zeros came in for the kill. It was a slightly closer match this time because all the earlier maneuvering during the *Hornet* squadron attack had caused the carriers to be strung out over a wider expanse of ocean. The *Hornet* planes had approached the Japanese force from one direction, and the *Enterprise* planes were coming in from another. The Zeros had to fly back to intercept the *Enterprise* squadron, so the attackers had a little more time. Also, the *Enterprise* fliers were more experienced, and they set up anvil attacks on both sides of *Kaga* as the Zeros arrived in force. However, skillful maneuvering by the *Kaga* captain and the erratic tracks of the US torpedoes resulted in no hits.

By 0950 most of Torpedo Six had been shot down. Another brave band of brothers went into the abyss of the Pacific Ocean. Only a few escaped. The Zeros landed to quickly rearm and refuel. Since 0710 the Zeros and antiaircraft fire of escorting cruisers and destroyers had beaten off a series of American attacks without the slightest damage to any of the Japanese ships.

---

285   Naval History, June 2017, Vol. 31, No. 3.

Meanwhile, Commander Ring and the rest of the *Hornet* air group, flying on course 241, had found nothing. Ring turned the *Hornet* dive-bombers and fighters to a southeast course, then to the northeast to again intercept the dead reckoning line of the Striking Force. If the Japanese carriers could have been ahead of the original dead reckoning estimate, there was a chance Ring's maneuver might have found them. However, the Striking Force was far behind, and Ring found nothing. It was not surprising that Ring found nothing because the dead reckoning projection had the Striking Force continuing on course at twenty-five knots, essentially its maximum speed, and it therefore was not possible for the Striking Force to be ahead of that projection. It also meant that any course or speed change would put it behind the dead reckoning projection. Running low on fuel, and by this time close to Midway, many of Ring's planes detached themselves from the formation and headed for the island. Other planes, particularly many of the Wildcat fighters, ran out of fuel and ditched in the ocean. Ring and some others made it back to *Hornet*.

At about 0950 a very worried Admiral Raymond Spruance stood on the *Enterprise* flag bridge and considered the situation. Both the *Hornet* and *Enterprise* squadrons had been consuming fuel since 0700 and should have found the Japanese carriers at least a half hour earlier. By this time, they were running low on fuel and would have to turn back very soon from wherever they were. With no radio messages, it was clear they had not found the Japanese. Fletcher had launched a strike from *Yorktown* later, about 0830, and there had been no word from those planes either.

For Spruance and his carriers, the situation was a crisis. Surprisingly, there had been no attack yet from Nagumo. That meant that Nagumo had recovered his Midway attack force. Refueled and rearmed, the entire Striking Force was surely being readied for a huge, coordinated assault on the Pacific Fleet carriers. Calculating from the time the Japanese attack on Midway would have ended, around 0700, Spruance estimated that Nagumo's Midway force would have returned to their carriers about 0830. Completing the landings would take until about 0900, rearming and refueling would take another hour, to 1000, and they would be spotted and launched in another thirty minutes—about 1030. Spruance assumed that Nagumo's carriers were about an hour's flying time from his own, so he could expect a first attack about 1130.

TF-16 planes had about four hours of total flying time, depending on the aircraft type, which meant they would be returning between 1100 and 1130. That meant that Nagumo's attack would hit his carriers just as the planes, low on fuel, were attempting to land. Spruance had ten Wildcats flying CAP, but they had little chance against a huge swarm of Zeros. He knew his and Fletcher's carriers were in deadly peril. Spruance thought about Nimitz's most fundamental directive: whatever else, don't lose the carriers. Now that was about to happen. If the *Enterprise* and *Hornet* attack failed, nothing would stop the Striking Force from launching a massive strike that would almost surely sink the three US carriers.

Also at 0950, Admiral Nagumo stood on the *Akagi* bridge and considered his situation. He had violated the fundamental axiom of carrier war—get off the first strike—in favor of recovering his Midway force. He gambled that he could delay an immediate but smaller attack, and then, with all his aircraft rearmed and refueled, make a massive, coordinated attack on the Pacific Fleet carriers.

It would be a smaller version of the Pearl Harbor attack—four carriers instead of six, minus some aircraft that had been lost in the Midway attack earlier in the day. But Nagumo had not weakened his attack by diverting some of his planes to scouting earlier in the morning. He would send about 200 planes in two waves. The first deck load would launch by 1045, and the second wave would go thirty minutes later. It would be a powerful, devastating attack. *Kaga* alone had twenty-seven torpedo planes ready for the first wave. The hothead Yamaguchi had wanted to do a small, piecemeal attack at the first sign of trouble. He would deal with

Yamaguchi's insolence after he had sunk the Americans. Another feeble attack by US torpedo planes was still ongoing, but the Zeros would send them all to their watery graves in short order.

Nagumo was now calm and supremely confident as he sent a message to Yamamoto and the other admirals who commanded the separate forces of the huge Japanese fleet:

> *Carried out air attack of [Midway] at 0630. Many enemy shore-based planes attacked us subsequent to 0715. We have suffered no damages. At 0728, enemy composed of 1 carrier, 7 cruisers and 5 destroyers . . . After destroying this [force] we plan to resume our [Midway] attack. Our . . . course [0]30 degrees, speed 24 knots.*[286]

At 0955 on June 4, it looked like Admiral Nagumo's gamble was going to pay off.

---

286   Parshall and Tully, 216.

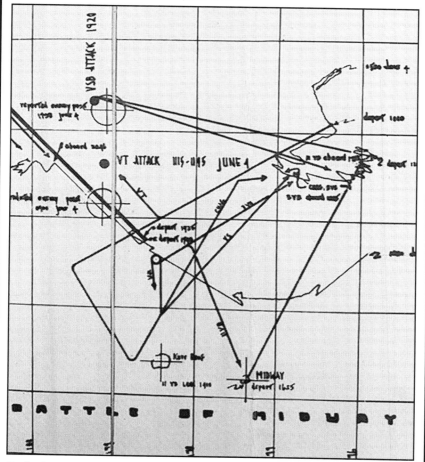

Attack of *Hornet* Planes
Battle of Midway
June 4, 1942

Track Chart of Planes of *USS Hornet* Planes, Battle of Midway, Enclosure (F), Excerpt, of Action. Report of Comanding Officer, *USS Hornet* to Commander-in-Chief, U.S. Pacific Fleet, via Commander Task Force Sixteen, Report of June 13, 1942. Included as Enclosure (G) of CINCPACFLT Action Report of June 15, 1942.

Attack of *Hornet* planes

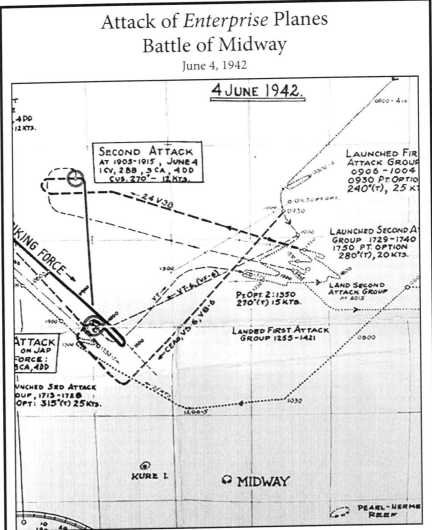

Attack of *Enterprise* Planes
Battle of Midway
June 4, 1942

Track Chart of Planes of USS *Enterprise*, Battle of Midway, June, 4, 1942, Enclosure (A), Excerpt, of Action Report of Comanding Officer, USS *Enterprise* to Commander-in-Chief, U.S. Pacific Fleet, via Commander Task Force Sixteen, Report of June 8, 1942. Included as Enclosure (B) of CINCPACFLT Action Report of June 15, 1942.

Attack of *Enterprise* planes

CHAPTER 25

Midway: The Finale

In the minutes just prior to 1000 on June 4, north of Midway, the admirals directly opposing each other were considering their separate situations. Spruance on *Enterprise* and Fletcher on *Yorktown* were very worried. Yamaguchi on *Hiryu* was cautiously hopeful, but concerned. Nagumo on *Akagi* was exulting in the prospect of another great victory.

Lieutenant Commander Wade McClusky, age 42, commander of the *Enterprise* air group, had been a fighter pilot, one of the best. His promotion to air group commander on *Enterprise* moved him to piloting the premier attack plane in the Navy arsenal, the Dauntless dive-bomber. Like the admirals on the flag bridges of the different carriers, he was considering his situation and that of the two squadrons of thirty-one dive-bombers he was leading into battle. The sixteen planes in the scouting squadron, VS-6, were each carrying a 500-pound bomb and two 100-pound bombs. The bomber squadron, VB-6, had fifteen planes each carrying a single 1,000-pound bomb. His air group had been in the air since shortly after 0700, and they were getting low on fuel.

They were flying southwest on a course of 240 degrees to intercept the Japanese carrier force, and McClusky calculated, after the earlier delay, that he should see it by 0925. His pilots had seen nothing but the low cumulus clouds and open ocean. He knew, as most of the senior aviators knew, that the Devastator torpedo planes would not succeed; against the Zeros they were like clay pigeons in a shooting gallery. Even if some got past the Zeros, flying slow and low over antiaircraft fire from the escorting destroyers and cruisers was another invitation to death. And, if any survived all that to launch a torpedo, Admiral Halsey's previous evaluations had shown the WWI-vintage torpedoes to be completely unreliable. He knew, as the other dive-bomber commanders knew, that it was up to the dive-bombers, or the Pacific Fleet was going to lose the Battle of Midway.

By 0930 he accepted that he should have intercepted the Japanese carriers if they had continued on the same course and speed after the 0603 report. Now all his experience and judgment were needed in this crucial moment. Facing the same situation as Ring, who turned the *Hornet* air group left to protect Midway, he analyzed the situation much the same way Waldron had, just minutes earlier. He decided to turn right about 90 degrees to the northwest and start a search pattern that would take him parallel to, but south of, the original Japanese course of 135 degrees. He executed the turn, and the two squadrons followed. If the Japanese had maintained their course but had been delayed for any reason, such as the need to take evasive maneuvers, flying back near that track would find them. McClusky and his air group were flying at 19,000 feet. At that altitude, one can see a vast expanse of ocean. But with 50 percent cumulus cloud cover at lower altitudes, visibility was difficult.

Still nothing, and the fuel situation was becoming serious. Some of the planes might have to ditch in the ocean when they ran out of fuel. McClusky would have been fully justified in turning back to *Enterprise* at this point, but he knew the Japanese carriers were out there and he had to find them. He hoped that all his years of training and flying experience could come together and give him the judgment needed to find them.

He led the two squadrons on the reverse of the Japanese course for about fifteen minutes until he had covered enough ocean to be confident the carriers were not on that track. He had begun the search south of the intercept point and so was sure the Japanese could not be farther south. He turned his group to the northeast to execute the first leg of a search pattern. Since he had not found the Striking Force carriers, it was possible their scouts had found the US task forces, and they had turned north to close the range.

Then, several minutes before 1000, McClusky, through an opening in the clouds, spotted a lone destroyer, which could only be Japanese, heading northeast at flank speed. It was the destroyer *Arashi*, which had been detached to counter the American submarine *Nautilus*. He turned his air group to parallel the track of the destroyer. After several minutes of flying, McClusky saw faint white slivers on the horizon indicating the wakes of ships. Following farther, and emerging from over a cloud layer, the Japanese carrier force was spread out below him. The yellow decks, each painted with a large red disc, identified the carriers. At 1002 the electrifying message went out to Spruance and Fletcher: "This is McClusky. Have sighted the enemy." McClusky's decision to persevere in his mission and decide on the search courses under the pressure of battle conditions and low fuel are some of the greatest moments of command leadership in the entire war.

Once dive-bombers nose over to begin their dives they are virtually unstoppable. If there was a weakness in the dive-bomber, it was the necessity to be almost directly over an enemy ship before starting their near-vertical dives. If the Japanese had maintained even a small portion of their CAP at high altitude around the Striking Force, they probably would have seen and attacked McClusky's Dauntlesses before they got close enough to make their dives. There were no Wildcats to defend McClusky's formation, and a high-altitude encounter with Zeros could have been very disruptive. Hitting a fast-moving, maneuvering carrier is difficult even in ideal conditions, and Zeros would have made it far more difficult for the *Enterprise* planes to get lined up over their targets. To carry out evasive maneuvers, some of the pilots would have been forced to jettison their bombs.

McClusky was surprised there were no Zeros opposing his squadrons. There was not even any indication they had been seen from the ships 19,000 feet below, and that gave him the opportunity to maneuver his squadrons around the Japanese force, so that when they began their dives they would be coming out of the sun. The bombing squadron, VB-6, was flying 5,000 feet lower than VS-6 because one of the pilots had a problem with his oxygen supply and had to breathe open air. This prevented the use of hand signals, and McClusky gave the orders by voice radio to the two squadrons to dive on the two closest carriers. He would lead the VS-6 squadron in a dive on *Kaga*. The action report of the Scouting Six (VS-6) squadron commander, Lieutenant Earl Gallaher, describes the action:[287]

> *The Enterprise Air Group Commander (CEAG) designated by voice radio one CV target for himself and VS-6 and another CV target for VB-6. Commander Scouting Six (Lt. Gallaher) followed the three-plane section led by CEAG on a CV of the Kaga or Akagi class and observed two of this section's bombs to be near misses – the impact of the third bomb was not observed. The CV at this time was undamaged. A clear view of the entire flight deck was observed and any damage by any bomb hits would have been observed. The bomb dropped by Commanding Officer of Scouting Six [Gallaher] was a direct hit in the center of the flight deck about 200 ft. from the stern. At least two more direct hits were scored by the first division and the CV was afire and smoking heavily.*

During retirement several more hits were observed on the CV attacked by Scouting Squadron Six and about five minutes after completion of the attack a terrific explosion was observed which completely enveloped the

---

287   Report of Action, June 4 – 6, 1942, From: Commander Scouting Squadron Six, To: Commanding Officer, U.S.S. ENTERPRISE, Via: Commander ENTERPRISE Air Group, June 10, 1942.

CV in flames. During retirement it was observed that three CV were on fire and smoking heavily.

The second division leader [Lieutenant C. E. Dickinson, Jr.] followed immediately after the last plane of the first division on the designated target scoring a direct hit with his 500 lb. bomb. At least two other hits were scored by this division. The third division was seen to follow the second division on the designated target. None of the pilots of this division returned but the second division leader stated that the third division made at least one direct hit.

Kaga became an inferno of multicolored flames, setting off secondary explosions from the fueled and armed aircraft. The twenty-seven torpedo planes ready to devastate the Pacific Fleet carriers were turned into flaming, exploding debris.

Lieutenant (junior grade) Norman "Dusty" Kleiss, in the fourth plane in the first division of the VS-6 squadron, wrote in his memoir, "[T]he SBD [dive-bomber] makes the scariest roller coaster on the planet seem like child's play."[288] Describing his dive on *Kaga*, Kleiss recalled:

> *I said to myself, "Here we go." My plane rolled into its dive, and in a few seconds all I could see was the enormous blue ocean, with the enemy carrier in the middle of it. . . . I felt the stomach-sinking feeling caused by the sharp drop . . . My plane knifed downward at 240 knots. The Rising Sun emblem on Kaga's bow made an inviting target, so I used it to sight my bombs. I picked out a spot on the ocean where I expected the big red orb to be in about forty-nine seconds, and dived for it.*

> *Accurate dive bombing requires a precise estimation of the target's lead. Any good dive bomber had to be able to size up a moving target's speed and direction during the first few seconds of the dive and aim for the position where it would be at the*

---

288   Kleiss, Lt. (jg) Jack "Dusty," *Never Call Me a Hero* (William Morrow, an imprint of Harper Collins, 2017), 202.

end. I did my best to maintain rudder trim and reduce yaw
while all the time monitoring the altimeter.

To release the bomb at 1,500 feet, Kleiss had to start pulling out of
the dive beginning at about 2,000 feet. He pulled back on his controls
and released his bombs, feeling the heavy g-forces as the plane pulled
out of the dive. The bombs dropped away. Looking back as his plane
pulled out, Kleiss could see them crash onto the bow of *Kaga* and the
enormous explosions that erupted, just about where he estimated they
would hit.

Bombing Six (VB-6) prepared to attack at the same time as VS-6. The
action report of its commander, Lieutenant Richard H. Best, records the
actions of his squadron:[289]

> *The Enterprise Air Group Commander designated by voice*
> *radio one CV target for himself and VS-6 and another*
> *target for VB-6. Commander Bombing Squadron Six [Best]*
> *understood his target to be the "left hand" CV. He gave the*
> *attack signal, releasing his other two division leaders for*
> *individual division maneuvering and led his (first) division*
> *towards the "left hand" CV. Almost at once he saw that VS-6*
> *was diving on the "left hand" CV and so led his division against*
> *the "right hand" CV which was of the "Kaga" type. It was*
> *launching planes as the attack was made. At least three 1,000*
> *lb bomb hits were observed on that target and it became a mass*
> *of flame and smoke. The first section of the first division joined*
> *up immediately after pull-out from the dive.*
>
> *The second division leader delayed attack momentarily. He*
> *observed misses near the "left hand" CV and decided to dive*
> *on that target. While in his dive he observed several hits on*
> *that target, starting fires. He scored a direct hit in the middle*

---

289   Report of Action, June 4–6, 1942, From: Commander Bombing Squadron Six, To: Commanding Officer, U.S.S. ENTERPRISE, Via: Commander ENTERPRISE Air Group, June 10, 1942.

of the carrier with his 1,000 lb bomb, and other 1,000 lb bomb hits were scored by planes following his. That CV appeared to suffer internal explosions in addition to bomb hits, and little of it remained visible in the midst of huge flames and smoke. The third division apparently attacked the same target as did the second division. Only one pilot from that division returned.

The remainder of Best's report deals primarily with the heavy losses of pilots and gunner crews, as planes either were shot down or ditched on the ocean when their fuel was exhausted. Some pilots that landed on the ocean were able to report an estimated position of their floating rafts, but in some cases searches by destroyers and other planes failed to find them. Only five planes out of fifteen of VB-6 returned to *Enterprise*. A crew gunner, Stuart J. Mason, Jr., was lauded for extraordinary performance.

The report also states that Best led the five-plane First Division in the attack and released the other two divisions for "individual maneuvering," which allowed the division commanders to assess the overall action and focus on targets of opportunity. The Second and Third Divisions, commanded by Lieutenant J. B. Penland and Lieutenant (junior grade) J. J. Van Buren respectively, were both composed of five planes. If either targeted carrier escaped destruction, the Second and Third Divisions of VB-6 could attack them, or go after other targets in the Japanese fleet once the carriers were destroyed.

The two reports show the attacks of the two squadrons on the targeted carriers were nearly simultaneous. The VB-6 Second Division commander, Lieutenant Penland, seeing the hits by Best and at least one other on *Akagi* and the initial miss by McClusky on *Kaga*, decided to target *Kaga* scant moments before Gallaher, Kleiss, and others made their hits on that carrier. Penland's and Van Buren's divisions of VB-6 followed the VS-6 dives. *Kaga* was hit by seven bombs from VS-6 and four more from sections two and three of VB-6. Van Buren, Third Division commander, continued the attack on *Kaga* even after it was obviously destroyed. The repeated hits on *Kaga* were similar to the hits on *Showa* by *Lexington* and *Yorktown* dive-bombers at the Coral Sea a month earlier. Best was mistaken in thinking his dive was on *Kaga*, as other records established that he and his division dove on *Akagi*, and their bombs destroyed that ship.

Nearly simultaneously with these attacks, the *Yorktown* air group entered the scene. It almost could have been planned. The *Yorktown* air group commander, Lieutenant Commander Max Leslie, divided the dive-bombers by squadron, with the VB-5 squadron attacking Soryu and VS-5 attacking Hiryu. He radioed Lieutenant Walter C. Short, the VS-5 commander, "How about you taking the one on the left [*Hiryu*], and I'll take the one on the right [*Soryu*]?" Leslie was one of the first to be launched from *Yorktown*. He did not realize, and would not have known without being informed, that the Short's VS-5 squadron had been held back aboard *Yorktown*.[290] There were no VS-5 planes in the formation and no planes available for a dive-bombing attack on *Hiryu*. Leslie's VB-5 dive-bombers dove on *Soryu*, and four hits on that ship turned it into a blazing hell.

The *Yorktown* torpedo planes came in against *Hiryu*, and yet again the Zeros swarmed over them. But this time Jimmy Thach's six Wildcats were on the scene. Though outnumbered, the Wildcats engaged in a ferocious dogfight against the Zeros employing the Thach Weave and, for the first time, a few Zeros went into the ocean. Thach and his fighter pilots did their best to protect the torpedo planes, and Thach himself was credited with three victories,[291] but there were too many Zeros and too few Wildcats. Ten of the twelve *Yorktown* torpedo planes were shot down, and no hits were scored on *Hiryu*.

---

290   Lundstrum, *Black Shoe Carrier Admiral*, 260.

291   Report of "Fighting Squadron Three Partial Bag for Battle of Midway," "Report of Action – June 4-6, 1942," Commanding Officer, U.S.S Hornet, Capt. M.A. Mitscher, To: Commander-in-Chief, U.S. Pacific Fleet, Via: Commander Task Force SIXTEEN, June 13, 1942.

In five minutes, three of the four ships of the Striking Force had been turned into pyrotechnic disasters. The flames on *Kaga* were as high as the 800-foot ship was long. Secondary explosions were erupting on *Akagi* and *Soryu* as ordnance on aircraft and stacked on racks in the hangar decks during the earlier changeover began to explode. Broken fuel lines spread flaming aviation fuel over the hangar decks. Hundreds of sailors were killed outright in the initial blasts. Japanese flight mechanics in the tropics typically worked in short-sleeved shirts and shorts, and the flaming fuel and explosions were now causing terrible burns over their bodies. The sailors who escaped or were less severely injured attempted to fight the fires, but their efforts were pitiful against the torrential flames and secondary explosions.

Kaga and *Soryu* were lost causes. For a while there was some hope that *Akagi* might be saved, but as continued explosions caused further damage, the battle to save the ship was abandoned. Nagumo was in a state of shock. His staff prevailed upon him to move to a cruiser. A vice admiral of the Imperial Japanese Navy had to crawl through a window on the bridge, slide down on a length of line, and finally down a rope ladder and onto a small boat sent from an escorting destroyer.

The battle scene had been transformed by the *Enterprise* attack. Had McClusky's determination and leadership not prevailed, *Akagi* and *Kaga* would have remained intact, and the escape of *Hiryu* would have meant that three Japanese carriers would have survived the attack, ready to launch their planes. Three fully armed and ready Japanese carriers were fully capable of destroying the three Pacific Fleet carriers, particularly while they were recovering planes. The result probably would have been a victory for the Japanese, but that was not the reality at 1030 on June 4. McClusky, wounded by Zero gunfire in the attack on *Kaga*, made it back flying with one hand and a scant amount of fuel left in his tanks. *Enterprise* commanding officer Captain G. D. Murray wrote in his official action report:

ENTERPRISE Air Group, both pilots and gunners, displayed a spirit of utter fearlessness, resolution, and determination throughout all air actions. This spirit, though shared by pilots and gunners alike, found its highest expression in the person of the Air Group commander, LtComdr C. W. McClusky, Jr., U.S.N. On June 4, prior to intercepting the main enemy forces, it was his decision, and his decision alone, that made the attack possible which led to the destruction of a major part of the main enemy forces. It is the considered opinion of the Commanding Officer that the success of our forces hinged on this attack. Any other action on the part of LtComdr McClusky would inevitably have led to irreparable loss to our forces. [292]

For his personal performance, courage, and leadership of the *Enterprise* air group at the Battle of Midway, Lieutenant Commander McClusky was awarded the Navy Cross.[293]

Within minutes of the cataclysm that destroyed *Akagi*, *Kaga*, and *Soryu*, Yamaguchi launched his own attack from *Hiryu*. The senior Striking Force admiral now was the screen commander, Rear Admiral Abe Hiroaki, but Yamaguchi did not wait for any orders from him. He also did not wait to mount a coordinated attack with his dive-bombers and torpedo planes because further attacks could come at any time. He was determined to get an attack off, just as he had been two hours earlier. The torpedo planes were not ready, but he got the *Hiryu* dive-bomber squadron into the air as quickly as possible.

By 1050, twenty minutes after the destruction of three Japanese carriers, *Hiryu* had spotted and launched sixteen dive-bombers and six Zero fighters. The scout aircraft was still on station over the American force and sent back range and bearing information to *Hiryu*. The Pacific

---

292   Commanding Officer, U.S.S. Enterprise, Capt G. D. Murray, Air Battle of the Pacific, June 4-6, 1942, Report of, To: Commander-in-Chief, U.S. Pacific Fleet, Via: Commander Task Force Sixteen (Rear Admiral R. A. Spruance, U.S.N.), June 13, 1942, 12.

293   *Dictionary of American Fighting Ships*: C. Wade McClusky.

Fleet carriers were only ninety miles away. While en route the attackers spotted several *Enterprise* dive-bombers flying toward their ship, and the hyperaggressive Zero pilots foolishly peeled off to make an attack. Two Zeros were damaged in that melee and were forced to return to *Hiryu*, resulting in the fighter protection being reduced to four. How many *Enterprise* dive-bombers were lost in that dogfight is unknown.

The closest ship was *Yorktown*, and the Japanese planes headed straight for it. Ship's radar picked up the attackers when they were more than thirty miles away. The *Yorktown* CAP was supplemented by fighters from *Hornet* and *Enterprise*. Ferocious fighting took place over *Yorktown* as the dive-bombers maneuvered to make their dives, and the Wildcats and the four outnumbered Zeros clashed in dogfights. The CAP tore into the Japanese formation and shot down or damaged several of the attacking dive-bombers and three of the Zeros.

The remaining dive-bombers converged on *Yorktown* from different angles to complicate defensive maneuvers. As they converged, several were shot down by anti-aircraft fire, but the surviving planes made three hits on *Yorktown*. Holes were torn in the flight deck, and damage extended to the hangar deck. At least one bomb penetrated to the engine spaces deep in the ship, and *Yorktown* went dead in the water. Damage to the bridge superstructure forced Admiral Fletcher and staff to transfer to the cruiser *Astoria*. The *Yorktown* VS-5 squadron, now damaged and unflyable, was still on the hangar deck.

As *Yorktown*'s crew battled to extinguish fires and get the ship underway again, the battered remains of *Hiryu*'s dive-bomber squadron headed back to their ship. Meanwhile, the torpedo planes were ready to launch. *Hiryu* had suffered extensive losses in the Midway attack earlier that day, but there were still ten torpedo planes ready to fly. Yamaguchi, receiving a report that one American carrier had been put out of action by the dive-bombers, came down to the flight deck to personally brief his fliers. He instructed the pilots to find a fresh carrier if they could. If the torpedo planes could disable another carrier, the battle would then become a one-on-one contest.

At 1400 Yamaguchi launched the torpedo bombers, commanded by the same Lieutenant Tomonaga who had led the Midway attack earlier that day. Only a few Zeros were available as escorts. The scout plane was still on station to guide them in, and within forty-five minutes Tomonaga saw a carrier making headway ahead and mistakenly thought it was a carrier that had not been hit by the dive-bombers. However, it was *Yorktown*. The fires had been put out in a superb job of damage control, and the ship was making headway. The torpedo planes split into two groups of five aircraft each to execute an anvil attack. Met by ten Wildcats, a dogfight with the Zeros ensued, but the Zeros were heavily outnumbered.

Tomonaga, as leader of his flight, was first to attack. Calculating the lead angle from the speed of *Yorktown*, he headed in on a course for his torpedo to hit the starboard side of *Yorktown*. Wildcats dove on his plane, and they riddled it with machine gun fire that ignited his fuel tanks. With the plane completely on fire, including the wings, he was losing altitude but somehow kept the plane horizontal. Closing in on *Yorktown*, he held on until the last possible instant to release his torpedo before he and his crew plunged to their deaths in the ocean. It missed.

Tomonaga's sacrifice was not wasted, however, as the Wildcats that were drawn to repel his plane opened another opportunity. On the port side, four torpedo planes were boring in for the kill. They dropped their torpedoes, and one, then another, hit *Yorktown* forward and then amidships with tremendous concussions. The ocean poured in, and *Yorktown* took a heavy list to port. In adjoining spaces to the engine rooms damaged bulkheads collapsed and more ocean water cascaded in. Electric power was lost, and there was no alternative for the sailors in the inky blackness of those flooded spaces but to drown. Others, farther from the impact area, wounded and choking, groped for fresh air. The ship, for the second time, went dead in the water.

After considering the situation on his ship, and concerned that *Yorktown* could capsize, Captain Buckmaster ordered Abandon Ship. Sailors came up from below decks, made difficult by the severe list. The edge of the flight deck on the port side was close to the water, and sailors started going over the side. The torpedo hits had ruptured fuel tanks, and there was a heavy fuel oil slick surrounding the ship. Destroyers and boats from other ships picked up men in the ocean as soon as they could, but some had swallowed fuel oil and were vomiting as they tried to swim. Wounded sailors were lowered over the side in stretchers fitted with floatation devices. Fletcher realized he could not control the American carrier force from his position on *Astoria* and signaled Spruance, "I will follow your movements." This shifted overall command to Spruance. At this point both senior admirals, Fletcher and Nagumo, had transferred to cruisers after their flagships suffered serious damage.

A shattered Yamamoto received the report of the destruction of three of his carriers but was still determined to turn the tables. He increased the speed of the main body and ordered Nagumo to close on the American force with his battleships. Yamamoto thought the Americans would continue west to pursue the remaining Japanese ships, and if he could get his battleships within range, he could destroy them in a night battle. Nagumo had two battleships in his force, plus cruisers and destroyers. In addition, Yamamoto with his battleships was coming up fast behind him.

Foolishly, Nagumo did not detach *Hiryu* from his force. It would have been smarter to send *Hiryu* to the west at flank speed as soon as the torpedo planes were launched. It was almost out of planes and was of no further value in the attempt to engage the Americans in a night surface action. Although Yamaguchi was desperately planning a final strike for 1700 with its few remaining aircraft, saving the ship was more important than launching another small, hopeless air operation.

The few remaining and exhausted *Hiryu* aircraft crews were given stimulants for yet another attempt against the Americans. But while this was taking place, a *Yorktown* scout found *Hiryu* and radioed the position of the ship. *Enterprise* and *Hornet* had lost almost all their torpedo planes earlier in the day, but a strike force of twenty-five dive-bombers was assembled and launched. McClusky was in sick bay, but the next senior officer, Lt. Earl Gallaher, led the attack. *Enterprise* aircraft found *Hiryu* just before 1700. *Hiryu* had only a few Zeros left for protection, and despite desperate maneuvering at thirty-four-knot flank speed, it was hit with four 1,000-pound bombs forward on the flight deck. Both Dick Best and Dusty Kleiss scored hits again in this attack. Since its planes were fueled and armed, the same secondary explosions erupted as they had on the other carriers earlier in the day. *Hiryu* was doomed, and all four carriers of the Striking Force were now destroyed.

On the sinking *Hiryu* the commanding officer ordered the crew to abandon ship. This they proceeded to do, with two exceptions. In the samurai ethic, honor is more important than life, and defeat in battle brings an intolerable shame. Despite the pleadings of his officers and crew, Admiral Yamaguchi, samurai to the end, could not accept the humiliation of a major, devastating defeat. Joined by the loyal *Hiryu* captain, he stayed aboard the ship as it sank.

Yamamoto continued on a high-speed, easterly course, intent on a night battle. Japanese forces had trained for years in the use of star shells and other incendiary devices to illuminate enemy ships at night. Destruction by the massive guns of *Yamato* and the other battleships could reverse the outcome of the battle. On board *Enterprise* some of the staff officers were urging Spruance to pursue westward to make an annihilating attack with his carriers at first light in the morning.

But Spruance had other thoughts. He had won the Midway battle. He knew at least two Japanese battleships were out there somewhere to the west, and he knew of their night-fighting capabilities. He also was concerned that the Japanese amphibious force might still attempt a landing on Midway, and he wanted to be in the proximity of Midway in that event. After recovering the planes that had demolished *Hiryu*, and despite the contrary advice he was receiving, he ordered his carrier force to take a course to the east.

As night fell, Yamamoto followed with his forces behind the two battleships of the Striking Force, and they steamed eastward at full speed into the night. Far ahead the destroyers went to flank speed to search for the US carriers. Lookouts, with the best night-vision binoculars in the world, swept the night horizon where the very dark sky meets the black ocean. The faintest shape, the tiniest pinprick of light, would show there was something out there, like the superstructure of a ship over the horizon. There was nothing. By midnight Yamamoto realized that, with his air cover destroyed, he would be vulnerable to an air attack from the American carriers at first light. The plan for a night surface battle had failed. Leaving four sunk or sinking carriers behind, a devastated Yamamoto reversed course to the west, and his entire fleet went into retreat.

The damage control crew on *Yorktown* did a heroic job of attempting to salvage the ship. The list had been largely corrected, but there was some delay getting an organized boarding party aboard with a line or cable and getting it towed out of the area. A line was attached to a small ship that attempted to tow *Yorktown*, but the carrier had been essentially dead in the water for most of a day. There was a small division of destroyers remaining to safeguard *Yorktown*, but most of the destroyer force stayed with the operating carriers as they pursued the retreating Japanese. A Japanese scout plane saw *Yorktown*, apparently drifting, and made its report to Yamamoto. Yamamoto contacted submarine *I-168*, which slipped through the screening destroyers and fired two torpedoes into *Yorktown* and one into the escorting destroyer *Hammann*.

Hammann was split in half and went down in a few minutes with nearly all hands. Terrible casualties to troops invading beaches and charging cliffs are readily understood; the unseen horrors of sailors inside a sinking ship as it plunges to the depths of the ocean are more difficult to visualize. The final attack was too much for *Yorktown*, and in a well-organized exercise of Abandon Ship the remaining crew was rescued with minimal additional casualties. The 800-foot *Yorktown* finally capsized and slowly slipped beneath the surface.

More than half of the *Enterprise* dive-bombers never made it back to their ship after the attack on *Akagi* and *Kaga*. How many were lost from Zero attacks or anti-aircraft fire, and how many ditched in the ocean after running out of fuel, will never be known. Some of the downed fliers floating on their life rafts would be picked up. Others would not.

The remnants of the huge Japanese fleet would be pursued over several days with comparatively minor action. But when Admiral Spruance turned the carrier force to the east late in the day on June 4, the Battle of Midway, for all intents and purposes, was over.

Epilogue

Winston Churchill said of the RAF fliers in the Battle of Britain, "Never in the field of human conflict was so much owed by so many to so few."[294] The same could be said of the fliers at Coral Sea and Midway. The Pacific Fleet victory at Midway eliminated any possibility of the Japanese winning the Pacific War. It is unfortunate that peace negotiations could not have been initiated after the Midway battle, but the state of human development did not, and probably still does not, allow for any such approach.

Even with the loss of four fleet carriers on June 4, 1942, the Japanese still retained powerful and deadly forces. Over the next three years, the Pacific Fleet, joined by Marine Corps and Army air and amphibious forces, would build to an enormous size that would overwhelm the Japanese—just as Admiral Yamamoto and the Total War Research Institute had predicted. Ferocious fighting and terrible casualties, including civilians, were suffered until, after two atomic blasts, the war finally ended on September 2, 1945, aboard the battleship *Missouri*, anchored in Tokyo Bay. Hardship and sorrow came to many in the United States, Japan, and other countries.

Admiral Yamamoto became a personal victim of the code breakers in 1943 when a message detailing his flight schedule in the northern Solomon Islands was decoded, and US interceptors shot him down. More than a million Japanese turned out for his funeral in Tokyo. Vice Admiral Nagumo, concluding in 1943 that the war was lost, and perhaps

---

294   Churchill, Winston S., Address to the House of Commons, August 20, 1940.

considering his own contributions to that end, committed suicide. The remaining Striking Force carrier division commander, Rear Admiral Hara Chuichi, was sentenced to six years in prison by the war crimes tribunal after the war. Following his release he spent the rest of his life aiding Japanese, Korean, and Taiwanese war veterans.

General and Prime Minister Tojo Hideki was found guilty of war crimes and executed. Prince Konoe Fumimaro also was to be brought before the war crimes tribunal but, unwilling to subject himself to a proceeding he felt was unjustified and humiliating, committed suicide at age fifty-four.

Admirals Nimitz, Halsey, and Spruance commanded huge naval forces in battles that were to follow Midway, but none had the world-shaping significance as did the events of June 4, 1942. They retired from the Navy with honor for their service to the United States. Lieutenant Commander Jimmy Thach, a hero of Midway, went on to four-star admiral rank and culminated his excellent service in the Navy as commander of NATO naval forces.

Lieutenant Commander Wade McClusky as a captain became commanding officer of escort carrier USS *Corregidor* and retired in 1956 with a promotion to rear admiral one day before he retired. A frigate, USS *McClusky* (FFG-41), was named in his honor. An award was established in his name that each year honors the best attack squadron in the Navy. Even with these noteworthy tributes, his crucial leadership that snatched victory from defeat in the last possible moments in the greatest of all naval victories has never been fully recognized.

Similarly, the sacrifices of the fliers from Midway Island have never been fully honored. Flying into the teeth of the Japanese defenses beginning just after 0700 on June 4, they caused unexpected confrontation and confusion in the Japanese command that prompted the disastrous command decisions that led to their defeat. In addition, it is likely the attacks of the Midway fliers drew down whatever high-altitude Japanese CAP was over the Striking Force, as there was no report of the B-17s encountering CAP when they bombed the Striking Force from high altitude around 0800. The dive-bombers that won the Battle of Midway would have faced much greater challenges had Japanese CAP been at high altitude.

In the attack of Torpedo Eight, Ensign George Gay was wounded from the machine guns and cannon of a Zero, but he still managed a crash landing on the ocean surface. After a day and night floating alone on the calm ocean he was picked up by a PBY amphibious plane.

Cordell Hull continued to serve as Secretary of State until 1944, when his ill health finally brought about his resignation. In 1945 he was awarded a Nobel Peace Prize for his contributions to the founding of the United Nations. Henry Stimson, having served five presidents in a long public career, left office for the last time in September 1945. Dean Acheson continued in the State Department through the war and served as Secretary of State from 1949 to 1953. Frank Knox continued as Navy Secretary until his death in 1944. Harold Ickes continued to serve as Interior Secretary until 1946. Stanley Hornbeck continued as an adviser to Cordell Hull, and near the end of the war in 1944 became ambassador to the Netherlands. All were feted and honored for the rest of their lives.

President Franklin D. Roosevelt, from his wheelchair in the White House, led the United States to victory in World War II. But like Moses, who would glimpse the Promised Land but never enter it, Roosevelt died in April 1945 when victory was assured, but a few months before the final surrenders of Germany and Japan.

Bibliography

BOOKS

Adams, John A. *If Mahan Ran the Great Pacific War: An Analysis of World War II Naval Strategy* (Indianapolis: Indiana University Press, 2008).

Asada, Sadao. *From Mahan to Pearl Harbor: The Imperial Japanese Navy and the United States* (Annapolis: Naval Institute Press, 2006).

Ballard, Robert D., and Rick Archbold. *Return to Midway* (Washington D.C.: Madison Publishing, 1999).

Bates, Richard W. *The Battle of Midway: Including the Aleutian Phase, June 3 to June 14, 1942: Strategical and Tactical Analysis* (U.S. Naval War College, 1948).

Batty, David. *Japan at War in Color* (London: Carlton Books, 2004).

Bauer, Conrad. *History's Greatest Spies: The Hidden Story of Richard Sorge* (USA: Maplewood Publishing, 2015).

Bishop, Chris. *Firepower: Sea Warfare* (New Jersey: Chartwell Books, Inc., 1999).

Borneman, Walter R. *The Admirals: Nimitz, Halsey, Leahy, and King— The Five-Star Admirals Who Won the War at Sea* (New York: Little, Brown and Company, 2012).

Bresnahan, Jim. *Refighting the Pacific War: An Alternative History of World War II* (Annapolis: Naval Institute Press, 2011).

Buell, Thomas B. *The Quiet Warrior: A Biography of Admiral Raymond A. Spruance* (Annapolis: Naval Institute Press, 1974).

Carlson, Elliot. *Joe Rochefort's War: The Odyssey of the Codebreaker Who Outwitted Yamamoto at Midway* (Annapolis: Naval Institute Press, 2011).

Chan, Jenny, and Barbara Halperin. *Prince Konoe Memoir: The Secret Negotiations Between Japan and the U.S. Before Pearl Harbor Presented with Related Materials by Pacific Atrocities Education* (San Francisco: Pacific Atrocities Education, 2020).

Costello, John. *The Pacific War* (New York: Rawson, Wade Publishers, Inc., 1981).

Cowley, Robert. *What If? The World's Foremost Military Historians Imagine What Might Have Been* (New York: Berkley Books, 1999).

Dallek, Robert. *Franklin D. Roosevelt: A Political Life* (Viking, 2017).

Devereux, James P.S. *Wake Island: An Eyewitness Account by the Commanding Officer* (Independently published, 2015).

Ditterich, Robert. *Before Pearl Harbor: Making the Pacific War* (Booksurge, LLC., 2008).

Evans, David C. *The Japanese Navy in World War II: In the Words of Former Japanese Naval Officers* (Annapolis: Naval Institute Press, 1969).

Evans, David C., and Mark R. Peattie. *Kaigun: Strategy, Tactics, and Technology in the Imperial Japanese Navy, 1887-1941* (Annapolis: Naval Institute Press, 1997).

Fawcett, Bill. *How to Lose WWII: Bad Mistakes of the Good War* (New York: Harper, 2010).

Fuchida, Mitsuo, and Masatake Okumiya. *Midway: The Battle That Doomed Japan, The Japanese Navy's Story* (Annapolis: Naval Institute Press, 1955).

Gay, George. *Sole Survivor: A Personal Story About the Battle of Midway* (Midway Publishers, 1979).

Gellman, Irwin F. *Secret Affairs: Franklin Roosevelt, Cordell Hull, and Summer Welles* (Baltimore: The Johns Hopkins University Press, 1995).

Gingrich, Newt, William R. Forstchen, and Albert S. Hanser. *Pearl Harbor: A Novel of December 8th, Book One of the Pacific War Series* (New York: Thomas Dunne Books, St. Martin's Press, 2007).

Grew, Joseph C. *Ten Years in Japan: A Contemporary Record Drawn from the Diaries and Private and Official Papers of Joseph C. Grew, United States Ambassador to Japan 1932-1942* (New York: Simon and Schuster, 1944).

Hamilton, Nigel. *Commander in Chief: FDR's Battle with Churchill 1943* (Great Britain: Biteback Publishing Ltd., 2016).

Hamilton, Nigel. *The Mantle of Command: FDR at War 1941-1942* (Boston: Mariner Books, Houghton Mifflin Harcourt, 2014).

Hamilton, Nigel. *War and Peace: FDR's Final Odyssey D-Day to Yalta, 1943-1945* (New York: Houghton Miller Harcourt, 2019).

Hanson, Victor Davis. *The Second World Wars: How the First Global Conflict Was Fought and Won* (New York: Basic Books, 2017).

Healy, Mark. *Midway 1942: Turning Point in the Pacific* (Connecticut: Osprey Publishing Limited, 2004).

Heinrichs, Waldo. *Threshold of War: Franklin D. Roosevelt and American Entry into World War II* (New York: Oxford University Press, 1988).

Henry, Chris. *Great Naval Battles: 2: Battle of the Coral Sea* (Annapolis: Naval Institute Press, 2003).

Hinton, Harold B. *Cordell Hull: A Biography* (New York: Doubleday, Doran & Company, Inc., 1942).

Holmes, Richard. *The Oxford Companion to Military History* (New York: Oxford University Press, 2001).

Hone, Thomas C. *The Battle of Midway: The Naval Institute Guide to the U.S. Navy's Greatest Victory* (Annapolis: Naval Institute Press, 2013).

Hotta, Eri. *Japan 1941: Countdown to Infamy* (New York: Alfred A. Knopf, 2013).

Hoyt, Edwin P. *Yamamoto: The Man Who Planned Pearl Harbor* (New York: McGraw-Hill Publishing Company, 1990).

Hughes, Wayne P. *Fleet Tactics and Coastal Combat* (Annapolis: Naval Institute Press, 2000).

Humble, Richard. *Naval Warfare: An Illustrated History* (New York: St. Martin's Press, 1983).

Kaiser, David. *No End Save Victory: How FDR Led the Nation Into War* (Philadelphia: Basic Books, 2014).

Keegan, John. *The Second World War* (New York: Penguin Books, 1989).

Kennedy, Paul. *Victory at Sea: Naval Power and the Transformation of the Global Order in World War II* (New Haven: Yale University Press, 2022).

Kieth, Phil. *Stay the Rising Sun: The True Story of USS Lexington, Her Valiant Crew, and Changing the Course of World War II* (Minneapolis: Zenith Press, 2015).

Kleiss, N. Jack "Dusty," and Timothy and Laura Orr. *Never Call Me a Hero: A Legendary American Dive Bomber Pilot Remembers the Battle of Midway* (New York: HarperCollins, 2017).

Koster, John. *Operation Snow: How a Soviet Mole in FDR's White House Triggered Pearl Harbor* (Washington, D.C.: Regnery Publishing, Inc., 2012).

Larrabee, Eric. *Commander in Chief: Franklin Delano Roosevelt, His Lieutenants, and Their War* (New York: Fitzhenry & Whiteside Limited, 1987).

Layton, Edwin T. *Reminiscences of Rear Admiral Edwin T. Latton U.S. Navy (Retired)* (Annapolis: U.S. Naval Institute, 1975).

Layton, Edwin T., Roger Pineau, and John Costello. *"And I was There:" Pearl Harbor and Midway—Breaking the Secrets* (Connecticut: Konecky & Konecky, 1985).

Lord, Walter. *Day of Infamy* (New York: Henry Holt and Company, Inc., 1957).

Lord, Walter. *Incredible Victory* (New York: Harper & Row, Publishers, 1967).

Lundstrom, John B. *Black Shoe Carrier Admiral: Frank Jack Fletcher at Coral Sea, Midway, and Guadalcanal* (Annapolis: Naval Institute Press, 2006).

Lundstrom, John B. *The First South Pacific Campaign: Pacific Fleet Strategy: December 1941-June 1942* (Annapolis: Naval Institute Press, 1976).

Mahan, A.T. *The Influence of Sea Power Upon History: 1660-1783* (Boston: Little, Brown and Company, 1890).

Matthews, Owen. *An Impeccable Spy: Richard Sorge, Stalin's Master Agent* (London: Bloomsbury Publishing, 2019).

Meacham, Jon. *Franklin and Winston: An Intimate Portrait of an Epic Friendship* (New York: Random House, 2003).

Miller, Edward S. *Bankrupting the Enemy: The U.S. Financial Siege of Japan before Pearl Harbor* (Annapolis: Naval Institute Press, 2007).

Millot, Bernard A. *The Battle of the Coral Sea* (USA: Naval Institute Press, 1974).

Morison, Samuel Eliot. *Coral Sea, Midway, and Submarine Actions: May 1942-August 1942* (Annapolis: Naval Institute Press, 1949).

Morison, Samuel Eliot. *The Rising Sun in the Pacific: 1931-April 1942* (Annapolis: Naval Institute Press, 1948).

Morison, Samuel Eliot. *The Two-Ocean War: A Short History of the United States Navy in the Second World War* (Boston: An Atlantic Monthly Press Book, Little, Brown and Company, 1963).

Nelson, Craig. *Pearl Harbor: From Infamy to Greatness* (New York: Scribner, 2016).

Nofi, Albert A. *To Train the Fleet for War: The U.S. Navy Fleet Problems* (Rhode Island: Naval War College Press, 2010).

O'Brien, Phillips Payson. *The Second Most Powerful Man in the World: The Life of Admiral William D. Leahy, Roosevelt's Chief of Staff* (Boston: Dutton, 2019).

Parshall, Jonathan B., and Anthony P. Tully. *Shattered Sword: The Untold Story of the Battle of Midway* (Sterling, Virginia: Potomac Books, 2007).

Perrett, Bryan. *Why the Japanese Lost: The Red Sun's Setting* (Barnsley, UK: Pen & Sword, 2014).

Potter, E.B. *Nimitz* (Annapolis: Naval Institute Press, 1976).

Prange, Gordon W., Donald M. Goldstein, and Katherine V. Dillon. *Miracle at Midway* (New York: McGraw-Hill Book Company, 1982).

Prange, Gordon W. *At Dawn We Slept: The Untold Story of Pearl Harbor* (New York: Penguin Books, 1981).

Pratt, Fletcher. *The Navy's War* (New York: Harper and Brothers Publishers, 1942).

Reynolds, Clark G. *Admiral John H. Towers: The Struggle for Naval Air Supremacy* (Annapolis: Naval Institute Press, 1991).

Rigby, David. *Wade McClusky and the Battle of Midway* (Oxford, UK: Osprey Publishing, 2019).

Roll, David L. *The Hopkins Touch: Harry Hopkins and the Forging of the Alliance to Defeat Hitler* (UK: Oxford University Press, 2013).

Roosevelt, Franklin. *The Fireside Chats* (New York: Sheba Blake Publishing, 2017).

Rowley, Hazel. *Franklin and Eleanor: An Extraordinary Marriage* (New York: Farrar, Strauss, and Giroux, 2010).

Showalter, Dennis, and Harold Deutsch. *If the Allies had Fallen: Sixty Alternate Scenarios of World War* (London: Frontline Books, 2010).

Smith, Douglas V. *Carrier Battles: Command Decision in Harm's Way* (Annapolis: Naval Institute Press, 2006).

Smith, Peter C. *Midway: Dauntless Victory: Fresh Perspectives on America's Seminal Naval Victory of World War II* (Great Britain: Pen and Sword Maritime, 2007).

Smith, Peter C. *The Dauntless in Battle: The Douglass SBD Dauntless Dive-Bomber in the Pacific 1941-1945* (Great Britain: Pen and Sword Aviation, 2019).

Spector, Ronald H. *At War at Sea: Sailors and Naval Combat in the Twentieth Century* (New York: Penguin Group, 2001).

Stafford, Edward P. *The Big E: The Story of the USS Enterprise* (Annapolis: Naval Institute Press, 1962).

Stille, Mark E. *The Imperial Japanese Navy in the Pacific War* (Great Britain: Osprey Publishing, 2014).

Stille, Mark. *Midway 1942: Turning Point in the Pacific* (Oxford, UK: Osprey Publishing, 2010).

Stillwell, Paul. *Air Raid: Pearl Harbor! Recollections of a Day of Infamy* (Annapolis: Naval Institute Press, 1981).

Stinnett, Robert B. *Day of Deceit: The Truth About FDR and Pearl Harbor* (New York: Touchstone, 2000).

Sweetman, Jack. *The Great Admirals: Command at Sea 1587-1945* (Annapolis: Naval Institute Press, 1997).

Symonds, Craig L. *Decisions at Sea: Five Naval Battles That Shaped American History* (New York: Oxford University Press, 2005).

Symonds, Craig L. *Nimitz at War: Command Leadership from Pearl Harbor to Tokyo Bay* (New York: Oxford University Press, 2022).

Symonds, Craig L. *The Naval Institute: Historical Atlas of the U.S. Navy* (Annapolis: Naval Institute Press, 1995).

Taylor, A.J.P. *The War Lords* (New York: Penguin Books Ltd., 1977).

Taylor, Theodore. *The Magnificent Mitscher* (New York: W.W. Norton & Company, Inc., 1954).

Thomas, Lowell. *These Men Shall Never Die* (Philadelphia: The John C. Winston Company, 1943).

Toland, John. Infamy: *Pearl Harbor and Its Aftermath* (New York: Doubleday & Company, Inc., 1972).

Toland, John. *The Rising Sun: The Decline and Fall of the Japanese Empire: 1936-1945* (New York: Random House, 1970).

Toll, Ian W. *Pacific Crucible: War at Sea in the Pacific, 1941-1942* (New York: W.W. Norton & Company, 2012).

Toye, Richard. *Churchill's Empire: The World That Made Him and the World He Made* (New York: A John Macrae Book, Henry Holt and Company, 2010).

Ugaki, Matome. *Fading Victory* (Annapolis: Naval Institute Press, 1991).

Walsh, George J. *The Battle of Midway: Searching for the Truth* (CreateSpace Independent Publishing Platform, 2015).

Ward, Geofrey C. *The War: An Intimate History 1941-1945* (New York: Alfred A. Knopf, 2007).

Warner, Oliver. *Great Sea Battles* (UK: The Hamlyn Publishing Group Ltd.).

Weisheit, Bowen P. *The Last Flight of Ensign C. Markland Kelly, Junior USNR, Battle of Midway, June 4, 1942* (Baltimore: The Ensign C. Markland Kelly, Jr., Memorial Foundation, Inc., 1993).

Welles, Benjamin. *Sumner Welles: FDR's Global Strategist* (New York: St. Martin's Press, 1997).

Whymant, Robert. *Stalin's Spy: Richard Sorge and the Tokyo Espionage Ring* (New York: St. Martin's Press, 1996).

Williford, G., and T. McGovern. *Defenses of Pearl Harbor and Oahu 1907-50* (Oxford, UK: Osprey Publishing, 2003).

Willmott, H.P. *Empires in the Balance: Japanese and Allied Pacific Strategies to April 1942* (Annapolis: Naval Institute Press, 1982).

Wohlstetter, Roberta. *Pearl Harbor: Warning and Decision* (California: Stanford University Press, 1962).

Woodman, Richard. *The History of the Ship: The Comprehensive Story of Seafaring from the Earliest Times to the Present Day* (Great Britain: Conway Maritime Press, 1997).

Wukovits, John. *Pacific Alamo: The Battle for Wake Island* (New York: New American Library, 2003).

Young, Edward M. *F4F Wildcat vs. A6M Zero-Sen: Pacific Theater 1942* (Great Britain: Osprey Publishing, 2013).

ARTICLES

Bergeron, David Lee. *"Fighting for Survival."* Naval History, Dec. 2019.

Borneman, Walter R. *"Brothers at the Attack's Epicenter."* Naval History, Dec. 2019.

Frank, Richard B. *"Picking Winners?"* Naval History, June 2011.

Giacomoro, Christopher M. *"How Japan Developed Carrier Aviation."* Naval History, Vol. 32, No. 32, April 2018.

Kaye, Richard. P. *"The Battle of Midway June, 1942: Its place in Naval History—Looking back and looking forward."* Harvard Club, Nov. 2012.

Petty, Bruce M. *"Jump-Starting Japanese Naval Aviation."* Naval History, Dec. 2019.

Rubel, Robert C. *"'The Voice of Mahan': The U.S. Naval Institute Proceedings 1890-1899."* www.usni.org, July 2014.

Scott, James M. *"Tokyo."* Naval History, April 2015.

Sears, David. *"Butch's Wingman."* Naval History, Aug. 2015.

Sears, David. *"Sam Morison's Long Campaign."* U.S. Naval Institute.

Sears, David. *"Sam Morison's War."* Naval History, Feb. 2020.

Stillwell, Paul. *"Plenty of Blame to Go Around."* www.usni.org, Dec. 2006.

Symonds, Craig L. *"Mitscher and the Mystery of Midway."* Naval History, June 2012.

Tillman, Barrett. *"The Plane that Won the War."* Naval History, Feb. 2017.

Zimm, Alan D. *"Commander Fuchida's Decision."* Naval History, Dec. 2016.

GOVERNMENT

Foreign Relations of the United States Diplomatic Papers

Action Reports of Commanders of Fleets, Task Forces, Ships, and Squadrons

Index

377

Acknowledgments

The excellent staff at the National Archives, College Park, Maryland, were professional and cooperative. They guided me to now-declassified original documents that included action reports of the Commander-in-Chief, Pacific Fleet, which enclosed the reports of commanders of ships and squadrons. The action reports and other associated original documents supplied the core information that allowed me to write the naval actions of *Diplomats & Admirals*.

Similarly, Irma Fink of the Dudley Knox Library at the Naval Postgraduate School, Monterey, California, assisted my credential approval process and provided access to the naval archives there. I also found a large cache of State Department records, including Papers as President, from the period just prior to Pearl Harbor.

At the US Naval Academy library at Annapolis, Maryland, David D'Onofrio brought out personal memorabilia donated to the library, including one by a Midway flier and Academy alumnus. These memorabilia further confirmed official records and added perspective to other accounts of the early Pacific carrier battles.

Steve Wills, a former naval officer, provided important basic research on Pearl Harbor and Wake Island. My long acquaintance with John Maurer at the US Naval War College provided constructive insights.

My very fortunate acquaintance with George J. Walsh, and through him Norman "Dusty" Kleiss, was particularly important. During World War II both were Navy pilots who flew dive bombers. George flew combat missions from carriers near the Philippines, Iwo Jima and Okinawa. Dusty Kleiss was a hero at Midway. Both survived the war, and in their senior years wrote accounts of their experiences that provided expert descriptions of the actions of Dauntless dive bombers in the war. Both accounts confirmed the action reports that are cited in *Diplomats & Admirals*. My many discussions with George added greatly to my understanding of the early Pacific carrier battles and naval aviation generally.

Through George I came to know Peter C. Smith, a prolific British writer and indefatigable researcher of Anglo-American naval history. His two books on the Dauntless dive-bomber are classic works on the subject, and these books together with Peter's observations were very helpful.

Finally, my wife Sandra, recently deceased brother Bob, and son Dave read the draft manuscript at various stages and made constructive observations. Daughters Francesca, Sunny, and Grace contributed with design advice, digital expertise, and their lively interest.

I am grateful for all of this.

About the Author

Dale Jenkins has had a lifelong interest in the Navy and international affairs. He is a former US Navy officer who served on a destroyer in the Pacific and for a time was home-ported in Yokosuka, Japan. Pacific Fleet commitments took him to the Philippines, Taiwan, South Korea, Hong Kong, and Singapore. While on active duty, he was awarded the Navy/Marine Corps Expeditionary Medal. His business career was primarily in international banking, and he was also a staff director at the Council on Foreign Relations in New York. Dale currently serves on the Samuel Eliot Morison Committee of the Naval Order of the United Sates, New York, and as a Regional Director of the Naval War College Foundation. As a result of his active-duty experience and new revelations, Dale provides insight into the diplomacy and strategies of the Pacific region. He has degrees in history and business from Harvard and Columbia.

Would You Leave a Review?

I hope you enjoyed *Diplomats & Admirals*. I would appreciate it if you would take a few moments and write a review on Amazon. Here is the link:

https://www.amazon.com/Diplomats-Admirals-Negotiations-Misjudgments-Powerful/dp/B0BMSKP9C7/